A Narrative of the Life of Mrs. Mary Jemison

by
James E. Seaver

A Narrative of the Life of Mrs. Mary Jemison
by James E. Seaver

Copyright © 2024

All Rights reserved.

No part of this publication may be reproduced, stored in a retrieval system, or transmitted in any form or by any means, electronic, mechanical, photocopying or Otherwise, without the written permission of the publisher.
The author/editor asserts the moral right to be identified as the author/editor of this work.

ISBN: 978-93-63053-83-0

Published by

DOUBLE 9 BOOKS

2/13-B, Ansari Road
Daryaganj, New Delhi – 110002
info@double9books.com
www.double9books.com
Tel. 011-40042856

This book is under public domain

ABOUT THE AUTHOR

James E. Seaver was an American author and historian who lived during the early 19th century. He is best known for his work "A Narrative of the Life of Mrs. Mary Jemison," which was first published in 1824. The book is based on the life of Mary Jemison, who was born in 1743 in what is now Pennsylvania. Mary Jemison's life took a dramatic turn when she was captured by a Shawnee raiding party during the French and Indian War at the age of fifteen. She was then adopted by a Seneca family and eventually assimilated into the Seneca tribe, adopting their language, customs, and way of life. Despite opportunities to return to European-American society, Mary chose to remain with the Seneca people, earning the respect and admiration of both Native Americans and European settlers. Seaver's narrative provides a detailed account of Mary Jemison's experiences, offering insights into Native American culture, colonial history, and the complex relationships between indigenous peoples and European settlers during the tumultuous period of American expansion. Seaver's work remains a valuable historical document, shedding light on the experiences of individuals who lived at the intersection of different cultures and societies during a pivotal era in American history.

CONTENTS

PREFACE 7

INTRODUCTION 10

LIFE OF MARY JEMISON

CHAPTER I 15

CHAPTER II 19

CHAPTER III 26

CHAPTER IV 34

CHAPTER V 39

CHAPTER VI 44

CHAPTER VII 48

CHAPTER VIII 54

CHAPTER IX 62

CHAPTER X 65

CHAPTER XI 69

CHAPTER XII 78

CHAPTER XIII 81

CHAPTER XIV 84

CHAPTER XV 89

CHAPTER XVI 92

APPENDIX 95

PREFACE

That to biographical writings we are indebted for the greatest and best field in which to study mankind, or human nature, is a fact duly appreciated by a well-informed community. In them we can trace the effects of mental operations to their proper sources; and by comparing our own composition with that of those who have excelled in virtue, or with that of those who have been sunk in the lowest depths of folly and vice, we are enabled to select a plan of life that will at least afford self-satisfaction, and guide us through the world in paths of morality.

Without a knowledge of the lives of the vile and abandoned, we should be wholly incompetent to set an appropriate value upon the charms, the excellence and the worth of those principles which have produced the finest traits in the character of the most virtuous.

Biography is a telescope of life, through which we can see the extremes and excesses of the varied properties of the human heart. Wisdom and folly, refinement and vulgarity, love and hatred, tenderness and cruelty, happiness and misery, piety and infidelity, commingled with every other cardinal virtue or vice, are to be seen on the variegated pages of the history of human events, and are eminently deserving the attention of those who would learn to walk in the "paths of peace."

The brazen statue and the sculptured marble, can commemorate the greatness of heroes, statesmen, philosophers, and blood-stained conquerors, who have risen to the zenith of human glory and popularity, under the influence of the mild sun of prosperity: but it is the faithful page of biography that transmits to future generations the poverty, pain, wrong, hunger, wretchedness and torment, and every nameless misery that has been endured by those who have lived in obscurity, and groped their lonely way through a long series of unpropitious events, with but little help besides the light of nature. While the gilded monument displays in brightest colors the vanity of pomp, and the emptiness of nominal greatness, the biographical page, that lives in every line, is giving lessons of fortitude in time of danger, patience in suffering, hope in distress, invention in necessity, and resignation to unavoidable evils. Here also may be learned, pity for the bereaved, benevolence for the destitute, and compassion for the helpless;

and at the same time all the sympathies of the soul will be naturally excited to sigh at the unfavorable result, or to smile at the fortunate relief.

In the great inexplicable chain which forms the circle of human events, each individual link is placed on a level with the others, and performs an equal task; but, as the world is partial, it is the situation that attracts the attention of mankind, and excites the unfortunate vociferous eclat of elevation, that raises the pampered parasite to such an immense height in the scale of personal vanity, as, generally, to deprive him of respect, before he can return to a state of equilibrium with his fellows, or to the place whence he started.

Few great men have passed from the stage of action, who have not left in the history of their lives indelible marks of ambition or folly, which produced insurmountable reverses, and rendered the whole a mere caricature, that can be examined only with disgust and regret. Such pictures, however, are profitable, for "by others' faults wise men correct their own."

The following is a piece of biography, that shows what changes may be effected in the animal and mental constitution of man; what trials may be surmounted; what cruelties perpetrated, and what pain endured, when stern necessity holds the reins, and drives the car of fate.

As books of this kind are sought and read with avidity, especially by children, and are well calculated to excite their attention, inform their understanding, and improve them in the art of reading, the greatest care has been observed to render the style easy, the language comprehensive, and the description natural. Prolixity has been studiously avoided. The line of distinction between virtue and vice has been rendered distinctly visible; and chastity of expression and sentiment have received due attention. Strict fidelity has been observed in the composition: consequently, no circumstance has been intentionally exaggerated by the paintings of fancy, nor by fine flashes of rhetoric: neither has the picture been rendered more dull than the original. Without the aid of fiction, what was received as matter of fact, only has been recorded.

It will be observed that the subject of this narrative has arrived at least to the advanced age of eighty years; that she is destitute of education; and that her journey of life, throughout its texture, has been interwoven with troubles, which ordinarily are calculated to impair the faculties of the mind; and it will be remembered, that there are but few old people who can recollect with precision the circumstances of their lives, (particularly those circumstances which transpired after middle age.) If, therefore, any error shall be discovered in the narration in respect to time, it will be overlooked by the kind reader, or charitably placed to the narrator's account, and not imputed to neglect, or to the want of attention in the compiler.

The appendix is principally taken from the words of Mrs. Jemison's statements. Those parts which were not derived from her, are deserving equal credit, having been obtained from authentic sources.

For the accommodation of the reader, the work has been divided into chapters, and a copious table of contents affixed. The introduction will facilitate the understanding of what follows; and as it contains matter that could not be inserted with propriety in any other place, will be read with interest and satisfaction.

Having finished my undertaking, the subsequent pages are cheerfully submitted to the perusal and approbation or animadversion of a candid, generous and indulgent public. At the same time it is fondly hoped that the lessons of distress that are portrayed, may have a direct tendency to increase our love of liberty; to enlarge our views of the blessings that are derived from our liberal institutions; and to excite in our breasts sentiments of devotion and gratitude to the great Author and finisher of our happiness.

THE AUTHOR.

Pembroke, March 1, 1824.

INTRODUCTION

The Peace of 1783, and the consequent cessation of Indian hostilities and barbarities, returned to their friends those prisoners, who had escaped the tomahawk, the gauntlet, and the savage fire, after their having spent many years in captivity, and restored harmony to society.

The stories of Indian cruelties which were common in the new settlements, and were calamitous realities previous to that, propitious event; slumbered in the minds that had been constantly agitated by them, and were only roused occasionally, to become the fearful topic of the fireside.

It is presumed that at this time there are but few native Americans that have arrived to middle age, who cannot distinctly recollect of sitting in the chimney corner when children, all contracted with fear, and there listening to their parents or visitors, while they related stories of Indian conquests, and murders, that would make their flaxen hair nearly stand erect, and almost destroy the power of motion.

At the close of the Revolutionary war; all that part of the State of New-York that lies west of Utica was uninhabited by white people, and few indeed had ever passed beyond Fort Stanwix, except when engaged in war against the Indians, who were numerous, and occupied a number of large towns Between the Mohawk river and lake Erie.

Sometime elapsed after this event, before the country about the lakes and on the Genesee river was visited, save by an occasional land speculator, or by defaulters who wished by retreating to what in those days was deemed almost the end of the earth, to escape the force of civil law.

At length, the richness and fertility of the soil excited emigration, and here and there a family settled down and commenced improvements in the country which had recently been the property of the aborigines. Those who settled near the Genesee river, soon became acquainted with "The White Woman," as Mrs. Jemison is called, whose history they anxiously sought, both as a matter of interest and curiosity. Frankness characterized her conduct, and without reserve she would readily gratify them by relating some of the most important periods of her life.

Although her bosom companion was an ancient Indian warrior, and notwithstanding her children and associates were all Indians, yet it was found that she possessed an uncommon share of hospitality, and that her friendship was well worth courting and preserving. Her house was the stranger's home; from her table the hungry were refreshed;—she made the naked as comfortable as her means would admit of; and in all her actions, discovered so much natural goodness of heart, that her admirers increases in proportion to the extension of her acquaintance, and she became celebrated as the friend of the distressed. She was the protectress of the homeless fugitive, and made welcome the weary wanderer. Many still live to commemorate her benevolence towards them, when prisoners during the war, and to ascribe their deliverance to the mediation of "The White Woman."

The settlements increased, and the whole country around her was inhabited by a rich and respectable people, principally from New-England, as much distinguished for their spirit of inquisitiveness as for their habits of industry and honesty, who had all heard from one source and another a part of her life in detached pieces, and had obtained an idea that the whole taken in connection would afford instruction and amusement.

Many gentlemen of respectability, felt anxious that her narrative might be laid before the public, with a view not only to perpetuate the remembrance of the atrocities of the savages in former times, but to preserve some historical facts which they supposed to be intimately connected with her life, and which otherwise must be lost.

Forty years had passed since the close of the Revolutionary war, and almost seventy years had seen Mrs. Jemison with the Indians, when Daniel W. Banister, Esq. at the instance of several gentlemen, and prompted by his own ambition to add something to the accumulating fund of useful knowledge, resolved, in the autumn of 1823, to embrace that time, while she was capable of recollecting and reciting the scenes through which she had passed, to collect from herself, and to publish to an accurate account of her life.

I was employed to collect the materials, and prepare the work for the press; and accordingly went to the house of Mrs. Jennet Whaley in the town of Castile, Genesee co. N.Y. in company with the publisher, who procured the interesting subject of the following narrative, to come to that place (a distance of four miles) and there repeat the story of her eventful life. She came on foot in company with Mr. Thomas Clute, whom she considers her protector, and tarried almost three days, which time was busily occupied in taking a sketch of her narrative as she recited it.

Her appearance was well calculated to excite a great degree of sympathy in a stranger, who had been partially informed of her origin, when comparing her present situation with what it probably would have been, had she been permitted to have remained with her friends, and to have enjoyed the blessings of civilization.

In stature she is very short, and considerably under the middle size, and stands tolerably erect, with her head bent forward, apparently from her having for a long time been accustomed to carrying heavy burdens in a strap placed across her forehead. Her complexion is very white for a woman of her age, and although the wrinkles of fourscore years are deeply indented in her cheeks, yet the crimson of youth is distinctly visible. Her eyes are light blue, a little faded by age, and naturally brilliant and sparkling. Her sight is quite dim, though she is able to perform her necessary labor without the assistance of glasses. Her cheek bones are high, and rather prominent, and her front teeth, in the lower jaw, are sound and good. When she looks up and is engaged in conversation her countenance is very expressive; but from her long residence with the Indians, she has acquired the habit of peeping from under eye-brows as they do with the head inclined downwards. Formerly her hair was of a light chestnut brown—it is now quite grey, a little curled, of middling length and tied in a bunch behind. She informed me that she had never worn a cap nor a comb.

She speaks English plainly and distinctly, with a little of the Irish emphasis, and has the use of words so well as to render herself intelligible on any subject with which she is acquainted. Her recollection and memory exceeded my expectation. It cannot be reasonably supposed, that a person of her age has kept the events of seventy years in so complete a chain as to be able to assign to each its proper time and place; she, however, made her recital with as few obvious mistakes as might be found in that of a person of fifty.

She walks with a quick step without a staff, and I was informed by Mr. Clute, that she could yet cross a stream on a log or pole as steadily as any other person.

Her passions are easily excited. At a number of periods in her narration, tears trickled down her grief worn cheek, and at the same time, a rising sigh would stop her utterance.

Industry is a virtue which she has uniformly practised from the day of her adoption to the present. She pounds her samp, cooks for herself, gathers and chops wood, feeds her cattle and poultry, and performs other laborious services. Last season she planted, tended and gathered corn—in short she is always busy.

Her dress at the time I saw her, was made and worn after, the Indian fashion, and consisted of a shirt, short gown, petticoat, stockings, moccasins, a blanket and a bonnet. The shirt was of cotton and made at the top, as I was informed, like a man's without collar or sleeves—was open before and extended down about midway of the hips.—The petticoat was a piece of broadcloth with the list at the top and bottom and the ends sewed together. This was tied on by a string that was passed over it and around the waist, in such a manner as to let the bottom of the petticoat down half way between the knee and ankle and leave one-fourth of a yard at the top to be turned down over the string—the bottom of the shift coming a little below, and on the outside of the top of the fold so as to leave the list and two or three inches of the cloth uncovered. The stockings, were of blue broadcloth, tied, or pinned on, which reached from the knees, into the mouth of the moccasins.—Around her toes only she had some rags, and over these her buckskin moccasins. Her gown was of undressed flannel, colored brown. It was made in old yankee style, with long sleeves, covered the top of the hips, and was tied before in two places with strings of deer skin. Over all this, she wore an Indian blanket. On her head she wore a piece of old brown woollen cloth made somewhat like a sun bonnet.

Such was the dress that this woman was contented to wear, and habit had rendered it convenient and comfortable. She wore it not as a matter of t necessity, but from choice, for it will be seen in the sequel, that her property is sufficient to enable her to dress in the best fashion, and to allow her every comfort of life.

Her house, in which she lives, is 20 by 28 feet; built of square timber, with a shingled roof, and a framed stoop. In the centre of the house is a chimney of stones and sticks, in which there are two fire places. She has a good framed barn, 26 by 36, well filled, and owns a fine stock of cattle and horses. Besides the buildings above mentioned, she owns a number of houses that are occupied by tenants, who work her flats upon shares. Her dwelling, is about one hundred rods north of the Great Slide, a curiosity that, will be described in its proper place, on the west side of the Genesee river.

Mrs. Jemison, appeared sensible of her ignorance of the manners of the white people, and for that reason, was not familiar, except with those with whom she was intimately acquainted. In fact she was (to appearance) so jealous of her rights, or that she should say something that would be injurious to herself or family, that if Mr. Clute had not been present, we should have been unable to have obtained her history. She, however, soon became free and unembarrassed in her conversation, and spoke with degree of mildness, candor and simplicity, that is calculated to remove all doubts as to the veracity of the speaker. The vices of the Indians, she appeared disposed not to aggravate, and seemed to take pride in extoling their virtues. A kind of family pride inclined her to withhold whatever would blot the character of her descendants, and perhaps induced her to keep back many things that would have been interesting.

For the life of her last husband, we are indebted to her cousin, Mr. George Jemison, to whom she referred us for information on that subject generally. The thoughts of his deeds, probably chilled her old heart, and made her dread to rehearse them, and at the same time she well knew they were no secret, for she had frequently heard him relate the whole, not only to her cousin, but to others.

Before she left us she was very sociable, and she resumed her naturally pleasant countenance, enlivened with a smile.

Her neighbors speak of her as possessing one of the happiest tempers and disposition, and give her the name of never having done a censurable act to their knowledge.

Her habits, are those of the Indians—she sleeps on skins without a bedstead, sits upon the floor or on a bench, and holds her victuals on her lap, or in her hands.

Her ideas of religion, correspond in every respect with those of the great mass of the Senecas. She applauds virtue, and despises vice. She believes in a future state, in which the good will be happy, and the bad miserable; and that the acquisition of that happiness, depends primarily upon human volition, and the consequent good deeds of the happy recipient of blessedness. The doctrines taught in the Christian religion, she is a stranger to.

Her daughters are said to be active and enterprizing women, and her grandsons, who arrived to manhood, are considered able, decent and respectable men in their tribe.

Having in this cursory manner, introduced the subject of the following pages, I proceed to the narration of a life that has been viewed with attention, for a great number of years by a few, and which will be read by the public the mixed sensations of pleasure and pain, and with interest, anxiety and satisfaction.

LIFE OF MARY JEMISON

CHAPTER I

Although I may have frequently heard the history of my ancestry, my recollection is too imperfect to enable me to trace it further back than my father and mother, whom I have often heard mention the families from whence they originated, as having possessed wealth and honorable stations under the government of the country in which they resided.

On the account of the great length of time that has elapsed since I was separated from my parents and friends, and having heard the story of their nativity only in the days of my childhood, I am not able to state positively, which of the two countries, Ireland or Scotland, was the land of my parents birth and education. It, however, is my impression, that they were born and brought up in Ireland.

My Father's name was Thomas Jemison, and my mother's before her marriage with him, was Jane Erwin. Their affection for each other was mutual, and of that happy kind which tends directly to sweeten the cup of life; to render connubial sorrows lighter; to assuage every discontentment and to promote not only their own comfort, but that of all who come within the circle of their acquaintance. Of their happiness I recollect to have heard them speak; and the remembrance I yet retain of their mildness and perfect agreement in the government of their children, together with their mutual attention to our common education, manners, religious instruction and wants, renders it a fact in my mind, that they were ornaments to the married state, and examples of connubial love, worthy of imitation. After my remembrance they were strict observers of religious duties; for it was the daily practice of my father, morning and evening, to attend, in his family, to the worship of God.

Resolved to leave the land of their nativity they removed from their residence to a port in Ireland, where they lived but a short time before they set sail for this country, in the year 1742 or 3 on board the ship Mary William, bound to Philadelphia, in the state of Pennsylvania.

The intestine divisions, civil wars, and ecclesiastical rigidity and domination that prevailed those days, were the causes of their leaving their mother country and a home in the American wilderness, under the mild and temperate government of the descendants of William Penn; where without fear they might worship God, and perform their usual avocations.

In Europe my parents had two sons and one daughter, whose names were John, Thomas and Betsey; with whom, after having put their effects on board, they embarked, leaving a large connexion of relatives and friends, under all those painful sensations, which are only felt when kindred souls give the parting hand and last farewell to those to whom they are endeared by every friendly tie.

In the course of their voyage I was born, to be the sport of fortune and almost an outcast to civil society; to stem the current of adversity through a long chain of vicissitudes, unsupported by the advice of tender parents, or the hand of an affectionate friend; and even without the enjoyment from others, of any of those tender sympathies that are adapted to the sweetening of society, except such as naturally flow from uncultivated minds, that have been calloused by ferocity.

Excepting my birth, nothing remarkable occurred to my parents on their passage, and they were safely landed at Philadelphia. My father being fond of rural life, and having been bred to agricultural pursuits, soon left the city, and removed his family to the then frontier settlements of Pennsylvania, to a tract of excellent land lying on Marsh creek. At that place he cleared a large farm, and for seven or eight years enjoyed the fruits of his industry. Peace attended their labors; and they had nothing to alarm them, save the midnight howl of the prowling wolf, or the terrifying shriek of the ferocious panther, as they occasionally visited their improvements, to take a lamb or a calf to satisfy their hunger.

During this period my mother had two sons, between whose ages there was a difference of about three years: the oldest was named Matthew, and the other Robert.

Health presided on every countenance, and vigor and strength characterized every exertion. Our mansion was a little paradise. The morning of my childish, happy days, will ever stand fresh in my remembrance, notwithstanding the many severe trials through which I have passed, in arriving at my present situation, at so advanced an age. Even at this remote period, the recollection of my pleasant home at my father's, of my parents, of my brothers and sister, and of the manner in which I was deprived of them all at once, affects me so powerfully, that I am almost overwhelmed with grief, that is seemingly insupportable. Frequently I dream of those happy days: but, alas! they are gone; they have left me to be carried through a long life, dependent for the little pleasures of nearly seventy years, upon the tender mercies of the Indians! In the spring of 1752, and through the succeeding seasons, the stories of Indian barbarities inflicted upon the whites in those days, frequently excited in my parents the most serious alarm for our safety.

The next year the storm gathered faster; many murders were committed; and many captives were exposed to meet death in its most frightful form, by having their bodies stuck full of pine splinters, which were immediately set on fire, while their tormentors, exulting in their distress, would rejoice at their agony!

In 1754, an army for the protection of the settlers, and to drive back the French and Indians, was raised from the militia of the colonial governments, and placed (secondarily) under the command of Col. George Washington. In that army I had an uncle, whose name was John Jemison who was killed at the battle at the Great Meadow or Fort Necessity. His wife had died some time before this, and left a young child, which my mother nursed in the most tender manner, till its mother's sister took it away, a few months after my uncle's death. The French and Indians, after the surrender of Fort Necessity by Col. Washington, (which happened the same season, and soon after his victory over them at that place,) grew more and more terrible. The death of the whites, and plundering and burning their property, was apparently their only object: But as yet we had not heard the death-yell, nor seen the smoke of a dwelling that had been lit by an Indian's hand.

The return of a new-year's day found us unmolested; and though we knew that the enemy was at no great distance from us, my father concluded that he would continue to occupy his land another season: expecting (probably from the great exertions which the government was then making) that as soon as the troops could commence their operations in the spring, the enemy would be conquered and compelled to agree to a treaty of peace.

In the preceding autumn my father either moved to another part of his farm, or to another neighborhood, a short distance from our former abode. I well recollect moving, and that the barn that was on the place we moved to was built of logs, though the house was a good one.

The winter of 1754-5 was as mild as a common fall season, and the spring presented a pleasant seed time, and indicated a plenteous harvest. My father, with the assistance of his oldest sons, repaired his farm as usual, and was daily preparing the soil for the reception of the seed. His cattle and sheep were numerous, and according to the best idea of wealth that I can now form, he was wealthy.

But alas! how transitory are all human affairs! how fleeting are riches! how brittle the invisible thread on which all earthly comforts are suspended! Peace in a moment can take an immeasurable flight; health can lose its rosy cheeks; and life will vanish like a vapor at the appearance of the sun! In one fatal day our prospects were all blasted; and death, by cruel hands, inflicted upon almost the whole of the family.

On a pleasant day in the spring of 1755, when my father was sowing flax-seed, and my brothers driving the teams, I was sent to a neighbor's house, a distance of perhaps a mile, to procure a horse and return with it the next morning. I went as I was directed. I was out of the house in the beginning of the evening, and saw a sheet wide spread approaching towards me, in which I was caught (as I have ever since believed) and deprived of my senses! The family soon found me on the ground, almost lifeless, (as they said,) took me in, and made use of every remedy in their power for my recovery, but without effect till day-break, when my senses returned, and I soon found myself in good health, so that I went home with the horse very early in the morning.

The appearance of that sheet, I have ever considered as a forerunner of the melancholy catastrophe that so soon afterwards happened to our family: and my being caught in it I believe, was ominous of my preservation from death at the time we were captured.

CHAPTER II

My education had received as much attention from my parents, as their situation in a new country would admit. I had been at school some, where I learned to read in a book that was about half as large as a Bible; and in the Bible I had read a little. I had also learned the Catechism, which I used frequently to repeat to my parents, and every night, before I went to bed, I was obliged to stand up before my mother and repeat some words that I suppose was a prayer.

My reading, Catechism and prayers, I have long since forgotten; though for a number of the first years that I lived with the Indians, I repeated the prayers as often as I had an opportunity. After the revolutionary war, I remembered the names of some of the letters when I saw them; but have never read a word since I was taken prisoner. It is but a few years since a Missionary kindly gave me a Bible, which I am very fond of hearing my neighbors read to me, and should be pleased to learn to read it myself; but my sight has been for a number of years, so dim that I have not been able to distinguish one letter from another.

As I before observed, I got home with the horse very early in the morning, where I found a man that lived in our neighborhood, and his sister-in-law who had three children, one son and two daughters. I soon learned that they had come there to live a short time; but for what purpose I cannot say. The woman's husband, however, was at that time in Washington's army, fighting, for his country; and as her brother-in-law had a house she had lived with him in his absence. Their names I have forgotten.

Immediately after I got home, the man took the horse to go to his house after a bag of grain, and took his gun in his hand for the purpose of killing game, if he should chance to see any.—Our family, as usual, was busily employed about their common business. Father was shaving an axe-helve at the side of the house; mother was making preparations for breakfast;—my two oldest brothers were at work near the barn; and the little ones, with myself, and the woman and her three children, were in the house.

Breakfast was not yet ready, when we were alarmed by the discharge of a number of guns, that seemed to be near. Mother and the women before mentioned, almost fainted at the report, and every one trembled with fear. On opening the door, the man and horse lay dead near the house, having just been shot by the Indians.

I was afterwards informed, that the Indians discovered him at his own house with his gun, and pursued him to father's, where they shot him as I have related. They first secured my father, and then rushed into the house, and without the least resistance made prisoners of my mother, Robert, Matthew, Betsey, the woman and her three children, and myself, and then commenced plundering.

My two brothers, Thomas and John, being at the barn, escaped and went to Virginia, where my grandfather Erwin then lived, as I was informed by a Mr. Fields, who was at my house about the close of the revolutionary war.

The party that took us consisted of six Indians and four Frenchmen, who immediately commenced plundering, as I just observed, and took what they considered most valuable; consisting principally of bread, meal and meat. Having taken as much provision as they could carry, they set out with their prisoners in great haste, for fear of detection, and soon entered the woods. On our march that day, an Indian went behind us with a whip, with which he frequently lashed the children to make them keep up. In this manner we travelled till dark without a mouthful of food or a drop of water; although we had not eaten since the night before. Whenever the little children cried for water, the Indians would make them drink urine or go thirsty. At night they encamped in the woods without fire and without shelter, where we were watched with the greatest vigilance. Extremely fatigued, and very hungry, we were compelled to lie upon the ground supperless and without a drop of water to satisfy the cravings of our appetites. As in the day time, so the little ones were made to drink urine in the night if they cried for water. Fatigue alone brought us a little sleep for the refreshment of our weary limbs; and at the dawn of day we were again started on our march in the same order that we had proceeded on the day before. About sunrise we were halted, and the Indians gave us a full breakfast of provision that they had brought from my father's house. Each of us being very hungry, partook of this bounty of the Indians, except father, who was so much overcome with his situation—so much exhausted by anxiety and grief, that silent despair seemed fastened upon his countenance, and he could not be prevailed upon to refresh his sinking nature by the use of a morsel of food. Our repast being finished, we again resumed our march, and, before noon passed a small fort that I heard my father say was called Fort Canagojigge.

That was the only time that I heard him speak from the time we were taken till we were finally separated the following night.

Towards evening we arrived at the border of a dark and dismal swamp, which was covered with small hemlocks, or some other evergreen, and other bushes, into which we were conducted; and having gone a short distance we stopped to encamp for the night.

Here we had some bread and meat for supper: but the dreariness of our situation, together with the uncertainty under which we all labored, as to our future destiny, almost deprived us of the sense of hunger, and destroyed our relish for food.

Mother, from the time we were taken, had manifested a great degree of fortitude, and encouraged us to support our troubles without complaining; and by her conversation seemed to make the distance and time shorter, and the way more smooth. But father lost all his ambition in the beginning of our trouble, and continued apparently lost to every care—absorbed in melancholy. Here, as before, she insisted on the necessity of our eating; and we obeyed her, but it was done with heavy hearts.

As soon as I had finished my supper, an Indian took off my shoes and stockings and put a pair of moccasins on my feet, which my mother observed; and believing that they would spare my life, even if they should destroy the other captives, addressed me as near as I can remember in the following words:—

"My dear little Mary, I fear that the time has arrived when we must be parted forever. Your life, my child, I think will be spared; but we shall probably be tomahawked here in this lonesome place by the Indians. O! how can I part with you my darling? What will become of my sweet little Mary? Oh! how can I think of your being continued in captivity without a hope of your being rescued? O that death had snatched you from my embraces in your infancy; the pain of parting then would have been pleasing to what it now is; and I should have seen the end of your troubles!—Alas, my dear! my heart bleeds at the thoughts of what awaits you; but, if you leave us, remember my child your own name, and the name of your father and mother. Be careful and not forget your English tongue. If you shall have an opportunity to get away from the Indians, don't try to escape; for if you do they will find and destroy you. Don't forget, my little daughter, the prayers that I have learned you—say them often; be a good child, and God will bless you. May God bless you my child, and make you comfortable and happy."

During this time, the Indians stripped the shoes and stockings from the little boy that belonged to the woman who was taken with us, and put moccasins on his feet, as they had done before on mine. I was crying. An Indian took the little boy and myself by the hand, to lead us off from the company, when my mother exclaimed, "Don't cry Mary—don't cry my child. God will bless you! Farewell—farewell!"

The Indian led us some distance into the bushes, or woods, and there lay down with us to spend the night. The recollection of parting with my tender mother kept me awake, while the tears constantly flowed from my eyes. A number of times in the night the little boy begged of me earnestly to run away with him and get clear of the Indians; but remembering the advice I had so lately received, and knowing the dangers to which we should be exposed, in travelling without a path and without a guide, through a wilderness unknown to us, I told him that I would not go, and persuaded him to lie still till morning.

Early the next morning the Indians and Frenchmen that we had left the night before, came to us; but our friends were left behind. It is impossible for any one to form a correct idea of what my feelings were at the sight of those savages, whom I supposed had murdered my parents and brothers, sister, and friends, and left them in the swamp to be devoured by wild beasts! But what could I do? A poor little defenceless girl; without the power or means of escaping; without a home to go to, even if I could be liberated; without a knowledge of the direction or distance to my former place of residence; and without a living friend to whom to fly for protection, I felt a kind of horror, anxiety, and dread, that, to me, seemed insupportable. I durst not cry—I durst not complain; and to inquire of them the fate of my friends (even if I could have mustered resolution) was beyond my ability, as I could not speak their language, nor they understand mine. My only relief was in silent stifled sobs.

My suspicions as to the fate of my parents proved too true; for soon after I left them they were killed and scalped, together with Robert, Matthew, Betsey, and the woman and her two children, and mangled in the most shocking manner.

Having given the little boy and myself some bread and meat for breakfast, they led us on as fast as we could travel, and one of them went behind and with a long staff, picked up all the grass and weeds that we trailed down by going over them. By taking that precaution they avoided detection; for each weed was so nicely placed in its natural position that no one would have suspected that we had passed that way. It is the custom of Indians when scouting, or on private expeditions, to step carefully and where no impression of their feet can be left—shunning wet or muddy ground. They seldom take hold of a bush or limb, and never break one; and by observing those precautions and that of setting up the weeds and grass which they necessarily lop, they completely elude the sagacity of their pursuers, and escape that punishment which they are conscious they merit from the hand of justice.

After a hard day's march we encamped in a thicket, where the Indians made a shelter of boughs, and then built a good fire to warm and dry our benumbed limbs and clothing; for it had rained some through the day. Here we were again fed as before. When the Indians had finished their supper they took from their baggage a number of scalps and went about preparing them for the market, or to keep without spoiling, by straining them over small hoops which they prepared for that purpose, and then drying and scraping them by the fire. Having put the scalps, yet wet and bloody, upon the hoops, and stretched them to their full extent, they held them to the fire till they were partly dried and then with their knives commenced scraping off the flesh; and in that way they continued to work, alternately drying and scraping them, till they were dry and clean. That being done they combed the hair in the neatest manner, and then painted it and the edges of the scalps yet on the hoops, red. Those scalps I knew at the time must have been taken from our family by the color of the hair. My mother's hair was red; and I could easily distinguish my father's and the children's from each other. That sight was most appaling; yet, I was obliged to endure it without complaining.

In the course of the night they made me to understand that they should not have killed the family if the whites had not pursued them.

Mr. Fields, whom I have before mentioned, informed me that at the time we were taken, he lived in the vicinity of my father; and that on hearing of our captivity, the whole neighborhood turned out in pursuit of the enemy, and to deliver us if possible: but that their efforts were unavailing. They however pursued us to the dark swamp, where they found my father, his family and companions, stripped and mangled in the most inhuman manner: That from thence the march of the cruel monsters could not be traced in any direction; and that they returned to their homes with the melancholy tidings of our misfortunes, supposing that we had all shared in the massacre.

The next morning we went on; the Indian going behind us and setting up the weeds as on the day before. At night we encamped on the ground in the open air, without a shelter or fire.

In the morning we again set out early, and travelled as on the two former days, though the weather was extremely uncomfortable, from the continual falling of rain and snow.

At night the snow fell fast, and the Indians built a shelter of boughs, and a fire, where we rested tolerably dry through that and the two succeeding nights.

When we stopped, and before the fire was kindled, I was so much fatigued from running, and so far benumbed by the wet and cold, that I expected that I must fail and die before I could get warm and comfortable. The fire, however, soon restored the circulation, and after I had taken my supper I felt so that I rested well through the night.

On account of the storm, we were two days at that place. On one of those days, a party consisting of six Indians who had been to the frontier settlements, came to where we were, and brought with them one prisoner, a young white man who was very tired and dejected. His name I have forgotten.

Misery certainly loves company. I was extremely glad to see him, though I knew from his appearance, that his situation was as deplorable as mine, and that he could afford me no kind of assistance. In the afternoon the Indians killed a deer, which they dressed, and then roasted it whole; which made them a full meal. We were each allowed a share of their venison, and some bread, so that we made a good meal also.

Having spent three nights and two days at that place, and the storm having ceased, early in the morning the whole company, consisting of twelve Indians, four Frenchmen, the young man, the little boy and myself, moved on at a moderate pace without an Indian behind us to deceive our pursuers.

In the afternoon we came in sight of Fort Pitt (as it is now called,) where we were halted while the Indians performed some customs upon their prisoners which they deemed necessary. That fort was then occupied by the

French and Indians, and was called Fort Du Quesne. It stood at the junction of the Monongahela, which is said to signify, in some of the Indian languages, the Falling-in-Banks, [Footnote: Navigator.] and the Alleghany [Footnote: The word Alleghenny, was derived from an ancient race of Indians called "Tallegawe." The Delaware Indians, instead of saying "Alleghenny," say "Allegawe," or "Allegawenink," *Western Tour*—p. 455.] rivers, where the Ohio river begins to take its name. The word O-hi-o, signifies bloody.

At the place where we halted, the Indians combed the hair of the young man, the boy and myself, and then painted our faces and hair red, in the finest Indian style. We were then conducted into the fort, where we received a little bread, and were then shut up and left to tarry alone through the night.

CHAPTER III

The night was spent in gloomy forebodings. What the result of our captivity would be, it was out of our power to determine or even imagine.—At times we could almost realize the approach of our masters to butcher and scalp us;—again we could nearly see the pile of wood kindled on which we were to be roasted; and then we would imagine ourselves at liberty; alone and defenceless in the forest, surrounded by wild beasts that were ready to devour us. The anxiety of our minds drove sleep from our eyelids; and it was with a dreadful hope and painful impatience that we waited for the morning to determine our fate.

The morning at length arrived, and our masters came early and let us out of the house, and gave the young man and boy to the French, who immediately took them away. Their fate I never learned; as I have not seen nor heard of them since.

I was now left alone in the fort, deprived of my former companions, and of every thing that was near or dear to me but life. But it was not long before I was in some measure relieved by the appearance of two pleasant looking squaws of the Seneca tribe, who came and examined me attentively for a short time, and then went out. After a few minutes absence they returned with my former masters, who gave me to them to dispose of as they pleased.

The Indians by whom I was taken were a party of Shawanees, if I remember right, that lived, when at home, a long distance down the Ohio.

My former Indian masters, and the two squaws, were soon ready to leave the fort, and accordingly embarked; the Indians in a large canoe, and the two squaws and myself in a small one, and went down the Ohio.

When we set off, an Indian in the forward canoe took the scalps of my former friends, strung them on a pole that he placed upon his shoulder, and in that manner carried them, standing in the stern of the canoe, directly before us as we sailed down the river, to the town where the two squaws resided.

On our way we passed a Shawanee town, where I saw a number of heads, arms, legs, and other fragments of the bodies of some white people who had just been burnt. The parts that remained were hanging on a pole which was supported at each end by a crotch stuck in the ground, and were roasted or burnt black as a coal. The fire was yet burning; and the whole appearances afforded a spectacle so shocking, that, even to this day, my blood almost curdles in my veins when I think of them!

At night we arrived at a small Seneca Indian town, at the mouth of a small river, that was called by the Indians, in the Seneca language, She-nan-jee, [Footnote: That town, according to the geographical description given by Mrs. Jemison, must have stood at the mouth of Indian Cross creek, which is about 76 miles by water, below Pittsburgh; or at the mouth of Indian Short creek, 87 miles below Pittsburgh, where the town of Warren now stands: But at which of those places I am unable to determine. *Author*.] where the two Squaws to whom I belonged resided. There we landed, and the Indians went on; which was the last I ever saw of them.

Having made fast to the shore, the Squaws left me in the canoe while they went to their wigwam or house in the town, and returned with a suit of Indian clothing, all new, and very clean and nice. My clothes, though whole and good when I was taken, were now torn in pieces, so that I was almost naked. They first undressed me and threw my rags into the river; then washed me clean and dressed me in the new suit they had just brought, in complete Indian style; and then led me home and seated me in the center of their wigwam.

I had been in that situation but a few minutes before all the Squaws in the town came in to see me. I was soon surrounded by them, and they immediately set up a most dismal howling, crying bitterly, and wringing their hands in all the agonies of grief for a deceased relative.

Their tears flowed freely, and they exhibited all the signs of real mourning. At the commencement of this scene, one of their number began, in a voice somewhat between speaking and singing, to recite some words to the following purport, and continued the recitation till the ceremony was ended; the company at the same time varying the appearance of their countenances, gestures and tone of voice, so as to correspond with the sentiments expressed by their leader:

"Oh our brother! Alas! He is dead—he has gone; he will never return! Friendless he died on the field of the slain, where his bones are yet lying unburied! Oh, who will not mourn his sad fate? No tears dropped around him; oh, no! No tears of his sisters were there! He fell in his prime, when his arm was most needed to keep us from danger! Alas! he has gone! and left us in sorrow, his loss to bewail: Oh where is his spirit? His spirit went naked, and hungry it wanders, and thirsty and wounded it groans to return! Oh helpless and wretched, our brother has gone! No blanket nor food to nourish and warm him; nor candles to light him, nor weapons of war:—Oh, none of those comforts had he! But well we remember his deeds!—The deer he could take on the chase! The panther shrunk back at the sight of his strength! His enemies fell at his feet! He was brave and courageous in war! As the fawn was harmless: his friendship was ardent: his temper was gentle: his pity was great! Oh! our friend, our companion is dead! Our brother, your brother, alas! he is gone! But why do we grieve for his loss? In the strength of a warrior, undaunted he left us, to fight by the side of the Chiefs! His war-whoop was shrill! His rifle well aimed laid his enemies low: his tomahawk drank of their blood: and his knife flayed their scalps while yet covered with gore! And why do we mourn? Though he fell on the field of the slain, with glory he fell, and his spirit went up to the land of his fathers in war! Then why do we mourn? With transports of joy they received him, and fed him, and clothed him, and welcomed him there! Oh friends, he is happy; then dry up your tears! His spirit has seen our distress, and sent us a helper whom with pleasure we greet. Dickewamis has come: then let us receive her with joy! She is handsome and pleasant! Oh! she is our sister, and gladly we welcome her here. In the place of our brother she stands in our tribe. With care we will guard her from trouble; and may she be happy till her spirit shall leave us."

In the course of that ceremony, from mourning they became serene—joy sparkled in their countenances, and they seemed to rejoice over me as over a long lost child. I was made welcome amongst them as a sister to the two Squaws before mentioned, and was called Dickewamis; which being interpreted, signifies a pretty girl, a handsome girl, or a pleasant, good thing. That is the name by which I have ever since been called by the Indians.

I afterwards learned that the ceremony I at that time passed through, was that of adoption. The two squaws had lost a brother in Washington's war, sometime in the year before and in consequence of his death went up to Fort Pitt, on the day on which I arrived there, in order to receive a prisoner or an enemy's scalp, to supply their loss.

It is a custom of the Indians, when one of their number is slain or taken prisoner in battle, to give to the nearest relative to the dead or absent, a prisoner, if they have chanced to take one, and if not, to give him the scalp of an enemy. On the return of the Indians from conquest, which is always announced by peculiar shoutings, demonstrations of joy, and the exhibition of some trophy of victory, the mourners come forward and make their claims. If they receive a prisoner, it is at their option either to satiate their vengeance by taking his life in the most cruel manner they can conceive of; or, to receive and adopt him into the family, in the place of him whom they have lost. All the prisoners that are taken in battle and carried to the encampment or town by the Indians, are given to the bereaved families, till their number is made good.

And unless the mourners have but just received the news of their bereavement, and are under the operation of a paroxysm of grief, anger and revenge; or, unless the prisoner is very old, sickly, or homely, they generally save him, and treat him kindly. But if their mental wound is fresh, their loss so great that they deem it irreparable, or if their prisoner or prisoners do not meet their approbation, no torture, let it be ever so cruel, seems sufficient to make them satisfaction. It is family, and not national, sacrifices amongst the Indians, that has given them an indelible stamp as barbarians, and identified their character with the idea which is generally formed of unfeeling ferocity, and the most abandoned cruelty.

It was my happy lot to be accepted for adoption; and at the time of the ceremony I was received by the two squaws, to supply the place of their brother in the family; and I was ever considered and treated by them as a real sister, the same as though I had been born of their mother.

During my adoption, I sat motionless, nearly terrified to death at the appearance and actions of the company, expecting every moment to feel their vengeance, and suffer death on the spot. I was, however, happily disappointed, when at the close of the ceremony the company retired, and my sisters went about employing every means for my consolation and comfort.

Being now settled and provided with a home, I was employed in nursing the children, and doing light work about the house. Occasionally I was sent out with the Indian hunters, when they went but a short distance, to help them carry their game.

My situation was easy; I had no particular hardships to endure. But still, the recollection of my parents, my brothers and sisters, my home, and my own captivity, destroyed my happiness, and made me constantly solitary, lonesome and gloomy.

My sisters would not allow me to speak English in their hearing; but remembering the charge that my dear mother gave me at the time I left her, whenever I chanced to be alone I made a business of repeating my prayer, catechism, or something I had learned in order that I might not forget my own language. By practising in that way I retained it till I came to Genesee flats, where I soon became acquainted with English people with whom I have been almost daily in the habit of conversing.

My sisters were diligent in teaching me their language; and to their great satisfaction I soon learned so that I could understand it readily, and speak it fluently. I was very fortunate in falling into their hands; for they were kind good natured women; peaceable and mild in their dispositions; temperate and decent in their habits, and very tender and gentle towards me. I have great reason to respect them, though they have been dead a great number of years.

The town where they lived was pleasantly situated on the Ohio, at the mouth of the Shenanjee: the land produced good corn; the woods furnished a plenty of game, and the waters abounded with fish. Another river emptied itself into the Ohio, directly opposite the mouth of the Shenanjee. We spent the summer at that place, where we planted, hoed, and harvested a large crop of corn, of an excellent quality.

About the time of corn harvest, Fort Pitt was taken from the French by the English. [Footnote: The above statement is apparently an error; and is to be attributed solely to the treachery of the old lady's memory; though she is confident that that event took place at the time above mentioned. It is certain that Fort Pitt was not evacuated by the French and given up to the English, till sometime in November, 1758. It is possible, however, that an armistice was agreed upon, and that for a time, between the spring of 1755 and 1758, both nations visited that post without fear of molestation. As the succeeding part of the narrative corresponds with the true historical chain of events, the public will overlook this circumstance, which appears unsupported by history. AUTHOR.]

The corn being harvested, the Indians took it on horses and in canoes, and proceeded down the Ohio, occasionally stopping to hunt a few days, till we arrived at the mouth of Sciota river; where they established their winter quarters, and continued hunting till the ensuing spring, in the adjacent wilderness. While at that place I went with the other children to assist the hunters to bring in their game. The forests on the Sciota were well stocked with elk, deer, and other large animals; and the marshes contained large numbers of beaver, muskrat, &c. which made excellent hunting for the Indians; who depended, for their meat, upon their success in taking elk and deer; and for ammunition and clothing, upon the beaver, muskrat, and other furs that they could take in addition to their peltry.

The season for hunting being passed, we all returned in the spring to the mouth of the river Shenanjee, to the houses and fields we had left in the fall before. There we again planted our corn, squashes, and beans, on the fields that we occupied the preceding summer.

About planting time, our Indians all went up to Fort Pitt, to make peace with the British, and took me with them. [Footnote: History is silent as to any treaty having been made between the English, and French and Indians, at that time; though it is possible that a truce was agreed upon, and that the parties met for the purpose of concluding a treaty of peace.] We landed on the opposite side of the river from the fort, and encamped for the night. Early the next morning the Indians took me over to the fort to see the white people that were there. It was then that my heart bounded to be liberated from the Indians and to be restored to my friends and my country. The white people were surprized to see me with the Indians, enduring the hardships of a savage life, at so early an age, and with so delicate a constitution as I appeared to possess. They asked me my name; where and when I was taken—and appeared very much interested on my behalf. They were continuing their inquiries, when my sisters became alarmed, believing that I should be taken from them, hurried me into their canoe and recrossed the river—took their bread out of the fire and fled with me, without stopping, till they arrived at the river Shenanjee. So great was their fear of losing me, or of my being given up in the treaty, that they never once stopped rowing till they got home.

Shortly after we left the shore opposite the fort, as I was informed by one of my Indian brothers, the white people came over to take me back; but after considerable inquiry, and having made diligent search to find where I was hid, they returned with heavy hearts. Although I had then been with the Indians something over a year, and had become considerably habituated to their mode of living, and attached to my sisters, the sight of white people who could speak English inspired me with an unspeakable anxiety to go home with them, and share in the blessings of civilization. My sudden departure and escape from them, seemed like a second captivity, and for a long time I brooded the thoughts of my miserable situation with almost as much sorrow and dejection as I had done those of my first sufferings. Time, the destroyer of every affection, wore away my unpleasant feelings, and I became as contented as before.

We tended our cornfields through the summer; and after we had harvested the crop, we again went down the river to the hunting ground on the Sciota, where we spent the winter, as we had done the winter before.

Early in the spring we sailed up the Ohio river, to a place that the Indians called Wiishto, [Footnote: Wiishto I suppose was situated near the mouth of Indian Guyundat, 327 miles below Pittsburgh, and 73 above Big Sciota; or at the mouth of Swan creek, 307 miles below Pittsburgh.] where one river emptied into the Ohio on one side, and another on the other. At that place the Indians built a town, and we planted corn.

We lived three summers at Wiishto, and spent each winter on the Sciota.

The first summer of our living at Wiishto, a party of Delaware Indians came up the river, took up their residence, and lived in common with us. They brought five white prisoners with them, who by their conversation, made my situation much more agreeable, as they could all speak English. I have forgotten the names of all of them except one, which was Priscilla Ramsay. She was a very handsome, good natured girl, and was married soon after she came to Wiishto to Capt. Little Billy's uncle, who went with her on a visit to her friends in the states. Having tarried with them as long as she wished to, she returned with her husband to Can-a-ah-tua, where he died. She, after his death, married a white man by the name of Nettles, and now lives with him (if she is living) on Grand River, Upper Canada.

Not long after the Delawares came to live with us, at Wiishto, my sisters told me that I must go and live with one of them, whose name was Sheninjee. Not daring to cross them, or disobey their commands, with a great degree of reluctance I went; and Sheninjee and I were married according to Indian custom.

Sheninjee was a noble man; large in stature; elegant in his appearance; generous in his conduct; courageous in war; a friend to peace, and a great lover of justice. He supported a degree of dignity far above his rank, and merited and received the confidence and friendship of all the tribes with whom he was acquainted. Yet, Sheninjee was an Indian. The idea of spending my days with him, at first seemed perfectly irreconcilable to my feelings: but his good nature, generosity, tenderness, and friendship towards me, soon gained my affection; and, strange as it may seem, I loved him!—To me he was ever kind in sickness, and always treated me with gentleness; in fact, he was an agreeable husband, and a comfortable companion.

We lived happily together till the time of our final separation, which happened two or three years after our marriage, as I shall presently relate.

In the second summer of my living at Wiishto, I had a child at the time that the kernels of corn first appeared on the cob. When I was taken sick, Sheninjee was absent, and I was sent to a small shed, on the bank of the river, which was made of boughs, where I was obliged to stay till my husband returned. My two sisters, who were my only companions, attended me, and on the second day of my confinement my child was born but it lived only two days. It was a girl: and notwithstanding the shortness of the time that I possessed it, it was a great grief to me to lose it.

After the birth of my child, I was very sick, but was not allowed to go into the house for two weeks; when, to my great joy, Sheninjee returned, and I was taken in and as comfortably provided for as our situation would admit of. My disease continued to increase for a number of days; and I became so far reduced that my recovery was despaired of by my friends, and I concluded that my troubles would soon be finished. At length, however, my complaint took a favorable turn, and by the time that the corn was ripe I was able to get about. I continued to gain my health, and in the fall was able to go to our winter quarters, on the Sciota, with the Indians.

From that time, nothing remarkable occurred to me till the fourth winter of my captivity, when I had a son born, while I was at Sciota: I had a quick recovery, and my child was healthy. To commemorate the name of my much lamented father, I called my son Thomas Jemison.

CHAPTER IV

In the spring, when Thomas was three or four moons [months] old, we returned from Sciota to Wiishto, and soon after set out to go to Fort Pitt, to dispose of our fur and skins, that we had taken in the winter, and procure some necessary articles for the use of our family.

I had then been with the Indians four summers and four winters, and had become so far accustomed to their mode of living, habits and dispositions, that my anxiety to get away, to be set at liberty, and leave them, had almost subsided. With them was my home; my family was there, and there I had many friends to whom I was warmly attached in consideration of the favors, affection and friendship with which they had uniformly treated me, from the time of my adoption. Our labor was not severe; and that of one year was exactly similar, in almost every respect, to that of the others, without that endless variety that is to be observed in the common labor of the white people. Notwithstanding the Indian women have all the fuel and bread to procure, and the cooking to perform, their task is probably not harder than that of white women, who have those articles provided for them; and their cares certainly are not half as numerous, nor as great. In the summer season, we planted, tended and harvested our corn, and generally had all our children with us; but had no master to oversee or drive us, so that we could work as leisurely as we pleased. We had no ploughs on the Ohio; but performed the whole process of planting and hoeing with a small tool that resembled, in some respects, a hoe with a very short handle.

Our cooking consisted in pounding our corn into samp or hommany, boiling the hommany, making now and then a cake and baking it in the ashes, and in boiling or roasting our venison. As our cooking and eating utensils consisted of a hommany block and pestle, a small kettle, a knife or two, and a few vessels of bark or wood, it required but little time to keep them in order for use.

Spinning, weaving, sewing, stocking knitting, and the like, are arts which have never been practised in the Indian tribes generally. After the revolutionary war, I learned to sew, so that I could make my own clothing after a poor fashion; but the other domestic arts I have been wholly ignorant of the application of, since my captivity. In the season of hunting, it was our business, in addition to our cooking, to bring home the game that was taken by the Indians, dress it, and carefully preserve the eatable meat, and prepare or dress the skins. Our clothing was fastened together with strings of deer skin, and tied on with the same.

In that manner we lived, without any of those jealousies, quarrels, and revengeful battles between families and individuals, which have been common in the Indian tribes since the introduction of ardent spirits amongst them.

The use of ardent spirits amongst the Indians, and the attempts which have been made to civilize and christianize them by the white people, has constantly made them worse and worse; increased their vices, and robbed them of many of their virtues; and will ultimately produce their extermination. I have seen, in a number of instances, the effects of education upon some of our Indians, who were taken when young, from their families, and placed at school before they had had an opportunity to contract many Indian habits, and there kept till they arrived to manhood; but I have never seen one of those but what was an Indian in every respect after he returned. Indians must and will be Indians, In spite of all the means that can be used for their cultivation in the sciences and arts.

One thing only marred my happiness, while I lived with them on the Ohio; and that was the recollection that I had once had tender parents, and a home that I loved. Aside from that consideration, or, if I had been taken in infancy, I should have been contented in my situation. Notwithstanding all that has been said against the Indians, in consequence of their cruelties to their enemies—cruelties that I have witnessed, and had abundant proof of— it is a fact that they are naturally kind, tender and peaceable towards their friends, and strictly honest; and that those cruelties have been practised, only upon their enemies, according to their idea of justice.

At the time we left Wiishto, it was impossible for me to suppress a sigh of regret on parting with those who had truly been my friends—with those whom I had every reason to respect. On account of a part of our family living at Genishau, we thought it doubtful whether we should return directly from Pittsburgh, or go from thence on a visit to see them.

Our company consisted of my husband, my two Indian brothers, my little son and myself. We embarked in a canoe that was large enough to contain ourselves, and our effects, and proceeded on our voyage up the river.

Nothing remarkable occurred to us on our way, till we arrived at the mouth of a creek which Sheninjee and my brother said was the outlet of Sandusky lake; where, as they said, two or three English traders in fur and skins had kept a trading house but a short time before, though they were then absent. We had passed the trading house but a short distance, when we met three white men floating down the river, with the appearance of having been recently murdered by the Indians, we supposed them to be the bodies of the traders, whose store we had passed the same day. Sheninjee being alarmed for fear of being apprehended as one of the murderers, if he should go on, resolved to put about immediately, and we accordingly returned to where the traders had lived, and there landed.

At the trading house we found a party of Shawnee Indians, who had taken a young white man prisoner, and had just begun to torture him for the sole purpose of gratifying their curiosity in exulting at his distress. They at first made him stand up, while they slowly pared his ears and split them into strings; they then made a number of slight incisions in his face; and then bound him upon the ground, rolled him in the dirt, and rubbed it in his wounds: some of them at the same time whipping him with small rods! The poor fellow cried for mercy and yelled most piteously.

The sight of his distress seemed too much for me to endure: I begged of them to desist—I entreated them with tears to release him. At length they attended to my intercessions, and set him at liberty. He was shockingly disfigured, bled profusely, and appeared to be in great pain: but as soon as he was liberated he made off in haste, which was the last I saw of him.

We soon learned that the same party of Shawnees had, but a few hours before, massacred the three white traders whom we saw in the river, and had plundered their store. We, however, were not molested by them, and after a short stay at that place, moved up the creek about forty miles to a Shawnee town, which the Indians called Gaw-gush-shaw-ga, (which being interpreted signifies a mask or a false face.) The creek that we went up was called Candusky.

It was now summer; and having tarried a few days at Gawgushshawga, we moved on up the creek to a place that was called Yis-kah-wa-na, (meaning in English open mouth.)

As I have before observed, the family to which I belonged was part of a tribe of Seneca Indians, who lived, at that time, at a place called Genishau, from the name of the tribe, that was situated on a river of the same name which is now called Genesee. The word Genishau signifies a shining, clear or open place. Those of us who lived on the Ohio, had frequently received invitations from those at Genishau, by one of my brothers, who usually went and returned every season, to come and live with them, and my two sisters had been gone almost two years.

While we were at Yiskahwana, my brother arrived there from Genishau, and insisted so strenuously upon our going home (as he called it) with him, that my two brothers concluded to go, and to take me with them.

By this time the summer was gone, and the time for harvesting corn had arrived. My brothers, for fear of the rainy season setting in early, thought it best to set out immediately that we might have good travelling. Sheninjee consented to have me go with my brothers; but concluded to go down the river himself with some fur and skins which he had on hand, spend the winter in hunting with his friends, and come to me in the spring following.

That was accordingly agreed upon, and he set out for Wiishto; and my three brothers and myself, with my little son on my back, at the same time set out for Genishau. We came on to Upper Sandusky, to an Indian town that we found deserted by its inhabitants, in consequence of their having recently murdered some English traders, who resided amongst them. That town was owned and had been occupied by Delaware Indians, who, when they left it, buried their provision in the earth, in order to preserve it from their enemies, or to have a supply for themselves if they should chance to return. My brothers understood the customs of the Indians when they were obliged to fly from their enemies; and suspecting that their corn at least must have been hid, made diligent search, and at length found a large quantity of it, together with beans, sugar and honey, so carefully buried that it was completely dry and as good as when they left it. As our stock of provision was scanty, we considered ourselves extremely fortunate in finding so seasonable a supply, with so little trouble. Having caught two or three horses, that we found there, and furnished ourselves with a good store of food, we travelled on till we came to the mouth of French Creek, where we hunted two days, and from thence came on to Conowongo Creek, where we were obliged to stay seven or ten days, in consequence of our horses having left us and straying into the woods. The horses, however, were found, and we again prepared to resume our journey. During our stay at that place the rain fell fast, and had raised the creek to such a height that it was seemingly impossible for us to cross it. A number of times we ventured in, but were compelled to return, barely escaping with our lives. At length we succeeded in swimming our horses and reached the opposite shore; though I but just escaped with my little boy from being drowned. From Sandusky the path that we travelled was crooked and obscure; but was tolerably well understood by my oldest brother, who had travelled it a number of times, when going to and returning from the Cherokee wars. The fall by this time was considerably advanced, and the rains, attended with cold winds, continued daily to increase the difficulties of travelling. From Conowongo we came to a place, called by the Indians Che-ua-shunggau-tau, and from that to U-na-waum-gwa, (which means an eddy, not strong), where the early frosts had destroyed the corn so that the Indians were in danger of starving for the want of bread. Having rested ourselves two days at that place, we came on to Caneadea and stayed one day, and then continued our march till we arrived at Genishau. Genishau at that time was a large Seneca town, thickly inhabited, lying on Genesee river, opposite what is now called the Free Ferry, adjoining Fall-Brook, and about south west of the present village of Geneseo, the county seat for the county of Livingston, in the state of New-York.

Those only who have travelled on foot the distance of five or six hundred miles, through an almost pathless wilderness, can form an idea of the fatigue and sufferings that I endured on that journey. My clothing was thin and illy calculated to defend me from the continually drenching rains with which I was daily completely wet, and at night with nothing but my wet blanket to cover me, I had to sleep on the naked ground, and generally without a shelter, save such as nature had provided. In addition to all that, I had to carry my child, then about nine months old, every step of the journey on my back, or in my arms, and provide for his comfort and prevent his suffering, as far as my poverty of means would admit. Such was the fatigue that I sometimes felt, that I thought it impossible for me to go through, and I would almost abandon the idea of even trying to proceed. My brothers were attentive, and at length, as I have stated, we reached our place of destination, in good health, and without having experienced a day's sickness from the time we left Yiskahwana.

We were kindly received by my Indian mother and the other members of the family, who appeared to make me welcome; and my two sisters, whom I had not seen in two years, received me with every expression of love and friendship, and that they really felt what they expressed, I have never had the least reason to doubt. The warmth of their feelings, the kind reception which I met with, and the continued favors that I received at their hands, rivetted my affection for them so strongly that I am constrained to believe that I loved them as I should have loved my own sister had she lived, and I had been brought up with her.

CHAPTER V

When we arrived at Genishau, the Indians of that tribe were making active preparations for joining the French, in order to assist them in retaking Fort Ne-a-gaw (as Fort Niagara was called in the Seneca language) from the British, who had taken it from the French in the month preceding. They marched off the next day after our arrival, painted and accoutred in all the habiliments of Indian warfare, determined on death or victory; and joined the army in season to assist in accomplishing a plan that had been previously concerted for the destruction of a part of the British army. The British feeling themselves secure in the possession of Fort Neagaw, and unwilling that their enemies should occupy any of the military posts in that quarter, determined to take Fort Schlosser, lying a few miles up the river from Neagaw, which they expected to effect with but little loss. Accordingly a detachment of soldiers, sufficiently numerous, as was supposed, was sent out to take it, leaving a strong garrison in the fort, and marched off, well prepared to effect their object. But on their way they were surrounded by the French and Indians, who lay in ambush to deceive them, and were driven off the bank of the river into a place called the "Devil's Hole," together with their horses, carriages, artillery, and every thing pertaining to the army. Not a single man escaped being driven off, and of the whole number one only was fortunate enough to escape with his life. [Footnote: For the particulars of that event, see Appendix, No. 1.] Our Indians were absent but a few days, and returned in triumph, bringing with them two white prisoners, and a number of oxen. Those were the first neat cattle that were ever brought to the Genesee flats.

The next day after their return to Genishau, was set apart as a day of feasting and frolicing, at the expence of the lives of their two unfortunate prisoners, on whom they purposed to glut their revenge, and satisfy their love for retaliation upon their enemies. My sister was anxious to attend the execution, and to take me with her, to witness the customs of the warriors, as it was one of the highest kind of frolics ever celebrated in their tribe, and one that was not often attended with so much pomp and parade as it was expected that would be. I felt a kind of anxiety to witness the scene, having never attended an execution, and yet I felt a kind of horrid dread that made my heart revolt, and inclined me to step back rather than support the idea of advancing. On the morning of the execution she made her intention of going to the frolic, and taking me with her, known to our mother, who in the most feeling terms, remonstrated against a step at once so rash and unbecoming the true dignity of our sex:

"How, my daughter, (said she, addressing my sister,) how can you even think of attending the feast and seeing the unspeakable torments that those poor unfortunate prisoners must inevitably suffer from the hands of our warriors? How can you stand and see them writhing in the warriors' fire, in all the agonies of a slow, a lingering death?

"How can you think of enduring the sound of their groanings and prayers to the Great Spirit for sudden deliverance from their enemies, or from life? And how can you think of conducting to that melancholy spot your poor sister Dickewamis, (meaning myself), who has so lately been a prisoner, who has lost her parents and brothers by the hands of the bloody warriors, and who has felt all the horrors of the loss of her freedom, in lonesome captivity? Oh! how can you think of making her bleed at the wounds which now are but partially healed? The recollection of her former troubles would deprive us of Dickewamis, and she would depart to the fields of the blessed, where fighting has ceased, and the corn needs no tending—where hunting is easy, the forests delightful, the summers are pleasant, and the winters are mild!—O! think once, my daughter, how soon you may have a brave brother made prisoner in battle, and sacrificed to feast the ambition of the enemies of his kindred, and leave us to mourn for the loss of a friend, a son and a brother, whose bow brought us venison, and supplied us with blankets!— Our task is quite easy at home, and our business needs our attention. With war we have nothing to do: our husbands and brothers are proud to defend us, and their hearts beat with ardor to meet our proud foes. Oh! stay then, my daughter; let our warriors alone perform on their victims their customs of war!"

This speech of our mother had the desired effect; we stayed at home and attended to our domestic concerns. The prisoners, however, were executed by having their heads taken off, their bodies cut in pieces and shockingly mangled, and then burnt to ashes!—They were burnt on the north side of Fall-brook, directly opposite the town which was on the south side, some time in the month of November, 1759.

I spent the winter comfortably, and as agreeably as I could have expected to, in the absence of my kind husband. Spring at length appeared, but Sheninjee was yet away; summer came on, but my husband had not found me. Fearful forebodings haunted my imagination; yet I felt confident that his affection for me was so great that if he was alive he would follow me and I should again see him. In the course of the summer, however, I received intelligence that soon after he left me at Yiskahwana he was taken sick and died at Wiishto. This was a heavy and an unexpected blow. I was now in my youthful days left a widow, with one son, and entirely dependent on myself for his and my support. My mother and her family gave me all the consolation in their power, and in a few months nay grief wore off and I became contented.

In a year or two after this, according to my best recollection of the time, the King of England offered a bounty to those who would bring in the prisoners that had been taken in the war, to some military post where they might be redeemed and set at liberty.

John Van Sice, a Dutchman, who had frequently been at our place, and was well acquainted with every prisoner at Genishau, resolved to take me to Niagara, that I might there receive my liberty and he the offered bounty. I was notified of his intention; but as I was fully determined not to be redeemed at that time, especially with his assistance, I carefully watched his movements in order to avoid falling into his hands. It so happened, however, that he saw me alone at work in a corn-field, and thinking probably that he could secure me easily, ran towards me in great haste. I espied him at some distance, and well knowing the amount of his errand, run from him with all the speed I was mistress of, and never once stopped till I reached Gardow. [Footnote: I have given this orthography, because it corresponds with the popular pronunciation.] He gave up the chase, and returned: but I, fearing that he might be lying in wait for me, stayed three days and three nights in an old cabin at Gardow, and then went back trembling at every step for fear of being apprehended. I got home without difficulty; and soon after, the chiefs in council having learned the cause of my elopement, gave orders that I should not be taken to any military post without my consent; and that as it was my choice to stay, I should live amongst them quietly and undisturbed. But, notwithstanding the will of the chiefs, it was but a few days before the old king of our tribe told one of my Indian brothers that I should be redeemed, and he would take me to Niagara himself. In reply to the old king, my brother said that I should not be given up; but that, as it was my wish, I should stay with the tribe as long as I was pleased to. Upon this a serious quarrel ensued between them, in which my brother frankly told him that sooner than I should be taken by force, he would kill me with his own hands!—Highly enraged at the old king; my brother came to my sister's house, where I resided, and informed her of all that had passed respecting me; and that, if the old king should attempt to take me, as he firmly believed he would, he would immediately take my life, and hazard the consequences.

He returned to the old king. As soon as I came in, my sister told me what she had just heard, and what she expected without doubt would befal me. Full of pity, and anxious for my preservation, she then directed me to take my child and go into some high weeds at no great distance from the house, and there hide myself and lay still till all was silent in the house, for my brother, she said, would return at evening and let her know the final conclusion of the matter, of which she promised to inform me in the following manner: If I was to be killed, she said she would bake a small cake and lay it at the door, on the outside, in a place that she then pointed out to me. When all was silent in the house, I was to creep softly to the door, and if the cake could not be found in the place specified, I was to go in: but if the cake was there, I was to take my child and; go as fast as I possibly could to a large spring on the south side of Samp's Creek, (a place that I had often seen,) and there wait till I should by some means hear from her.

Alarmed for my own safety, I instantly followed her advice, and went into the weeds, where I lay in a state of the greatest anxiety, till all was silent in the house, when I crept to the door, and there found, to my great distress, the little cake! I knew my fate was fixed, unless I could keep secreted till the storm was over, and accordingly crept back to the weeds, where my little Thomas lay, took him on my back, and laid my course for the spring as fast as my legs would carry me. Thomas was nearly three years old, and very large and heavy. I got to the spring early in the morning, almost overcome with fatigue, and at the same time fearing that I might be pursued and taken, I felt my life an almost insupportable burthen. I sat down with my child at the spring, and he and I made a breakfast of the little cake, and water of the spring, which I dipped and supped with the only implement which I possessed, my hand.

In the morning after I fled, as was expected, the old King came to our house in search of me, and to take me off; but, as I was not to be found, he gave me up, and went to Niagara with the prisoners he had already got into his possession.

As soon as the old King was fairly out of the way, my sister told my brother where he could find me. He immediately set out for the spring, and found me about noon. The first sight of him made me tremble with the fear of death; but when he came near, so that I could discover his countenance, tears of joy flowed down my cheeks, and I felt such a kind of instant relief as no one can possibly experience, unless when under the absolute sentence of death he receives an unlimited pardon. We were both rejoiced at the event of the old King's project; and after staying at the spring through the night, set out together for home early in the morning. When we got to a cornfield near the town, my brother secreted me till he could go and ascertain how my case stood; and finding that the old King was absent, and that all was peaceable, he returned to me, and I went home joyfully.

Not long after this, my mother went to Johnstown, on the Mohawk river, with five prisoners, who were redeemed by Sir William Johnson, and set at liberty.

When my son Thomas was three or four years old, I was married to an Indian, whose name was Hiokatoo, commonly called Gardow, by whom I had four daughters and two sons. I named my children, principally, after my relatives, from whom I was parted, by calling my girls Jane, Nancy, Betsey and Polly, and the boys John and Jesse. Jane died about twenty-nine years ago, in the month of August, a little before the great Council at Big-Tree, aged about fifteen years. My other daughters are yet living, and have families.

CHAPTER VI

After the conclusion of the French war, our tribe had nothing to trouble it till the commencement of the Revolution. For twelve or fifteen years the use of the implements of war was not known, nor the war-whoop heard, save on days of festivity, when the achievements of former times were commemorated in a kind of mimic warfare, in which the chiefs and warriors displayed their prowess, and illustrated their former adroitness, by laying the ambuscade, surprizing their enemies, and performing many accurate manoeuvres with the tomahawk and scalping knife; thereby preserving and handing to their children, the theory of Indian warfare. During that period they also pertinaciously observed the religious rites of their progenitors, by attending with the most scrupulous exactness and a great degree of enthusiasm to the sacrifices, at particular times, to appease the anger of the evil deity, or to excite the commisseration and friendship of the Great Good Spirit, whom they adored with reverence, as the author, governor, supporter and disposer of every good thing of which they participated.

They also practised in various athletic games, such as running, wrestling, leaping, and playing ball, with a view that their bodies might be more supple, or rather that they might not become enervated, and that they might be enabled to make a proper selection of Chiefs for the councils of the nation and leaders for war.

While the Indians were thus engaged in their round of traditionary performances, with the addition of hunting, their women attended to agriculture, their families, and a few domestic concerns of small consequence, and attended with but little labor.

No people can live more happy than the Indians did in times of peace, before the introduction of spirituous liquors amongst them. Their lives were a continual round of pleasures. Their wants were few, and easily satisfied; and their cares were only for to-day; the bounds of their calculations for future comfort not extending to the incalculable uncertainties of to-morrow. If peace ever dwelt with men, it was in former times, in the recesses from war, amongst what are now termed barbarians. The moral character of the Indians was (if I may be allowed the expression) uncontaminated. Their fidelity was perfect, and became proverbial; they were strictly honest; they despised deception and falsehood; and chastity was held in high veneration, and a violation of it was considered sacrilege. They were temperate in their desires, moderate in their passions, and candid and honorable in the expression of their sentiments on every subject of importance.

Thus, at peace amongst themselves, and with the neighboring whites, though there were none at that time very near, our Indians lived quietly and peaceably at home, till a little before the breaking out of the revolutionary war, when they were sent for, together with the Chiefs and members of the Six Nations generally, by the people of the States, to go to the German Flats, and there hold a general council, in order that the people of the states might ascertain, in good season, who they should esteem and treat as enemies, and who as friends, in the great war which was then upon the point of breaking out between them and the King of England.

Our Indians obeyed the call, and the council was holden, at which the pipe of peace was smoked, and a treaty made, in which the Six Nations solemnly agreed that if a war should eventually break out, they would not take up arms on either side; but that they would observe a strict neutrality. With that the people of the states were satisfied, as they had not asked their assistance, nor did not wish it. The Indians returned to their homes well pleased that they could live on neutral ground, surrounded by the din of war, without being engaged in it.

About a year passed off, and we, as usual, were enjoying ourselves in the employments of peaceable times, when a messenger arrived from the British Commissioners, requesting all the Indians of our tribe to attend a general council which was soon to be held at Oswego. The council convened, and being opened, the British Commissioners informed the Chiefs that the object of calling a council of the Six Nations, was, to engage their assistance in subduing the rebels, the people of the states, who had risen up against the good King, their master, and were about to rob him of a great part of his possessions and wealth, and added that they would amply reward them for all their services.

The Chiefs then arose, and informed the Commissioners of the nature and extent of the treaty which they had entered into with the people of the states, the year before, and that they should not violate it by taking up the hatchet against them.

The Commissioners continued their entreaties without success, till they addressed their avarice, by telling our people that the people of the states were few in number, and easily subdued; and that on the account of their disobedience to the King, they justly merited all the punishment that it was possible for white men and Indians to inflict upon them; and added, that the King was rich and powerful, both in money and subjects: That his rum was as plenty as the water in lake Ontario: that his men were as numerous as the sands upon the lake shore:—and that the Indians, if they would assist in the war, and persevere in their friendship to the King, till it was closed, should never want for money or goods. Upon this the Chiefs concluded a treaty with the British Commissioners, in which they agreed to take up arms against the rebels, and continue in the service of his Majesty till they were subdued, in consideration of certain conditions which were stipulated in the treaty to be performed by the British government and its agents.

As soon as the treaty was finished, the Commissioners made a present to each Indian of a suit of clothes, a brass kettle, a gun and tomahawk, a scalping knife, a quantity of powder and lead a piece of gold, and promised a bounty on every scalp that should be brought in. Thus richly clad and equipped, they returned home, after an absence of about two weeks, full of the fire of war, and anxious to encounter their enemies. Many of the kettles which the Indians received at that time are now in use on the Genesee Flats.

Hired to commit depredations upon the whites, who had given them no offence, they waited impatiently to commence their labor, till sometime in the spring of 1776, when a convenient opportunity offered for them to make an attack. At that time, a party of our Indians were at Cau-te-ga, who shot a man that was looking after his horse, for the sole purpose, as I was informed by my Indian brother, who was present, of commencing hostilities.

In May following, our Indians were in their first battle with the Americans; but at what place I am unable to determine. While they were absent at that time, my daughter Nancy was born.

The same year, at Cherry Valley, our Indians took a woman and her three daughters prisoners, and brought them on, leaving one at Canandaigua, one at Honeoy, one at Cattaraugus, and one (the woman) at Little Beard's Town, where I resided. The woman told me that she and her daughters might have escaped, but that they expected the British army only, and therefore made no effort. Her husband and sons got away. Sometime having elapsed, they were redeemed at Fort Niagara by Col. Butler, who clothed them well, and sent them home.

In the same expedition, Joseph Smith was taken prisoner at or near Cherry Valley, brought to Genesee, and detained till after the revolutionary war. He was then liberated, and the Indians made him a present, in company with Horatio Jones, of 6000 acres of land lying in the present town of Leicester, in the county of Livingston.

One of the girls just mentioned, was married to a British officer at Fort Niagara, by the name of Johnson, who at the time she was taken, took a gold ring from her finger, without any compliments or ceremonies. When he saw her at Niagara he recognized her features, restored the ring that he had so impolitely borrowed, and courted and married her.

Previous to the battle at Fort Stanwix, the British sent for the Indians to come and see them whip the rebels; and, at the same time stated that they did not wish to have them fight, but wanted to have them just sit down smoke their pipes, and look on. Our Indians went, to a man; but contrary to their expectation, instead of smoking and looking on, they were obliged to fight for their lives, and in the end of the battle were completely beaten, with a great loss in killed and wounded. Our Indians alone had thirty-six killed, and a great number wounded. Our town exhibited a scene of real sorrow and distress, when our warriors returned and recounted their misfortunes, and stated the real loss they had sustained in the engagement. The mourning was excessive, and was expressed by the most doleful yells, shrieks, and howlings, and by inimitable gesticulations.

During the revolution, my house was the home of Col's Butler and Brandt, whenever they chanced to come into our neighborhood as they passed to and from Fort Niagara, which was the seat of their military operations. Many and many a night I have pounded samp for them from sun-set till sun-rise, and furnished them with necessary provision and clean clothing for their journey.

CHAPTER VII

For four or five years we sustained no loss in the war, except in the few who had been killed in distant battles; and our tribe, because of the remoteness of its situation, from the enemy, felt secure from an attack. At length, in the fall of 1779, intelligence was received that a large and powerful army of the rebels, under the command of General Sullivan, was making rapid progress towards our settlement, burning and destroying the huts and corn-fields; killing the cattle, hogs and horses, and cutting down the fruit trees belonging to the Indians throughout the country.

Our Indians immediately became alarmed, and suffered every thing but death from fear that they should be taken by surprize, and totally destroyed at a single blow. But in order to prevent so great a catastrophe, they sent out a few spies who were to keep themselves at a short distance in front of the invading army, in order to watch its operations, and give information of its advances and success.

Sullivan arrived at Canandaigua Lake, and had finished his work of destruction there, and it was ascertained that he was about to march to our flats, when our Indians resolved to give him battle on the way, and prevent, if possible, the distresses to which they knew we should be subjected, if he should succeed in reaching our town. Accordingly they sent all their women and children into the woods a little west of Little Beard's Town, in order that we might make a good retreat if it should be necessary, and then, well armed, set out to face the conquering enemy. The place which they fixed upon for their battle ground lay between Honeoy Creek and the head of Connessius Lake.

At length a scouting party from Sullivan's army arrived at the spot selected, when the Indians arose from their ambush with all the fierceness and terror that it was possible for them to exercise, and directly put the party upon a retreat. Two Oneida Indians were all the prisoners that were taken in that skirmish. One of them was a pilot of Gen. Sullivan, and had been very active in the war, rendering to the people of the states essential services. At the commencement of the revolution he had a brother older than himself, who resolved to join the British service, and endeavored by all the art that he was capable of using to persuade his brother to accompany him; but his arguments proved abortive. This went to the British, and that joined the

American army. At this critical juncture they met, one in the capacity of a conqueror, the other in that of a prisoner; and as an Indian seldom forgets a countenance that he has seen, they recognized each other at sight. Envy and revenge glared in the features of the conquering savage, as he advanced to his brother (the prisoner) in all the haughtiness of Indian pride, heightened by a sense of power, and addressed him in the following manner:

"Brother, you have merited death! The hatchet or the war-club shall finish your career!—When I begged of you to follow me in the fortunes of war, you was deaf to my cries—you spurned my entreaties!

"Brother! you have merited death and shall have your deserts! When the rebels raised their hatchets to fight their good master, you sharpened your knife, you brightened your rifle and led on our foes to the fields of our fathers'—You have merited death and shall die by our hands! When those rebels had drove us from the fields of our fathers to seek out new homes, it was you who could dare to step forth as their pilot, and conduct them even to the doors of our wigwams, to butcher our children and put us to death! No crime can be greater!—But though you have merited death and shall die on this spot, my hands shall not be stained in the blood of a brother! *Who will strike?*"

Little Beard, who was standing by, as soon as the speech was ended, struck the prisoner on the head with his tomahawk, and despatched him at once!

Little Beard then informed the other Indian prisoner that as they were at war with the whites only, and not with the Indians, they would spare his life, and after a while give him his liberty in an honorable manner. The Oneida warrior, however, was jealous of Little Beard's fidelity; and suspecting that he should soon fall by his hands, watched for a favorable opportunity to make his escape; which he soon effected. Two Indians were leading him, one on each side, when he made a violent effort, threw them upon the ground, and run for his life towards where the main body of the American army was encamped. The Indians pursued him without success; but in their absence they fell in with a small detachment of Sullivan's men, with whom they had a short but severe skirmish, in which they killed a number of the enemy, took Capt. or Lieut. William Boyd and one private, prisoners, and brought them to Little Beard's Town, where they were soon after put to death in the most shocking and cruel manner. Little Beard, in this, as in all other scenes of cruelty that happened at his town, was master of ceremonies, and principal actor. Poor Boyd was stripped of his clothing, and then tied to a sapling, where the Indians menaced his life by throwing their tomahawks at the tree, directly over his head, brandishing their scalping knives around him in the most frightful manner, and accompanying their ceremonies with terrific shouts of joy. Having punished him sufficiently in this way, they made a small opening in his abdomen, took out an intestine, which they tied to the sapling, and then unbound him from the tree, and drove him round it till he had drawn out the whole of his intestines. He was then beheaded, his head was stuck upon a pole, and his body left on the ground unburied.

Thus ended the life of poor William Boyd, who, it was said, had every appearance of being an active and enterprizing officer, of the first talents. The other prisoner was (if I remember distinctly) only beheaded and left near Boyd.

This tragedy being finished, our Indians again held a short council on the expediency of giving Sullivan battle, if he should continue to advance, and finally came to the conclusion that they were not strong enough to drive him, nor to prevent his taking possession of their fields: but that if it was possible they would escape with their own lives, preserve their families, and leave their possessions to be overrun by the invading army.

The women and children were then sent on still further towards Buffalo, to a large creek that was called by the Indians Catawba, accompanied by a part of the Indians, while the remainder secreted themselves in the woods back of Beard's Town, to watch the movements of the army.

At that time I had three children who went with me on foot, one who rode on horse back, and one whom I carried on my back.

Our corn was good that year; a part of which we had gathered and secured for winter.

In one or two days after the skirmish at Connissius lake, Sullivan and his army arrived at Genesee river, where they destroyed every article of the food kind that they could lay their hands on. A pan of our corn they burnt, and threw the remainder into the river. They burnt our houses, killed what few cattle and horses they could find, destroyed our fruit trees, and left nothing but the bare soil and timber. But the Indians had eloped and were not to be found.

Having crossed and recrossed the river, and finished the work of destruction, the army marched off to the east. Our Indians saw them move off, but suspecting that it was Sullivan's intention to watch our return, and then to take us by surprize, resolved that the main body of our tribe should hunt where we then were, till Sullivan had gone so far that there would be no danger of his returning to molest us.

This being agreed to, we hunted continually till the Indians concluded that there could be no risk in our once more taking possession of our lands.

Accordingly we all returned; but what were our feelings when we found that there was not a mouthful of any kind of sustenance left, not even enough to keep a child one day from perishing with hunger.

The weather by this time had become cold and stormy; and as we were destitute of houses and food too, I immediately resolved to take my children and look out for myself, without delay. With this intention I took two of my little ones on my back, bade the other three follow, and the same night arrived on the Gardow flats, where I have ever since resided.

At that time, two negroes, who had run away from their masters sometime before, were the only inhabitants of those flats. They lived in a small cabin and had planted and raised a large field of corn, which they had not yet harvested. As they were in want of help to secure their crop, I hired to them to husk corn till the whole was harvested.

I have laughed a thousand times to myself when I have thought of the good old negro, who hired me, who fearing that I should get taken or injured by the Indians, stood by me constantly when I was husking, with a loaded gun in his hand, in order to keep off the enemy, and thereby lost as much labor of his own as he received from me, by paying good wages. I, however, was not displeased with his attention; for I knew that I should need all the corn that I could earn, even if I should husk the whole. I husked enough for them, to gain for myself, at every tenth string, one hundred strings of ears, which were equal to twenty-five bushels of shelled corn. This seasonable supply made my family comfortable for samp and cakes through the succeeding winter, which was the most severe that I have witnessed since my remembrance. The snow fell about five feet deep, and remained so for a long time, and the weather was extremely cold; so much so indeed, that almost all the game upon which the Indians depended for subsistence, perished, and reduced them almost to a state of starvation through that and three or four succeeding years. When the snow melted in the spring, deer were found dead upon the ground in vast numbers; and other animals, of every description, perished from the cold also, and were found dead, in multitudes. Many of our people barely escaped with their lives, and some actually died of hunger and freezing.

But to return from this digression: Having been completely routed at Little Beard's Town, deprived of a house, and without the means of building one in season, after I had finished my husking, and having found from the short acquaintance which I had had with the negroes, that they were kind and friendly, I concluded, at their request, to take up my residence with them for a while in their cabin, till I should be able to provide a hut for myself. I lived more comfortable than I expected to through the winter, and the next season made a shelter for myself.

The negroes continued on my flats two or three years after this, and then left them for a place that they expected would suit them much better. But as that land became my own in a few years, by virtue of a deed from the Chiefs of the Six Nations, I have lived there from that to the present time.

My flats were cleared before I saw them; and it was the opinion of the oldest Indians that were at Genishau, at the time that I first went there, that all the flats on the Genesee river were improved before any of the Indian tribes ever saw them. I well remember that soon after I went to Little Beard's Town, the banks of Fall-Brook were washed off, which left a large number of human bones uncovered. The Indians then said that those were not the bones of Indians, because they had never heard of any of their dead being buried there; but that they were the bones of a race of men who a great many moons before, cleared that land and lived on the flats.

The next summer after Sullivan's campaign, our Indians, highly incensed at the whites for the treatment they had received, and the sufferings which they had consequently endured, determined to obtain some redress by destroying their frontier settlements. Corn Planter, otherwise called John O'Bail, led the Indians, and an officer by the name of Johnston commanded the British in the expedition. The force was large, and so strongly bent upon revenge and vengeance, that seemingly nothing could avert its march, nor prevent its depredations. After leaving Genesee they marched directly to some of the head waters of the Susquehannah river, and Schoharie Creek, went down that creek to the Mohawk river, thence up that river to Fort Stanwix, and from thence came home. In their route they burnt a number of places; destroyed all the cattle and other property that fell in their way; killed a number of white people, and brought home a few prisoners.

In that expedition, when they came to Fort Plain, on the Mohawk river, Corn Planter and a party of his Indians took old John O'Bail, a white man, and made him a prisoner. Old John O'Bail, in his younger days had frequently passed through the Indian settlements that lay between the Hudson and Fort Niagara, and in some of his excursions had become enamored with a squaw, by whom he had a son that was called Corn Planter.

Corn Planter, was a chief of considerable eminence; and having been informed of his parentage and of the place of his father's residence, took the old man at this time, in order that he might make an introduction leisurely, and become acquainted with a man to whom, though a stranger, he was satisfied that he owed his existence.

After he had taken the old man, his father, he led him as a prisoner ten or twelve miles up the river, and then stepped before him, faced about, and addressed him in the following terms:—

"My name is John O'Bail, commonly called Corn Planter. I am your son! you are my father! You are now my prisoner, and subject to the customs of Indian warfare: but you shall not be harmed; you need not fear. I am a warrior! Many are the scalps which I have taken! Many prisoners I have tortured to death! I am your son! I am a warrior! I was anxious to see you, and to greet you in friendship. I went to your cabin and took you by force! But your life shall be spared. Indians love their friends and their kindred, and treat them with kindness. If now you choose to follow the fortune of your yellow son, and to live with our people, I will cherish your old age with plenty of venison, and you shall live easy: But if it is your choice to return to your fields and live with your white children, I will send a party of my trusty young men to conduct you back in safety. I respect you, my father; you have been friendly to Indians, and they are your friends."

Old John chose to return. Corn Planter, as good as his word, ordered an escort to attend him home, which they did with the greatest care.

Amongst the prisoners that were brought to Genesee, was William Newkirk, a man by the name of Price, and two negroes.

Price lived a while with Little Beard, and afterwards with Jack Berry, an Indian. When he left Jack Berry he went to Niagara, where he now resides.

Newkirk was brought to Beard's Town, and lived with Little Beard and at Fort Niagara about one year, and then enlisted under Butler, and went with him on an expedition to the Monongahela.

CHAPTER VIII

Sometime near the close of the revolutionary war, a white man by the name of Ebenezer Allen, left his people in the state of Pennsylvania on the account of some disaffection towards his countrymen, and came to the Genesee river, to reside with the Indians. He tarried at Genishau a few days, and came up to Gardow, where I then resided.—He was, apparently, without any business that would support him; but he soon became acquainted with my son Thomas, with whom he hunted for a long time, and made his home with him at my house; winter came on, and he continued his stay.

When Allen came to my house, I had a white man living on my land, who had a Nanticoke squaw for his wife, with whom he had lived very peaceably; for he was a moderate man commonly, and she was a kind, gentle, cunning creature. It so happened that he had no hay for his cattle; so that in the winter he was obliged to drive them every day, perhaps half a mile from his house, to let them feed on rushes, which in those days were so numerous as to nearly cover the ground.

Allen having frequently seen the squaw in the fall, took the opportunity when her husband was absent with his cows, daily to make her a visit; and in return for his kindnesses she made and gave him a red cap finished and decorated in the highest Indian style.

The husband had for some considerable length of time felt a degree of jealousy that Allen was trespassing upon him with the consent of his squaw; but when he saw Allen dressed in so fine an Indian cap, and found that his dear Nanticoke had presented it to him, his doubts all left him, and he became so violently enraged that he caught her by the hair of her head, dragged her on the ground to my house, a distance of forty rods, and threw her in at the door. Hiokatoo, my husband, exasperated at the sight of so much inhumanity, hastily took down his old tomahawk, which for awhile had lain idle, shook it over the cuckold's head, and bade him jogo (i. e. go off.) The enraged husband, well knowing that he should feel a blow if he waited to hear the order repeated, instantly retreated, and went down the river to his cattle. We protected the poor Nanticoke woman, and gave her victuals; and Allen sympathized with her in her misfortunes till spring, when her husband came to her, acknowledged his former errors, and that he had abused her without a cause, promised a reformation, and she received him with every mark of a renewal of her affection. They went home lovingly, and soon after removed to Niagara.

The same spring, Allen commenced working my flats, and continued to labor there till after the peace in 1783. He then went to Philadelphia on some business that detained him but a few days, and returned with a horse and some dry goods, which he carried to a place that is now called Mount Morris, where he built or bought a small house.

The British and Indians on the Niagara frontier, dissatisfied with the treaty of peace, were determined, at all hazards, to continue their depredations upon the white settlements which lay between them and Albany. They actually made ready, and were about setting out on an expedition to that effect, when Allen (who by this time understood their customs of war) took a belt of wampum, which he had fraudulently procured, and carried it as a token of peace from the Indians to the commander of the nearest American military post.

The Indians were soon answered by the American officer that the wampum was cordially accepted and, that a continuance of peace was ardently wished for. The Indians, at this, were chagrined and disappointed beyond measure; but as they held the wampum to be a sacred thing, they dared not to go against the import of its meaning, and immediately buried the hatchet as it respected the people of the United State; and smoked the pipe of peace. They, however, resolved to punish Allen for his officiousness in meddling with their national affairs, by presenting the sacred wampum without their knowledge, and went about devising means for his detection. A party was accordingly despatched from Fort Niagara to apprehend him; with orders to conduct him to that post for trial, or for safe keeping, till such time as his fate should be determined upon in a legal manner.

The party came on; but before it arrived at Gardow, Allen got news of its approach, and fled for safety, leaving the horse and goods that he had brought from Philadelphia, an easy prey to his enemies. He had not been long absent when they arrived at Gardow, where they made diligent search for him till they were satisfied that they could not find him, and then seized the effects which he had left, and returned to Niagara. My son Thomas, went with them, with Allen's horse, and carried the goods.

Allen, on finding that his enemies had gone, came back to my house, where he lived as before; but of his return they were soon notified at Niagara, and Nettles (who married Priscilla Ramsay) with a small party of Indians came on to take him. He, however, by some means found that they were near, and gave me his box of money and trinkets to keep safely, till he called for it, and again took to the woods.

Nettles came on determined at all events to take him before he went back; and, in order to accomplish his design, he, with his Indians, hunted in the day time and lay by at night at my house, and in that way they practised for a number of days. Allen watched the motion of his pursuers, and every night after they had gone to rest, came home and got some food, and then returned to his retreat. It was in the fall, and the weather was cold and rainy, so that he suffered extremely. Some nights he sat in my chamber till nearly day-break, while his enemies were below, and when the time arrived I assisted him to escape unnoticed.

Nettles at length abandoned the chase—went home, and Allen, all in tatters, came in. By running in the woods his clothing had become torn into rags, so that he was in a suffering condition, almost naked. Hiokatoo gave him a blanket, and a piece of broadcloth for a pair of trowsers. Allen made his trowsers himself, and then built a raft, on which he went down the river to his own place at Mount Morris.

About that time he married a squaw, whose name was Sally.

The Niagara people finding that he was at his own house, came and took him by surprize when he least expected them, and carried him to Niagara. Fortunately for him, it so happened that just as they arrived at the fort, a house took fire and his keepers all left him to save the building, if possible. Allen had supposed his doom to be nearly sealed; but finding himself at liberty he took to his heels, left his escort to put out the fire, and ran to Tonnawanta. There an Indian gave him some refreshment, and a good gun, with which he hastened on to Little Beard's Town, where he found his squaw. Not daring to risk himself at that place for fear of being given up, he made her but a short visit, and came immediately to Gardow.

Just as he got to the top of the hill above the Gardow flats, he discovered a party of British soldiers and Indians in pursuit of him; and in fact they were so near that he was satisfied that they saw him, and concluded that it would be impossible for him to escape. The love of liberty, however, added to his natural swiftness, gave him sufficient strength to make his escape to his former castle of safety. His pursuers came immediately to my house, where they expected to have found him secreted, and under my protection. They told me where they had seen him but a few moments before, and that they were confident that it was within my power to put him into their hands. As I was perfectly clear of having had any hand in his escape, I told them plainly that I had not seen him since he was taken to Niagara, and that I could give them no information at all respecting him. Still unsatisfied, and doubting my veracity, they advised my Indian brother to use his influence to draw from me the secret of his concealment, which they had an idea that I considered of great importance, not only to him but to myself. I persisted in my ignorance of his situation, and finally they left me.

Although I had not seen Allen, I knew his place of security, and was well aware that if I told them the place where he had formerly hid himself, they would have no difficulty in making him a prisoner.

He came to my house in the night, and awoke me with the greatest caution, fearing that some of his enemies might be watching to take him at a time when, and in a place where it would be impossible for him to make his escape. I got up and assured him that he was then safe; but that his enemies would return early in the morning and search him out if it should be possible. Having given him some victuals, which he received thankfully, I told him to go, but to return the next night to a certain corner of the fence near my house where he would find a quantity of meal that I would have well prepared and deposited there for his use.

Early the next morning, Nettles and his company came in while I was pounding the meal for Allen, and insisted upon my giving him up. I again told them that I did not know where he was, and that I could not, neither would I, tell them any thing about him. I well knew that Allen considered his life in my hands; and although it was my intention not to lie, I was fully determined to keep his situation a profound secret. They continued their labor and examined (as they supposed) every crevice, gully, tree and hollow log in the neighboring woods, and at last concluded that he had left the country, and gave him up for lost, and went home.

At that time Allen lay in a secret place in the gulph a short distance above my flats, in a hole that he accidentally found in the rock near the river. At night he came and got the meal at the corner of the fence as I had directed him, and afterwards lived in the gulph two weeks. Each night he came to the pasture and milked one of my cows, without any other vessel in which to receive the milk than his hat, out of which he drank it. I supplied him with meal, but fearing to build a fire he was obliged to eat it raw and wash it down with the milk. Nettles having left our neighborhood, and Allen considering himself safe, left his little cave and came home. I gave him his box of money and trinkets, and he went to his own house at Mount Morris. It was generally considered by the Indians of our tribe, that Allen was an innocent man, and that the Niagara people were persecuting him without a just cause. Little Beard, then about to go to the eastward on public business, charged his Indians not to meddle with Allen, but to let him live amongst them peaceably, and enjoy himself with his family and property if he could. Having the protection of the chief, he felt himself safe, and let his situation be known to the whites from whom he suspected no harm. They, however, were more inimical than our Indians and were easily bribed by Nettles to assist in bringing him to justice. Nettles came on, and the whites, as they had agreed, gave poor Allen up to him. He was bound and carried to Niagara, where he was confined in prison through the winter. In the spring he was taken to Montreal or Quebec for trial, and was honorably acquitted. The crime for which he was tried was, for his having carried the wampum to the Americans, and thereby putting too sudden a stop to their war.

From the place of his trial he went directly to Philadelphia, and purchased on credit, a boat load of goods which he brought by water to Conhocton, where he left them and came to Mount Morris for assistance to get them brought on. The Indians readily went with horses and brought them to his house, where he disposed of his dry goods; but not daring to let the Indians begin to drink strong liquor, for fear of the quarrels which would naturally follow, he sent his spirits to my place and we sold them. For his goods he received ginseng roots, principally, and a few skins. Ginseng at that time was plenty, and commanded a high price. We prepared the whole that he received for the market, expecting that he would carry them to Philadelphia. In that I was disappointed; for when he had disposed of, and got pay for all his goods, he took the ginseng and skins to Niagara, and there sold them and came home.

Tired of dealing in goods, he planted a large field of corn on or near his own land, attended to it faithfully, and succeeded in raising a large crop, which he harvested, loaded into canoes and carried down the river to the mouth of Allen's Creek, then called by the Indians Gin-is-a-ga, where he unloaded it, built him a house, and lived with his family.

The next season he planted corn at that place and built a grist and saw mill on Genesee Falls, now called Rochester.

At the time Allen built the mills, he had an old German living with him by the name of Andrews, whom he sent in a canoe down the river with his mill irons. Allen went down at the same time; but before they got to the mills Allen threw the old man overboard and drowned him, as it was then generally believed, for he was never seen or heard of afterwards.

In the course of the season in which Allen built his mills, he became acquainted with the daughter of a white man, who was moving to Niagara. She was handsome, and Allen soon got into her good graces, so that he married and took her home, to be a joint partner with Sally, the squaw, whom she had never heard of till she got home and found her in full possession; but it was too late for her to retrace the hasty steps she had taken, for her father had left her in the care of a tender husband and gone on. She, however, found that she enjoyed at least an equal half of her husband's affections, and made herself contented. Her father's name I have forgotten, but her's was Lucy.

Allen was not contented with two wives, for in a short time after he had married Lucy he came up to my house, where he found a young woman who had an old husband with her. They had been on a long journey, and called at my place to recruit and rest themselves. She filled Allen's eye, and he accordingly fixed upon a plan to get her into his possession. He praised his situation, enumerated his advantages, and finally persuaded them to go home and tarry with him a few days at least, and partake of a part of his comforts. They accepted his generous invitation and went home with him. But they had been there but two or three days when Allen took the old gentleman out to view his flats; and as they were deliberately walking on the bank of the river, pushed him into the water. The old man, almost strangled, succeeded in getting out; but his fall and exertions had so powerful an effect upon his system that he died in two or three days, and left his young widow to the protection of his murderer. She lived with him about one year in a state of concubinage and then left him.

How long Allen lived at Allen's Creek I am unable to state; but soon after the young widow left him, he removed to his old place at Mount Morris, and built a house, where he made Sally, his squaw, by whom he had two daughters, a slave to Lucy, by whom he had had one son; still, however, he considered Sally to be his wife.

After Allen came to Mt. Morris at that time, he married a girl by the name of Morilla Gregory, whose father at the time lived on Genesee Flats. The ceremony being over, he took her home to live in common with his other wives; but his house was too small for his family; for Sally and Lucy, conceiving that their lawful privileges would be abridged if they received a partner, united their strength and whipped poor Morilla so cruelly that he was obliged to keep her in a small Indian house a short distance from his own, or lose her entirely. Morilla, before she left Mt. Morris, had four children.

One of Morilla's sisters lived with Allen about a year after Morilla was married, and then quit him.

A short time after they all got to living at Mt. Morris, Allen prevailed upon the Chiefs to give to his Indian children, a tract of land four miles square, where he then resided. The Chiefs gave them the land, but he so artfully contrived the conveyance, that he could apply it to his own use, and by alienating his right, destroy the claim of his children.

Having secured the land, in that way, to himself, he sent his two Indian girls to Trenton, (N.J.) and his white son to Philadelphia, for the purpose of giving each of them a respectable English education.

While his children were at school, he went to Philadelphia, and sold his right to the land which he had begged of the Indians for his children to Robert Morris. After that, he sent for his daughters to come home, which they did.

Having disposed of the whole of his property on the Genesee river, he took his two white wives and their children, together with his effects, and removed to a Delaware town on the river De Trench, in Upper Canada. When he left Mt. Morris, Sally, his squaw, insisted upon going with him, and actually followed him, crying bitterly, and praying for his protection some two or three miles, till he absolutely bade her leave him, or he would punish her with severity.

At length, finding her case hopeless, she returned to the Indians.

At the great treaty at Big Tree, one of Allen's daughters claimed the land which he had sold to Morris. The claim was examined and decided against her in favor of Ogden, Trumbull, Rogers and others, who were the creditors of Robert Morris. Allen yet believed that his daughter had an indisputable right to the land in question, and got me to go with mother Farly, a half Indian woman, to assist him by interceding with Morris for it, and to urge the propriety of her claim. We went to Thomas Morris, and having stated to him our business, he told us plainly that he had no land to give away, and that as the title was good, he never would allow Allen, nor his heirs, one foot, or words to that effect. We returned to Allen the answer we had received, and he, conceiving all further attempts to be useless, went home.

He died at the Delaware town, on the river De Trench, in the year 1814 or 15, and left two white widows and one squaw, with a number of children, to lament his loss.

By his last will he gave all his property to his last wife (Morilla,) and her children, without providing in the least for the support of Lucy, or any of the other members of his family. Lucy, soon after his death, went with her children down the Ohio river, to receive assistance from her friends.

In the revolutionary war, Allen was a tory, and by that means became acquainted with our Indians, when they were in the neighborhood of his native place, desolating the settlements on the Susquehannah. In those predatory battles, he joined them, and (as I have often heard the Indians say,) for cruelty was not exceeded by any of his Indian comrades!

At one time, when he was scouting with the Indians in the Susquehannah country, he entered a house very early in the morning, where he found a man, his wife, and one child, in bed. The man, as he entered the door, instantly sprang on the floor, for the purpose of defending himself and little family; but Allen dispatched him at one blow. He then cut off his head and threw it bleeding into the bed with the terrified woman; took the little infant from its mother's breast, and holding it by its legs, dashed its head against the jamb, and left the unhappy widow and mother to mourn alone over her murdered family. It has been said by some, that after he had killed the child, he opened the fire and buried it under the coals and embers: But of that I am not certain. I have often heard him speak of that transaction with a great degree of sorrow, and as the foulest crime he had ever committed—one for which I have no doubt he repented.

CHAPTER IX

Soon after the close of the revolutionary war, my Indian brother, Kaujises-tau-ge-au (which being interpreted signifies Black Coals,) offered me my liberty, and told me that if it was my choice I might go to my friends.

My son, Thomas, was anxious that I should go; and offered to go with me and assist me on the journey, by taking care of the younger children, and providing food as we travelled through the wilderness. But the Chiefs of our tribe, suspecting from his appearance, actions, and a few warlike exploits, that Thomas would be a great warrior, or a good counsellor, refused to let him leave them on any account whatever.

To go myself, and leave him, was more than I felt able to do; for he had been kind to me, and was one on whom I placed great dependence. The Chiefs refusing to let him go, was one reason for my resolving to stay; but another, more powerful, if possible, was, that I had got a large family of Indian children, that I must take with me; and that if I should be so fortunate as to find my relatives, they would despise them, if not myself; and treat us as enemies; or, at least with a degree of cold indifference, which I thought I could not endure.

Accordingly, after I had duly considered the matter, I told my brother that it was my choice to stay and spend the remainder of my days with my Indian friends, and live with my family as I had heretofore done. He appeared well pleased with my resolution, and informed me, that as that was my choice, I should have a piece of land that I could call my own, where I could live unmolested, and have something at my decease to leave for the benefit of my children.

In a short time he made himself ready to go to Upper Canada; but before he left us, he told me that he would speak to some of the Chiefs at Buffalo, to attend the great Council, which he expected would convene in a few years at farthest, and convey to me such a tract of land as I should select. My brother left us, as he had proposed, and soon after died at Grand River.

Kaujisestaugeau, was an excellent man, and ever treated me with kindness. Perhaps no one of his tribe at any time exceeded him in natural mildness of temper, and warmth and tenderness of affection. If he had taken my life at the time when the avarice of the old King inclined him to procure my emancipation, it would have been done with a pure heart and from good motives. He loved his friends; and was generally beloved. During the time that I lived in the family with him, he never offered the most trifling abuse; on the contrary, his whole conduct towards me was strictly honorable. I mourned his loss as that of a tender brother, and shall recollect him through life with emotions of friendship and gratitude.

I lived undisturbed, without hearing a word on the subject of my land, till the great Council was held at Big Tree, in 1797, when Farmer's Brother, whose Indian name is Ho-na-ye-wus, sent for me to attend the council. When I got there, he told me that my brother had spoken to him to see that I had a piece of land reserved for my use; and that then was the time for me to receive it.—He requested that I would choose for myself and describe the bounds of a piece that would suit me. I accordingly told him the place of beginning, and then went round a tract that I judged would be sufficient for my purpose, (knowing that it would include the Gardow Flats,) by stating certain bounds with which I was acquainted.

When the Council was opened, and the business afforded a proper opportunity, Farmer's Brother presented my claim, and rehearsed the request of my brother. Red Jacket, whose Indian name is Sagu-yu-what-hah, which interpreted, as Keeper-awake, opposed me or my claim with all his influence and eloquence. Farmer's Brother insisted upon the necessity, propriety and expediency of his proposition, and got the land granted. The deed was made and signed, securing to me the title to all the land I had described; under the same restrictions and regulations that other Indian lands are subject to.

That land has ever since been known by the name of the Gardow Tract.

Red Jacket not only opposed my claim at the Council, but he withheld my money two or three years, on the account of my lands having been granted without his consent. Parrish and Jones at length convinced him that it was the white people, and not the Indians who had given me the land, and compelled him to pay over all the money which he had retained on my account.

My land derived its name, Gardow, from a hill that is within its limits, which is called in the Seneca language Kau-tam. Kautam when interpreted signifies up and down, or down and up, and is applied to a hill that you will ascend and descend in passing it; or to a valley. It has been said that Gardow was the name of my husband Hiokatoo, and that my land derived its name from him; that however was a mistake, for the old man always considered Gardow a nickname, and was uniformly offended when called by it.

About three hundred acres of my land, when I first saw it, was open flats, lying on the Genesee River, which it is supposed was cleared by a race of inhabitants who preceded the first Indian settlements in this part of the country. The Indians are confident that many parts of this country were settled and for a number of years occupied by people of whom their fathers never had any tradition, as they never had seen them. Whence those people originated, and whither they went, I have never heard one of our oldest and wisest Indians pretend to guess. When I first came to Genishau, the bank of Fall Brook had just slid off and exposed a large number of human bones, which the Indians said were buried there long before their fathers ever saw the place; and that they did not know what kind of people they were. It however was and is believed by our people, that they were not Indians.

My flats were extremely fertile; but needed more labor than my daughters and myself were able to perform, to produce a sufficient quantity of grain and other necessary productions of the earth, for the consumption of our family. The land had lain uncultivated so long that it was thickly covered with weeds of almost every description. In order that we might live more easy, Mr. Parrish, with the consent of the chiefs, gave me liberty to lease or my land to white people to till on shares. I accordingly let it out, and have continued to do so, which makes my task less burthensome, while at the same time I am more comfortably supplied with the means of support.

CHAPTER X

I have frequently heard it asserted by white people, and can truly say from my own experience that the time at which parents take the most satisfaction and comfort with their families is when their children are young, incapable of providing for their own wants, and are about the fireside, where they can be daily observed and instructed.

Few mothers, perhaps, have had less trouble with their children during their minority than myself. In general, my children were friendly to each other, and it was very seldom that I knew them to have the least difference or quarrel: so far, indeed, were they from rendering themselves or me uncomfortable, that I considered myself happy—more so than commonly falls to the lot of parents, especially to women.

My happiness in this respect, however, was not without alloy; for my son Thomas, from some cause unknown to me, from the time he was a small lad, always called his brother John, a witch, which was the cause, as they grew towards manhood, of frequent and severe quarrels between them, and gave me much trouble and anxiety for their safety. After Thomas and John arrived to manhood, in addition to the former charge, John got two wives, with whom he lived till the time of his death. Although polygamy was tolerated in our tribe, Thomas considered it a violation of good and wholesome rules in society, and tending directly to destroy that friendly social intercourse and love, that ought to be the happy result of matrimony and chastity. Consequently, he frequently reprimanded John, by telling him that his conduct was beneath the dignity, and inconsistent with the principles of good Indians; indecent and unbecoming a gentleman; and, as he never could reconcile himself to it, he was frequently, almost constantly, when they were together, talking to him on the same subject. John always resented such reprimand, and reproof, with a great degree of passion, though they never quarrelled, unless Thomas was intoxicated.

In his fits of drunkenness, Thomas seemed to lose all his natural reason, and to conduct like a wild or crazy man, without regard to relatives, decency or propriety. At such times he often threatened to take my life for having raised a witch, (as he called John,) and has gone so far as to raise his tomahawk to split my head. He, however, never struck me; but on John's account he struck Hiokatoo, and thereby excited in John a high degree of indignation, which was extinguished only by blood.

For a number of years their difficulties, and consequent unhappiness, continued and rather increased, continually exciting in my breast the most fearful apprehensions, and greatest anxiety for their safety. With tears in my eyes, I advised them to become reconciled to each other, and to be friendly; told them the consequences of their continuing to cherish so much malignity and malice, that it would end in their destruction, the disgrace of their families, and bring me down to the grave. No one can conceive of the constant trouble that I daily endured on their account—on the account of my two oldest sons, whom I loved equally, and with all the feelings and affection of a tender mother, stimulated by an anxious concern for their fate. Parents, mothers especially, will love their children, though ever so unkind and disobedient. Their eyes of compassion, of real sentimental affection, will be involuntarily extended after them, in their greatest excesses of iniquity; and those fine filaments of consanguinity, which gently entwine themselves around the heart where filial love and parental care is equal, will be lengthened, and enlarged to cords seemingly of sufficient strength to reach and reclaim the wanderer. I know that such exercises are frequently unavailing; but, notwithstanding their ultimate failure, it still remains true, and ever will, that the love of a parent for a disobedient child, will increase, and grow more and more ardent, so long as a hope of its reformation is capable of stimulating a disappointed breast.

My advice and expostulations with my sons were abortive; and year after year their disaffection for each other increased. At length, Thomas came to my house on the 1st day of July, 1811, in my absence, somewhat intoxicated, where he found John, with whom he immediately commenced a quarrel on their old subjects of difference.—John's anger became desperate. He caught Thomas by the hair of his head, dragged him out at the door and there killed him, by a blow which he gave him on the head with his tomahawk!

I returned soon after, and found my son lifeless at the door, on the spot where he was killed! No one can judge of my feelings on seeing this mournful spectacle; and what greatly added to my distress, was the fact that he had fallen by the murderous hand of his brother! I felt my situation unsupportable. Having passed through various scenes of trouble of the most cruel and trying kind, I had hoped to spend my few remaining days in quietude, and to die in peace, surrounded by my family. This fatal event, however, seemed to be a stream of woe poured into my cup of afflictions, filling it even to overflowing, and blasting all my prospects.

As soon as I had recovered a little from the shock which I felt at the sight of my departed son, and some of my neighbors had come in to assist in taking care of the corpse, I hired Shanks, an Indian, to go to Buffalo, and carry the sorrowful news of Thomas' death, to our friends at that place, and request the Chiefs to hold a Council, and dispose of John as they should think proper. Shanks set out on his errand immediately,—and John, fearing that he should be apprehended and punished for the crime he had committed, at the same time went off towards Caneadea.

Thomas was decently interred in a style corresponding with his rank.

The Chiefs soon assembled in council on the trial of John, and after having seriously examined the matter according to their laws, justified his conduct, and acquitted him. They considered Thomas to have been the first transgressor, and that for the abuses which he had offered, he had merited from John the treatment that he had received.

John, on learning the decision of the council, returned to his family.

Thomas (except when intoxicated, which was not frequent,) was a kind and tender child, willing to assist me in my labor, and to remove every obstacle to my comfort. His natural abilities were said to be of a superior cast, and he soared above the trifling subjects of revenge, which are common amongst Indians, as being far beneath his attention. In his childish and boyish days, his natural turn was to practise in the art of war, though he despised the cruelties that the warriors inflicted upon their subjugated enemies. He was manly in his deportment, courageous and, active; and commanded respect. Though he appeared well pleased with peace, he was cunning in Indian warfare, and succeeded to admiration in the execution of his plans.

At the age of fourteen or fifteen years, he went into the war with manly fortitude, armed with a tomahawk and scalping knife; and when he returned, brought one white man a prisoner, whom he had taken with his own hands, on the west branch of the Susquehannah river. It so happened, that as he was looking out for his enemies, he discovered two men boiling sap in the woods. He watched them unperceived, till dark when he advanced with a noiseless step to where they were standing, caught one of them before they were apprized of danger, and conducted him to the camp. He was well treated while a prisoner, and redeemed at the close of the war.

At the time Kaujisestaugeau gave me my liberty to go to my friends, Thomas was anxious to go with me; but as I have before observed, the Chiefs would not suffer him to leave them on the account of his courage and skill in war: expecting that they should need his assistance. He was a great Counsellor and a Chief when quite young; and in the last capacity, went two or three times to Philadelphia to assist in making treaties with the people of the states.

Thomas had four wives, by whom he had eight children. Jacob Jemison, his second son by his last wife, who is at this time twenty-seven or twenty-eight years of age, went to Dartmouth college, in the spring of 1816, for the purpose of receiving a good education, where it was said that he was an industrious scholar, and made great proficiency in the study of the different branches to which he attended. Having spent two years at that Institution, he returned in the winter of 1818, and is now at Buffalo; where I have understood that he contemplates commencing the study of medicine, as a profession.

Thomas, at the time he was killed, was a few moons over fifty-two years old, and John was forty-eight. As he was naturally good natured, and possessed a friendly disposition, he would not have come to so untimely an end, had it not been far his intemperance. He fell a victim to the use of ardent spirits—a poison that will soon exterminate the Indian tribes in this part of the country, and leave their names without a root or branch. The thought is melancholy; but no arguments, no examples, however persuasive or impressive, are sufficient to deter an Indian for an hour from taking the potent draught, which he knows at the time will derange his faculties, reduce him to a level with the beasts, or deprive him of life!

CHAPTER XI

In the month of November 1811, my husband Hiokatoo, who had been sick four years of the consumption, died at the advanced age of one hundred and three years, as nearly as the time could be estimated. He was the last that remained to me of our family connection, or rather of my old friends with whom I was adopted, except a part of one family, which now lives at Tonewanta.

Hiokatoo was buried decently, and had all the insignia of a veteran warrior buried with him; consisting of a war club, tomahawk and scalping knife, a powder-flask, flint, a piece of spunk, a small cake and a cup; and in his best clothing.

Hiokatoo was an old man when I first saw him; but he was by no means enervated. During the term of nearly fifty years that I lived with him, I received, according to Indian customs, all the kindness and attention that was my due as his wife.—Although war was his trade from his youth till old age and decrepitude stopt his career, he uniformly treated me with tenderness, and never offered an insult.

I have frequently heard him repeat the history of his life from his childhood; and when he came to that part which related to his actions, his bravery and his valor in war; when he spoke of the ambush, the combat, the spoiling of his enemies and the sacrifice of the victims, his nerves seemed strung with youthful ardor, the warmth of the able warrior seemed to animate his frame, and to produce the heated gestures which he had practised in middle age. He was a man of tender feelings to his friends, ready and willing to assist them in distress, yet, as a warrior, his cruelties to his enemies perhaps were unparalleled, and will not admit a word of palliation.

Hiokatoo, was born in one of the tribes of the Six Nations that inhabited the banks of the Susquehannah; or, rather he belonged to a tribe of the Senecas that made, at the time of the great Indian treaty, a part of those nations. He was own cousin to Farmer's Brother, a Chief who has been justly celebrated for his worth. Their mothers were sisters, and it was through the influence of Farmer's Brother, that I became Hiokatoo's wife.

In early life, Hiokatoo showed signs of thirst for blood, by attending only to the art of war, in the use of the tomahawk and scalping knife; and in practising cruelties upon every thing that chanced to fall into his hands, which was susceptible of pain. In that way he learned to use his implements of war effectually, and at the same time blunted all those fine feelings and tender sympathies that are naturally excited, by hearing or seeing, a fellow being in distress. He could inflict the most excruciating tortures upon his enemies, and prided himself upon his fortitude, in having performed the most barbarous ceremonies and tortures, without the least degree of pity or remorse. Thus qualified, when very young he was initiated into scenes of carnage, by being engaged in the wars that prevailed amongst the Indian tribes.

In the year 1731, he was appointed a runner, to assist in collecting an army to go against the Cotawpes, Cherokees and other southern Indians. A large army was collected, and after a long and fatiguing march, met its enemies in what was then called the "low, dark and bloody lands," near the mouth of Red River, in what is now called the state of Kentucky. [Footnote: Those powerful armies met near the place that is now called Clarksville, which is situated at the fork where Red River joins the Cumberland, a few miles above the line between Kentucky and Tennessee.] The Cotawpes [Footnote: The Author acknowledges himself unacquainted, from Indian history, with a nation of this name; but as 90 years have elapsed since the date of this occurrence, it is highly probable that such a nation did exist, and that it was absolutely exterminated at that eventful period.] and their associates, had, by some means, been apprized of their approach, and lay in ambush to take them at once, when they should come within their reach, and destroy the whole army. The northern Indians, with their usual sagacity, discovered the situation of their enemies, rushed upon the ambuscade and massacred 1200 on the spot. The battle continued for two days and two nights, with the utmost severity, in which the northern Indians were victorious, and so far succeeded in destroying the Cotawpes that they at that time ceased to be a nation. The victors suffered an immense loss in killed; but gained the hunting ground, which was their grand object, though the Cherokees would not give it up in a treaty, or consent to make peace. Bows and arrows, at that time were in general use, though a few guns were employed.

From that time he was engaged in a number of battles in which Indians only were engaged, and that made fighting his business, till the commencement of the French war. In those battles he took a number of Indians prisoners, whom he killed by tying them to trees and then setting small Indian boys to shooting at them with arrows, till death finished the misery of the sufferers; a process that frequently took two days for its completion!

During the French war he was in every battle that was fought on the Susquehannah and Ohio rivers; and was so fortunate as never to have been taken prisoner.

At Braddock's defeat he took two white prisoners, and burnt them alive in a fire of his own kindling.

In 1777, he was in the battle at Fort Freeland, in Northumberland county, Penn. The fort contained a great number of women and children, and was defended only by a small garrison. The force that went against it consisted of 100 British regulars, commanded by a Col. McDonald, and 300 Indians under Hiokatoo. After a short but bloody engagement, the fort was surrendered; the women and children were sent under an escort to the next fort below, and the men and boys taken off by a party of British to the general Indian encampment. As soon as the fort had capitulated and the firing had ceased, Hiokatoo with the help of a few Indians tomahawked every wounded American while earnestly begging with uplifted hands for quarters.

The massacre was but just finished when Capts. Dougherty and Boon arrived with a reinforcement to assist the garrison. On their arriving in sight of the fort they saw that it had surrendered, and that an Indian was holding the flag. This so much inflamed Capt. Dougherty that he left his command, stept forward and shot the Indian at the first fire. Another took the flag, and had no sooner got it erected than Dougherty dropt him as he had the first. A third presumed to hold it, who was also shot down by Dougherty. Hiokatoo, exasperated at the sight of such bravery, sallied out with a party of his Indians, and killed Capts. Dougherty, Boon, and fourteen men, at the first fire. The remainder of the two companies escaped by taking to flight, and soon arrived at the fort which they had left but a few hours before.

In an expedition that went out against Cherry Valley and the neighboring settlements, Captain David, a Mohawk Indian, was first, and Hiokatoo the second in command. The force consisted of several hundred Indians, who were determined on mischief, and the destruction of the whites. A continued series of wantonness and barbarity characterized their career, for they plundered and burnt every thing that came in their way, and killed a number of persons, among whom were several infants, whom Hiokatoo butchered or dashed upon the stones with his own hands. Besides the instances which have been mentioned, he was in a number of parties during the revolutionary war, where he ever acted a conspicuous part.

The Indians having removed the seat of their depredations and war to the frontiers of Pennsylvania, Ohio, Kentucky and the neighboring territories, assembled a large force at Upper Sandusky, their place of general rendezvous, from whence they went out to the various places which they designed to sacrifice.

Tired of the desolating scenes that were so often witnessed, and feeling a confidence that the savages might be subdued, and an end put to their crimes, the American government raised a regiment, consisting of 300 volunteers, for the purpose of dislodging them from their cantonment and preventing further barbarities. Col. William Crawford and Lieut. Col. David Williamson, men who had been thoroughly tried and approved, were commissioned by Gen. Washington to take the command of a service that seemed all-important to the welfare of the country. In the month of July, 1782, well-armed and provided with a sufficient quantity of provision, this regiment made an expeditious march through the wilderness to Upper Sandusky, where, as had been anticipated, they found the Indians assembled in full force at their encampment, prepared to receive an attack.

As Col. Crawford and his brave band advanced, and when they had got within a short distance from the town, they were met by a white man, with a flag of truce from the Indians, who proposed to Col. Crawford that if he would surrender himself and his men to the Indians, their lives should be spared; but, that if they persisted in their undertaking, and attacked the town, they should all be massacred to a man.

Crawford, while hearing the proposition, attentively surveyed its bearer, and recognized in his features one of his former schoolmates and companions, with whom he was perfectly acquainted, by the name of Simon Gurty. Gurty, but a short time before this, had been a soldier in the American army, in the same regiment with Crawford; but on the account of his not having received the promotion that he expected, he became disaffected—swore an eternal war with his countrymen, fled to the Indians, and joined them, as a leader well qualified to conduct them to where they could satiate their thirst for blood, upon the innocent, unoffending and defenceless settlers.

Crawford sternly inquired of the traitor if his name was not Simon Gurty; and being answered in the affirmative, he informed him that he despised the offer which he had made; and that he would not surrender his army unless he should be compelled to do so, by a superior force.

Gurty returned, and Crawford immediately commenced an engagement that lasted till night, without the appearance of victory on either side, when the firing ceased, and the combatants on both sides retired to take refreshment, and to rest through the night. Crawford encamped in the woods near half a mile from the town, where, after the centinels were placed, and each had taken his ration, they slept on their arms, that they might be instantly ready in case they should be attacked. The stillness of death hovered over the little army, and sleep relieved the whole, except the wakeful centinels who vigilantly attended to their duty.—But what was their surprise, when they found late in the night, that they were surrounded by the Indians on every side, except a narrow space between them and the town? Every man was under arms, and the officers instantly consulted each other on the best method of escaping; for they saw that to fight, would be useless, and that to surrender, would be death.

Crawford proposed a retreat through the ranks of the enemy in an opposite direction from the town, as being the most sure course to take. Lt. Col. Williamson advised to march directly through the town, where there appeared to be no Indians, and the fires were yet burning.

There was no time or place for debates: Col. Crawford, with sixty followers retreated on the route that he had proposed by attempting to rush through the enemy; but they had no sooner got amongst the Indians, than every man was killed or taken prisoner! Amongst the prisoners, were Col. Crawford, and Doct. Night, surgeon of the regiment.

Lt. Col. Williamson, with the remainder of the regiment, together with the wounded, set out at the same time that Crawford did, went through the town without losing a man, and by the help of good guides arrived at their homes in safety.

The next day after the engagement the Indians disposed of all their prisoners to the different tribes, except Col. Crawford and Doct. Night; but those unfortunate men were reserved for a more cruel destiny. A council was immediately held on Sandusky plains, consisting of all the Chiefs and warriors, ranged in their customary order, in a circular form; and Crawford and Night were brought forward and seated in the centre of the circle.

The council being opened, the Chiefs began to examine Crawford on various subjects relative to the war. At length they enquired who conducted the military operations of the American army on the Ohio and Susquehannah rivers, during the year before; and who had led that army against them with so much skill and so uniform success? Crawford very honestly and without suspecting any harm from his reply promptly answered that he was the man who had led his countrymen to victory, who had driven the enemy from the settlements, and by that means had procured a great degree of happiness to many of his fellow-citizens. Upon hearing this, a Chief, who had lost a son in the year before, in a battle where Colonel Crawford commanded, left his station in the council, stepped to Crawford, blacked his face, and at the same time told him that the next day he should be burnt.

The council was immediately dissolved on its hearing the sentence from the Chief, and the prisoners were taken off the ground, and kept in custody through the night. Crawford now viewed his fate as sealed; and despairing of ever returning to his home or his country, only dreaded the tediousness of death, as commonly inflicted by the savages, and earnestly hoped that he might be despatched at a single blow.

Early the next morning, the Indians assembled at the place of execution, and Crawford was led to the post—the goal of savage torture, to which he was fastened. The post was a stick of timber placed firmly in the ground, having an arm framed in at the top, and extending some six or eight feet from it, like the arm of a sign post. A pile of wood containing about two cords, lay a few feet from the place where he stood, which he was informed was to be kindled into a fire that would burn him alive, as many had been burnt on the same spot, who had been much less deserving than himself.

Gurty stood and supposedly looked on the preparations that were making for the funeral of one his former playmates; a hero by whose side he had fought; of a man whose valor had won laurels which, if he could have returned, would have been strewed upon his grave, by his grateful countrymen. Dreading the agony that he saw he was about to feel, Crawford used every argument which his perilous situation could suggest to prevail upon Gurty to ransom him at any price, and deliver him (as it was in his power,) from the savages, and their torments. Gurty heard his prayers, and expostulations, and saw his tears with indifference, and finally told the forsaken victim that he would not procure him a moment's respite, nor afford him the most trifling assistance.

The Col. was then bound, stripped naked and tied by his wrists to the arm, which extended horizontally from the post, in such a manner that his arms were extended over his head, with his feet just standing upon the ground. This being done, the savages placed the wood in a circle around him at the distance of a few feet, in order that his misery might be protracted to the greatest length, and then kindled it in a number of places at the same time. The flames arose and the scorching heat became almost insupportable. Again he prayed to Gurty in all the anguish of his torment, to rescue him from the fire, or shoot him dead upon the spot. A demoniac smile suffused the countenance of Gurty, while he calmly replied to the dying suppliant, that he had no pity for his sufferings; but that he was then satisfying that spirit of revenge, which for a long time he had hoped to have an opportunity to wreak upon him. Nature now almost exhausted from the intensity of the heat, he settled down a little, when a squaw threw coals of fire and embers upon him, which made him groan most piteously, while the whole camp rung with exultation. During the execution they manifested all the exstacy of a complete triumph. Poor Crawford soon died and was entirely consumed.

Thus ended the life of a patriot and hero, who had been an intimate with Gen. Washington, and who shared in an eminent degree the confidence of that great, good man, to whom, in the time of revolutionary perils, the sons of legitimate freedom looked with a degree of faith in his mental resources, unequalled in the history of the world.

That tragedy being ended, Doct. Night was informed that on the next day he should be burnt in the same manner that his comrade Crawford had been, at Lower Sandusky. Hiokatoo, who out had been a leading chief in the battle with, and in the execution of Crawford, painted Doct. Night's face black, and then bound and gave him up to two able bodied Indians to conduct to the place of execution.

They set off with him immediately, and travelled till towards evening, when they halted to encamp till morning. The afternoon had been very rainy, and the storm still continued, which rendered it very difficult for the Indians to kindle a fire. Night observing the difficulty under which they labored, made them to understand by signs, that if they would unbind him, he would assist them.—They, accordingly unbound him, and he soon succeeded in making a fire by the application of small dry stuff which he was at considerable trouble to procure. While the Indians were warming themselves, the Doct. continued to gather wood to last through the night, and in doing this, he found a club which he placed in a situation from whence he could take it conveniently whenever an opportunity should present itself in which he could use it effectually. The Indians continued warming, till at length the Doct. saw that they had placed themselves in a favorable position for the execution of his design, when, stimulated by the love of life, he cautiously took his club and at two blows knocked them both down. Determined to finish the work of death which he had so well begun, he drew one of their scalping knives, with which he beheaded and scalped them both! He then took a rifle, tomahawk, and some ammunition, and directed his course for home, where he arrived without having experienced any difficulty on his journey.

The next morning, the Indians took the track of their victim and his attendants, to go to Lower Sandusky, and there execute the sentence which they had pronounced upon him. But what was their surprise and disappointment, when they arrived at the place of encampment, where they found their trusty friends scalped and decapitated, and that their prisoner had made his escape?—Chagrined beyond measure, they immediately separated, and went in every direction in pursuit of their prey; but after having spent a number of days unsuccessfully, they gave up the chase, and returned to their encampment. [Footnote: I have understood, (from unauthenticated sources however,) that soon after the revolutionary war, Doct. Night published a pamphlet, containing an account of the battle at Sandusky, and of his own sufferings. My information on this subject, was derived from a different quarter.

The subject of this narrative in giving the account of her last husband, Hiokatoo, referred us to Mr. George Jemison, who, (as it will be noticed) lived on her land a number of years, and who had frequently heard the old Chief relate the story of his life; particularly that part which related to his military career. Mr. Jemison; on being enquired of, gave the foregoing account, partly from his own personal knowledge, and the remainder, from the account given by Hiokatoo.

Mr. Jemison was in the battle, was personally acquainted with Col. Crawford, and one that escaped with Lt. Col. Williamson. We have no doubt of the truth of the statement, and have therefore inserted the whole account, as an addition to the historical facts which are daily coming into a state of preservation, in relation to the American Revolution.

AUTHOR.]

In the time of the French war, in an engagement that took place on the Ohio river, Hiokatoo took a British Col. by the name of Simon Canton, whom he carried to the Indian encampment. A council was held, and the Col. was sentenced to suffer death, by being tied on a wild colt, with his face towards its tail, and then having the colt turned loose to run where it pleased. He was accordingly tied on, and the colt let loose, agreeable to the sentence. The colt run two days, and then returned with its rider yet alive. The Indians, thinking that he would never die in that way, took him off, and made him run the gauntlet three times; but in the last race a squaw knocked him down, and he was supposed to have been dead. He, however, recovered, and was sold for fifty dollars to a Frenchman, who sent him as a prisoner to Detroit. On the return of the Frenchman to Detroit, the Col. besought him to ransom him, and give, or set him at liberty, with so much warmth, and promised with so much solemnity, to reward him as one of the best of benefactors, if he would let him go, that the Frenchman took his word, and sent him home to his family. The Col. remembered his promise, and in a short time sent his deliverer one hundred and fifty dollars, as a reward for his generosity.

Since the commencement of the revolutionary war, Hiokatoo has been in seventeen campaigns, four of which were in the Cherokee war. He was so great an enemy to the Cherokees, and so fully determined upon their subjugation, that on his march to their country, he raised his own army for those four campaigns, and commanded it; and also superintended its subsistence. In one of those campaigns, which continued two whole years without intermission, he attacked his enemies on the Mobile, drove them to the country of the Creek Nation, where he continued to harrass them, till being tired of war, he returned to his family. He brought home a great number of scalps, which he had taken from the enemy, and ever seemed to possess an unconquerable will that the Cherokees might be utterly destroyed. Towards the close of his last fighting in that country, he took two squaws, whom he sold on his way home for money to defray the expense of his journey.

Hiokatoo was about six feet four or five inches high, large boned, and rather inclined to leanness. He was very stout and active, for a man of his size, for it was said by himself and others, that he had never found an Indian who could keep up with him on a race, or throw him at wrestling. His eye was quick and penetrating; and his voice was of that harsh and powerful kind, which, amongst, Indians, always commands attention. His health had been uniformly good. He never was confined by sickness, till he was attacked with the consumption, four years before his death. And, although he had, from his earliest days, been inured to almost constant fatigue, and exposure to every inclemency of the weather, in the open air he seemed to lose the vigor of the prime of life only by the natural decay occasioned by old age.

CHAPTER XII

Being now left a widow in my old age, to mourn the loss of a husband, who had treated me well and with whom I had raised five children, and having suffered the loss of an affectionate son, I fondly fostered the hope that my melancholy vicissitudes had ended, and that the remainder of my time would be characterized by nothing unpropitious. My children, dutiful and kind, lived near me, and apparently nothing obstructed our happiness.

But a short time, however, elapsed after my husband's death, before my troubles were renewed with redoubled severity.

John's hands having been once stained in the blood of a brother, it was not strange that after his acquital, every person of his acquaintance should shun him, from a fear of his repeating upon them the same ceremony that he had practised upon Thomas. My son Jesse, went to Mt. Morris, a few miles from home, on business, in the winter after the death of his father; and it so happened that his brother John was there, who requested Jesse to come home with him. Jesse, fearing that John would commence a quarrel with him on the way, declined the invitation, and tarried over night.

From that time John conceived himself despised by Jesse, and was highly enraged at the treatment which he had received. Very little was said, however, and it all passed off, apparently, till sometime in the month of May, 1812, at which time Mr. Robert Whaley, who lived in the town of Castile, within four miles of me, came to my house early on Monday morning, to hire George Chongo, my son-in-law, and John and Jesse, to go that day and help him slide a quantity of boards from the top of the hill to the river, where he calculated to build a raft of them for market.

They all concluded to go with Mr. Whaley, and made ready as soon as possible. But before they set out I charged them not to drink any whiskey; for I was confident that if they did, they would surely have a quarrel in consequence of it. They went and worked till almost night, when a quarrel ensued between Chongo and Jesse, in consequence of the whiskey that they had drank through the day, which terminated in a battle, and Chongo got whipped.

When Jesse had got through with Chongo, he told Mr. Whaley that he would go home, and directly went off. He, however, went but a few rods before he stopped and lay down by the side of a log to wait, (as was supposed,) for company. John, as soon as Jesse was gone, went to Mr. Whaley with his knife in his hand and bade him jogo (i. e. be gone,) at the same time telling him that Jesse was a bad man. Mr. Whaley, seeing that his countenance was changed, and that he was determined upon something desperate, was alarmed for his own safety, and turned towards home, leaving Chongo on the ground drunk, near to where Jesse had lain, who by this time had got up, and was advancing towards John. Mr. Whaley was soon out of hearing of them; but some of his workmen staid till it was dark. Jesse came up to John, and said to him, you want more whiskey, and more fighting, and after a few words went at him, to try in the first place to get away his knife. In this he did not succeed, and they parted. By this time the night had come on, and it was dark. Again they clenched and at length in their struggle they both fell. John, having his knife in his hand, came under, and in that situation gave Jesse a fatal stab with his knife, and repeated the blows till Jesse cried out, brother, you have killed me, quit his hold and settled back upon the ground. Upon hearing this, John left him and came to Thomas' widow's house, told them that he had been fighting with their uncle, whom he had killed, and showed them his knife.

Next morning as soon as it was light, Thomas' and John's children came and told me that Jesse was dead in the woods, and also informed me how he came by his death. John soon followed them and informed me himself of all that had taken place between him and his brother, and seemed to be somewhat sorrowful for his conduct. You can better imagine what my feelings were than I can describe them. My darling son, my youngest child, him on whom I depended, was dead; and I in my old age left destitute of a helping hand!

As soon as it was consistent for me, I got Mr. George Jemison, (of whom I shall have occasion to speak,) to go with his sleigh to where Jesse was, and bring him home, a distance of 3 or 4 miles. My daughter Polly arrived at the fatal spot first: we got there soon after her; though I went the whole distance on foot. By this time, Chongo, (who was left on the ground drunk the night before,) had become sober and sensible of the great misfortune which had happened to our family.

I was overcome with grief at the sight of my murdered son, and so far lost the command of myself as to be almost frantic; and those who were present were obliged to hold me from going near him.

On examining the body it was found that it had received eighteen wounds so deep and large that it was believed that either of them would have proved mortal. The corpse was carried to my house, and kept till the

Thursday following, when it was buried after the manner of burying white people.

Jesse was twenty-seven or eight years old when he was killed. His temper had been uniformly very mild and friendly; and he was inclined to copy after the white people; both in his manners and dress. Although he was naturally temperate, he occasionally became intoxicated; but never was quarrelsome or mischievous. With the white people he was intimate, and learned from them their habits of industry, which he was fond of practising, especially when my comfort demanded his labor. As I have observed, it is the custom amongst the Indians, for the women to perform all the labor in, and out of doors, and I had the whole to do, with the help of my daughters, till Jesse arrived to a sufficient age to assist us. He was disposed to labor in the cornfield, to chop my wood, milk my cows, and attend to any kind of business that would make my task the lighter. On the account of his having been my youngest child, and so willing to help me, I am sensible that I loved him better than I did either of my other children. After he began to understand my situation, and the means of rendering it more easy, I never wanted for anything that was in his power to bestow; but since his death, as I have had all my labor to perform alone, I have constantly seen hard times.

Jesse shunned the company of his brothers, and the Indians generally; and never attended their frolics; and it was supposed that this, together with my partiality for him, were the causes which excited in John so great a degree of envy, that nothing short of death would satisfy it.

CHAPTER XIII

A year or two before the death of my husband, Capt. H. Jones sent me word that a cousin of mine was then living in Leicester, (a few miles from Gardow,) by the name of George Jemison, and as he was very poor, thought it advisable for me to go and see him, and take him home to live with me on my land. My Indian friends were pleased to hear that one of my relatives was so near, and also advised me to send for him and his family immediately. I accordingly had him and his family moved into one of my houses, in the month of March, 1810.

He said that he was my father's brother's son—that his father did not leave Europe, till after the French war in America, and that when he did come over, he settled in Pennsylvania, where he died. George had no personal knowledge of my father; but from information, was confident that the relationship which he claimed between himself and me, actually existed. Although I had never before heard of my father having had but one brother, (him who was killed at Fort Necessity,) yet I knew that he might have had others, and, as the story of George carried with it a probability that it was true, I received him as a kinsman, and treated him with every degree of friendship which his situation demanded. [Footnote: Mrs. Jemison is now confident that George Jemison is not her cousin, and thinks that he claimed the relationship, only to gain assistance: But the old gentleman, who is now living, is certain that his and her father were brothers, as before stated.]

I found that he was destitute of the means of subsistence, and in debt to the amount of seventy dollars, without the ability to pay one cent. He had no cow, and finally, was completely poor, I paid his debts to the amount of seventy-two dollars, and bought him a cow, for which I paid twenty dollars, and a sow and pigs, that I paid eight dollars for. I also paid sixteen dollars for pork that I gave him, and furnished him with other provisions and furniture; so that his family was comfortable. As he was destitute of a team, I furnished him with one, and also supplied him with tools for farming. In addition to all this, I let him have one of Thomas' cows, for two seasons.

My only object in mentioning his poverty, and the articles with which I supplied him, is to show how ungrateful a person can be for favors, and how soon a kind benefactor will, to all appearance, be forgotten.

Thus furnished with the necessary implements of husbandry, a good team, and as much land as he could till, he commenced farming on my flats, and for some time labored well. At length, however, he got an idea that if he could become the owner of a part of my reservation, he could live more easy, and certainly be more rich, and accordingly set himself about laying a plan to obtain it, in the easiest manner possible.

I supported Jemison and his family eight years, and probably should have continued to have done so to this day, had it not been for the occurrence of the following circumstance.

When he had lived with me some six or seven years, a friend of mine told me that as Jemison was my cousin, and very poor, I ought to give him a piece of land that he might have something whereon to live, that he would call his own. My friend and Jemison were then together at my house, prepared to complete a bargain. I asked how much land he wanted? Jemison said that he should be glad to receive his old field (as he called it) containing about fourteen acres, and a new one that contained twenty-six.

I observed to them that as I was incapable of transacting business of that nature, I would wait till Mr. Thomas Clute, (a neighbor on whom I depended,) should return from Albany, before I should do any thing about it. To this Jemison replied that if I waited till Mr. Clute returned, he should not get the land at all, and appeared very anxious to have the business closed without delay. On my part, I felt disposed to give him some land, but knowing my ignorance of writing, feared to do it alone, lest they might include as much land they pleased, without my knowledge.

They then read the deed which my friend had prepared before he came from home, describing a piece of land by certain bounds that were a specified number of chains and links from each other. Not understanding the length of a chain or link, I described the bounds of a piece of land that I intended Jemison should have, which they said was just the same that the deed contained and no more. I told them that the deed must not include a lot that was called the Steele place, and they assured me that it did not. Upon this, putting confidence in them both, I signed the deed to George Jemison, containing, and conveying to him as I supposed, forty acres of land. The deed being completed they charged me never to mention the bargain which I had then made to any person; because if I did, they said it would spoil the contract. The whole matter was afterwards disclosed; when it was found that that deed instead of containing only forty acres, contained four hundred, and that one half of it actually belonged to my friend, as it had been given to him by Jemison as a reward for his trouble in procuring the deed, in the fraudulent manner above mentioned.

My friend, however, by the advice of some well disposed people, awhile afterwards gave up his claim; but Jemison held his till he sold it for a trifle to a gentleman in the south part of Genesee county.

Sometime after the death of my son Thomas, one of his sons went to Jemison to get the cow that I had let him have two years; but Jemison refused to let her go, and struck the boy so violent a blow as to almost kill him. Jemison then run to Jellis Clute, Esq. to procure a warrant to take the boy; but Young King, an Indian Chief, went down to Squawky hill to Esq. Clute's, and settled the affair by Jemison's agreeing never to use that club again. Having satisfactorily found out the friendly disposition of my cousin towards me, I got him off my premises as soon as possible.

CHAPTER XIV

Trouble seldom comes single. While George Jemison was busily engaged in his pursuit of wealth at my expence, another event of a much more serious nature occurred, which added greatly to my afflictions, and consequently destroyed, at least a part of the happiness that I had anticipated was laid up in the archives of Providence, to be dispensed on my old age.

My son John, was a doctor, considerably celebrated amongst the Indians of various tribes, for his skill in curing their diseases, by the administration of roots and herbs, which he gathered in the forests, and other places where they had been planted by the hand of nature.

In the month of April, or first of May, 1817, he was called upon to go to Buffalo, Cattaraugus and Allegany, to cure some who were sick. He went, and was absent about two months. When he returned, he observed the Great Slide of the bank of Genesee river, a short distance above my house, which had taken place during his absence; and conceiving that circumstance to be ominous of his own death, called at his sister Nancy's, told her that he should live but a few days, and wept bitterly at the near approach of his dissolution. Nancy endeavored to persuade him that his trouble was imaginary, and that he ought not to be affected by a fancy which was visionary. Her arguments were ineffectual, and afforded no alleviation to his mental sufferings. From his sister's, he went to his own house, where he stayed only two nights, and then went to Squawky Hill to procure money, with which to purchase flour for the use of his family.

While at Squawky Hill he got into the company of two Squawky Hill Indians, whose names were Doctor and Jack, with whom he drank freely, and in the afternoon had a desperate quarrel, in which his opponents, (as it was afterwards understood,) agreed to kill him. The quarrel ended, and each appeared to be friendly. John bought some spirits, of which they all drank, and then set out for home. John and an Allegany Indian were on horseback, and Doctor and Jack were on foot. It was dark when they set out. They had not proceeded far, when Doctor and Jack commenced another quarrel with John, clenched and dragged him off his horse, and then with a stone gave him so severe a blow on his head, that some of his brains were discharged from the wound. The Allegany Indian, fearing that his turn would come next, fled for safety as fast as possible.

John recovered a little from the shock he had received, and endeavored to get to an old hut that stood near; but they caught him, and with an axe cut his throat, and beat out his brains, so that when he was found the contents of his skull were lying on his arms.

Some squaws, who heard the uproar, ran to find out the cause of it; but before they had time to offer their assistance, the murderers drove them into a house, and threatened to take their lives if they did not stay there, or if they made any noise.

Next morning, Esq. Clute sent me word that John was dead, and also informed me of the means by which his life was taken. A number of people went from Gardow to where the body lay, and Doct. Levi Brundridge brought it up home, where the funeral was attended after the manner of the white people. Mr. Benjamin Luther, and Mr. William Wiles, preached a sermon, and performed the funeral services; and myself and family followed the corpse to the grave as mourners. I had now buried my three sons, who had been snatched from me by the hands of violence, when I least expected it.

Although John had taken the life of his two brothers, and caused me unspeakable trouble and grief, his death made a solemn impression upon my mind, and seemed, in addition to my former misfortunes, enough to bring down my grey hairs with sorrow to the grave. Yet, on a second thought, I could not mourn for him as I had for my other sons, because I knew that his death was just, and what he had deserved for a long time, from the hand of justice.

John's vices were so great and so aggravated, that I have nothing to say in his favor: yet, as a mother, I pitied him while he lived, and have ever felt a great degree of sorrow for him, because of his bad conduct.

From his childhood, he carried something in his features indicative of an evil disposition, that would result in the perpetration of enormities of some kind; and it was the opinion and saying of Ebenezer Allen, that he would be a bad man, and be guilty of some crime deserving of death. There is no doubt but what the thoughts of murder rankled in his breast, and disturbed his mind even in his sleep; for he dreamed that he had killed Thomas for a trifling offence, and thereby forfeited his own life. Alarmed at the revelation, and fearing that he might in some unguarded moment destroy his brother, he went to the Black Chief, to whom he told the dream, and expressed his fears that the vision would be verified. Having related the dream, together with his feelings on the subject, he asked for the best advice that his old friend was capable of giving, to prevent so sad an event. The Black Chief, with his usual promptitude, told him, that from the nature of the dream, he was fearful that something serious would take place between him and Thomas; and advised him by all means to govern his temper, and avoid any quarrel which in future he might see arising, especially if Thomas was a party. John, however, did not keep the good counsel of the Chief; for soon after he killed Thomas, as I have related.

John left two wives with whom he had lived at the same time, and raised nine children. His widows are now living at Caneadea with their father, and keep their children with, and near them. His children are tolerably white, and have got light colored hair. John died about the last day of June, 1817, aged 54 years.

Doctor and Jack, having finished their murderous design, fled before they could be apprehended, and lay six weeks in the woods back of Canisteo. They then returned and sent me some wampum by Chongo, (my son-in-law,) and Sun-ge-waw (that is Big Kettle) expecting that I would pardon them, and suffer them to live as they had done with their tribe. I however, would not accept their wampum, but returned it with a request, that, rather than have them killed, they would run away and keep out of danger.

On their receiving back the wampum, they took my advice, and prepared to leave their country and people immediately. Their relatives accompanied them a short distance on their journey, and when about to part, their old uncle, the Tall Chief, addressed them in the following pathetic and sentimental speech:

"Friends, hear my voice!—When the Great Spirit made Indians, he made them all good, and gave them good corn-fields; good rivers, well stored with fish; good forests, filled with game and good bows and arrows. But very soon each wanted more than his share, and Indians quarrelled with Indians, and some were killed, and others were wounded. Then the Great Spirit made a very good word, and put it in every Indians breast, to tell us when we have done good, or when we have done bad; and that word has never told a lie.

"Friends! whenever you have stole, or got drunk, or lied, that good word has told you that you were bad Indians, and made you afraid of good Indians; and made you ashamed and look down.

"Friends! your crime is greater than all those:—you have killed an Indian in a time of peace; and made the wind hear his groans, and the earth drink his blood. You are bad Indians! Yes, you are very bad Indians; and what can you do? If you go into the woods to live alone, the ghost of John Jemison will follow you, crying, blood! blood! and will give you no peace! If you go to the land of your nation, there that ghost will attend you, and say to your relatives, see my murderers! If you plant, it will blast your corn; if you hunt, it will scare your game; and when you are asleep, its groans, and the sight of an avenging tomahawk, will awake you! What can you do? Deserving of death, you cannot live here; and to fly from your country, to leave all your relatives, and to abandon all that you have known to be pleasant and dear, must be keener than an arrow, more bitter than gall, more terrible than death! And how must we feel?—Your path will be muddy; the woods will be dark; the lightnings will glance down the trees by your side, and you will start at every sound! peace has left you, and you must be wretched.

"Friends, hear me, and take my advice. Return with us to your homes. Offer to the Great Spirit your best wampum, and try to be good Indians! And, if those whom you have bereaved shall claim your lives as their only satisfaction, surrender them cheerfully, and die like good Indians. And—" Here Jack, highly incensed, interrupted the old man, and bade him stop speaking or he would take his life. Affrighted at the appearance of so much desperation, the company hastened towards home, and left Doctor and Jack to consult their own feelings.

As soon as they were alone, Jack said to Doctor, "I had rather die here, than leave my country and friends! Put the muzzle of your rifle into my mouth, and I will put the muzzle of mine into yours, and at a given signal we will discharge them, and rid ourselves at once of all the troubles under which we now labor, and satisfy the claims which justice holds against us."

Doctor heard the proposition, and after a moment's pause, made the following reply:—"I am as sensible as you can be of the unhappy situation in which we have placed ourselves. We are bad Indians. We have forfeited our lives, and must expect in some way to atone for our crime: but, because we are bad and miserable, shall we make ourselves worse? If we were now innocent, and in a calm reflecting moment should kill ourselves, that act would make us bad, and deprive us of our share of the good hunting in the land where our fathers have gone! What would Little Beard [Footnote: Little Bears was a Chief who died in 1806.] say to us on our arrival at his cabin? He would say, 'Bad Indians! Cowards! You were afraid to wait till we wanted your help! Go (Jogo) to where snakes will lie in your path; where the panthers will starve you, by devouring the venison; and where you will be naked and suffer with the cold! Jogo, (go,) none but the brave and good Indians live here!' I cannot think of performing an act that will add to my wretchedness. It is hard enough for me to suffer here, and have good hunting hereafter—worse to lose the whole."

Upon this, Jack withdrew his proposal. They went on about two miles, and then turned about and came home. Guilty and uneasy, they lurked about Squawky Hill near a fortnight, and then went to Cattaraugus, and were gone six weeks. When they came back, Jack's wife earnestly requested him to remove his family to Tonnewonta; but he remonstrated against her project, and utterly declined going. His wife and family, however, tired of the tumult by which they were surrounded, packed up their effects in spite of what he could say, and went off.

Jack deliberated a short time upon the proper course for himself to pursue, and finally, rather than leave his old home, he ate a large quantity of muskrat root, and died in 10 or 12 hours. His family being immediately notified of his death, returned to attend the burial, and is yet living at Squawky Hill.

Nothing was ever done with Doctor, who continued to live quietly at Squawky Hill till sometime in the year 1819, when he died of Consumption.

CHAPTER XV

In 1816, Micah Brooks, Esq. of Bloomfield, Ontario county, was recommended to me (as it was said) by a Mr. Ingles, to be a man of candor, honesty and integrity, who would by no means cheat me out of a cent. Mr. Brooks soon after, came to my house and informed me that he was disposed to assist me in regard to my land, by procuring a legislative act that would invest me with full power to dispose of it for my own benefit, and give as ample a title as could be given by any citizen of the state. He observed that as it was then situated, it was of but little value, because it was not in my power to dispose of it, let my necessities be ever so great. He then proposed to take the agency of the business upon himself, and to get the title of one half of my reservation vested in me personally, upon the condition that, as a reward for his services, I would give him the other half.

I sent for my son John, who on being consulted, objected to my going into any bargain with Mr. Brooks, without the advice and consent of Mr. Thomas Clute, who then lived on my land and near me. Mr. Clute was accordingly called on, to whom Mr. Brooks repeated his former statement, and added, that he would get an act passed in the Congress of the United States, that would invest me with all the rights and immunities of a citizen, so far as it respected my property. Mr. Clute, suspecting that some plan was in operation that would deprive me of my possessions, advised me to have nothing to say on the subject to Mr. Brooks, till I had seen Esquire Clute, of Squawky Hill. Soon after this Thomas Clute saw Esq. Clute, who informed him that the petition for my naturalization would be presented to the Legislature of this State, instead of being sent to Congress; and that the object would succeed to his and my satisfaction. Mr. Clute then observed to his brother, Esq. Clute, that as the sale of Indian lands, which had been reserved, belonged exclusively to the United States, an act of the Legislature of New-York could have no effect in securing to me a title to my reservation, or in depriving me of my property. They finally agreed that I should sign a petition to Congress, praying for my naturalization, and for the confirmation of the title of my land to me, my heirs, &c.

Mr. Brooks came with the petition: I signed it, and it was witnessed by Thomas Clute, and two others, and then returned to Mr. Brooks, who presented it to the Legislature of this state at its session in the winter of 1816-17. On the 19th of April, 1817, an act was passed for my naturalization, and ratifying and confirming the title of my land, agreeable to the tenor of the petition, which act Mr. Brooks presented to me on the first day of May following.

Thomas Clute having examined the law, told me that it would probably answer, though it was not according to the agreement made by Mr. Brooks, and Esq. Clute and himself, for me. I then executed to Micah Brooks and Jellis Clute, a deed of all my land lying east of the picket line on the Gardow reservation, containing about 7000 acres.

It is proper in this place to observe, in relation to Mr. Thomas Clute, that my son John, a few months before his death, advised me to take him for my guardian, (as I had become old and incapable of managing my property,) and to compensate him for his trouble by giving him a lot of land on the west side of my reservation where he should choose it. I accordingly took my son's advice, and Mr. Clute has ever since been faithful and honest in all his advice and dealings with, and for, myself and family.

In the month of August, 1817, Mr. Brooks and Esq. Clute again came to me with a request that I would give them a lease of the land which I had already deeded to them, together with the other part of my reservation, excepting and reserving to myself only about 4000 acres.

At this time I informed Thomas Clute of what John had advised, and recommended me to do, and that I had consulted my daughters on the subject, who had approved of the measure. He readily agreed to assist me; whereupon I told him he was entitled to a lot of land, and might select as John had mentioned. He accordingly at that time took such a piece as he chose, and the same has ever since been reserved for him in all the land contracts which I have made.

On the 24th of August, 1817, I leased to Micah Brooks and Jellis Clute, the whole of my original reservation, except 4000 acres, and Thomas Clute's lot. Finding their title still incomplete, on account of the United States government and Seneca Chiefs not having sanctioned my acts, they solicited me to renew the contract, and have the conveyance made to them in such a manner as that they should thereby be constituted sole proprietors of the soil.

In the winter of 1822-3, I agreed with them, that if they would get the chiefs of our nation, and a United States Commissioner of Indian Lands, to meet in council at Moscow, Livingston county, N. Y. and there concur in my agreement, that I would sell to them all my right and title to the Gardow reservation, with the exception of a tract for my own benefit, two miles long, and one mile wide, lying on the river where I should choose it; and also reserving Thomas Clute's lot. This arrangement was agreed upon, and the council assembled at the place appointed, on the 3d or 4th day of September, 1823.

That council consisted of Major Carrol, who had been appointed by the President to dispose of my lands, Judge Howell and N. Gorham, of Canandaigua, (who acted in concert with Maj. Carrol,) Jasper Parrish, Indian Agent, Horatio Jones, Interpreter, and a great number of Chiefs.

The bargain was assented to unanimously, and a deed given to H. B. Gibson, Micah Brooks and Jellis Clute, of the whole Gardow tract, excepting the last mentioned reservations, which was signed by myself and upwards of twenty Chiefs.

The land which I now own, is bounded as follows:—Beginning at the center of the Great Slide [Footnote: The Great Slide of the bank of Genesee river is a curiosity worthy of the attention of the traveller. In the month of May, 1817, a portion of land thickly covered with timber, situated at the upper end of the Gardow flats, on the west side of the river, all of a sudden gave way, and with a tremendous crash, slid into the bed of the river, which it so completely filled, that the stream formed a new passage on the east side of it, where it continues to run, without overflowing the slide. This slide, as it now lies, contains 22 acres, and has a considerable share of the timber that formerly covered it, still standing erect upon it, and growing.] and running west one mile, thence north two miles, thence east about one mile to Genesee river, thence south on the west bank of Genesee river to the place of beginning.

In consideration of the above sale, the purchasers have bound themselves, their heirs, assigns, &c. to pay to me, my heirs or successors, three hundred dollars a year forever.

Whenever the land which I have reserved, shall be sold, the income of it is to be equally divided amongst the members of the Seneca nation, without any reference to tribes or families.

CHAPTER XVI

When I review my life, the privations that I have suffered, the hardships I have endured, the vicissitudes I have passed, and the complete revolution that I have experienced in my manner of living; when I consider my reduction from a civilized to a savage state, and the various steps by which that process has been effected, and that my life has been prolonged, and my health and reason spared, it seems a miracle that I am unable to account for, and is a tragical medley that I hope will never be repeated.

The bare loss of liberty is but a mere trifle when compared with the circumstances that necessarily attend, and are inseparably connected with it. It is the recollection of what we once were, of the friends, the home, and the pleasures that we have left or lost; the anticipation of misery, the appearance of wretchedness, the anxiety for freedom, the hope of release, the devising of means of escaping, and the vigilance with which we watch our keepers, that constitute the nauseous dregs of the bitter cup of slavery. I am sensible, however, that no one can pass from a state of freedom to that of slavery, and in the last situation rest perfectly contented; but as every one knows that great exertions of the mind tend directly to debilitate the body, it will appear obvious that we ought, when confined, to exert all our faculties to promote our present comfort, and let future days provide their own sacrifices. In regard to ourselves, just as we feel, we are.

For the preservation of my life to the present time I am indebted to an excellent constitution, with which I have been blessed in as great a degree as any other person. After I arrived to years of understanding, the care of my own health was one of my principal studies; and by avoiding exposures to wet and cold, by temperance in eating, abstaining from the use of spirits, and shunning the excesses to which I was frequently exposed, I effected my object beyond what I expected. I have never once been sick till within a year or two, only as I have related. Spirits and tobacco I have never used, and I have never once attended an Indian frolic. When I was taken prisoner, and for sometime after that, spirits was not known; and when it was first introduced, it was in small quantities, and used only by the Indians; so that it was a long time before the Indian women begun to even taste it.

After the French war, for a number of years, it was the practice of the Indians of our tribe to send to Niagara and get two or three kegs of rum, (in all six or eight gallons,) and hold a frolic as long as it lasted. When the rum was brought to the town, all the Indians collected, and before a drop was drank, gave all their knives, tomahawks, guns, and other instruments of war, to one Indian, whose business it was to bury them in a private place, keep them concealed, and remain perfectly sober till the frolic was ended. Having thus divested themselves, they commenced drinking, and continued their frolic till every drop was consumed, If any of them became quarrelsome, or got to fighting, those who were sober enough bound them upon the ground, where they were obliged to lie till they got sober, and then were unbound. When the fumes of the spirits had left the company, the sober Indian returned to each the instruments with which they had entrusted him, and all went home satisfied. A frolic of that kind was held but once a year, and that at the time the Indians quit their hunting, and come in with their deer-skins.

In those frolics the women never participated. Soon after the revolutionary war, however, spirits became common in our tribe, and has been used indiscriminately by both sexes; though there are not so frequent instances of intoxication amongst the squaws as amongst the Indians.

To the introduction and use or that baneful article, which has made such devastation in our tribes, and threatens the extinction of our people, (the Indians,) I can with the greatest propriety impute the whole of my misfortune in losing my three sons. But as I have before observed, not even the love of life will restrain an Indian from sipping the poison that he knows will destroy him. The voice of nature, the rebukes of reason, the advice of parents, the expostulations of friends, and the numerous instances of sudden death, are all insufficient to reclaim an Indian, who has once experienced the exhilarating and inebriating effects of spirits, from seeking his grave in the bottom of his bottle!

My strength has been great for a woman of my size, otherwise I must long ago have died under the burdens which I was obliged to carry. I learned to carry loads on my back, in a strap placed across my forehead, soon after my captivity; and continue to carry in the same way. Upwards of thirty years ago, with the help of my young children, I backed all the boards that were used about my house from Allen's mill at the outlet of Silver Lake, a distance of five miles. I have planted, hoed, and harvested corn every season but one since I was taken prisoner. Even this present fall (1823) I have husked my corn and backed it into the house.

The first cow that I ever owned, I bought of a squaw sometime after the revolution. It had been stolen from the enemy. I had owned it but a few days when it fell into a hole, and almost died before we could get it out. After this, the squaw wanted to be recanted, but as I would not give up the cow, I gave her money enough to make, when added to the sum which I paid her at first, thirty-five dollars. Cows were plenty on the Ohio, when I lived there, and of good quality.

For provisions I have never suffered since I came upon the flats; nor have I ever been in debt to any other hands than my own for the plenty that I have shared.

My vices, that have been suspected, have been but few. It was believed for a long time, by some of our people, that I was a great witch; but they were unable to prove my guilt, and consequently I escaped the certain doom of those who are convicted of that crime, which, by Indians, is considered as heinous as murder. Some of my children had light brown hair, and tolerable fair skin, which used to make some say that I stole them; yet as I was ever conscious of my own constancy, I never thought that any one really believed that I was guilty of adultery.

I have been the mother of eight children; three of whom are now living, and I have at this time thirty-nine grand children, and fourteen great-grand children, all living in the neighborhood of Genesee River, and at Buffalo.

I live in my own house, and on my own land with my youngest daughter, Polly, who is married to George Chongo, and has three children.

My daughter Nancy, who is married to Billy Green, lives about 80 rods south of my house, and has seven children.

My other, daughter, Betsey, is married to John Green, has seven children, and resides 80 rods north of my house.

Thus situated in the midst of my children, I expect I shall soon leave the world, and make room for the rising generation. I feel the weight of years with which I am loaded, and am sensible of my daily failure in seeing, hearing and strength; but my only anxiety is for my family. If my family will live happily, and I can be exempted from trouble while I have to stay, I feel as though I could lay down in peace a life that has been checked in almost every hour, with troubles of a deeper dye, than are commonly experienced by mortals.

APPENDIX

An account of the destruction of a part of the British Army, by the Indians, at a place called the Devil's Hole, on the Niagara River, in the year 1763.

It is to be regretted that an event of so tragical a nature as the following, should have escaped the pens of American Historians, and have been suffered to slide down the current of time, to the verge of oblivion, without having been snatched almost from the vortex of forgetfulness, and placed on the faithful page, as a memorial of premeditated cruelties, which, in former times, were practised upon the white people, by the North American Savages.

Modern History, perhaps, cannot furnish a parallel so atrocious in design and execution, as the one before us, and it may be questioned, even if the history of ancient times, when men fought hand to hand, and disgraced their nature by inventing engines of torture, can more than produce its equal.

It will be observed in the preceding narrative, that the affair at the Devil's Hole is said to have happened in November, 1759. That Mrs. Jemison arrived at Genesee about that time, is rendered certain from a number of circumstances; and that a battle was fought on the Niagara in Nov. 1759, in which two prisoners and some oxen were taken, and brought to Genesee, as she has stated, is altogether probable. But it is equally certain that the event which is the subject of this article, did not take place till the year 1763.

In the time of the French war, the neighborhood of Forts Niagara and Sclusser, (or Schlosser, as it was formerly written,) on the Niagara river, was a general battle-ground, and for this reason, Mrs. Jemison's memory ought not to be charged with treachery, for not having been able to distinguish accurately, after the lapse of sixty years, between the circumstances of one engagement and those of another. She resided on the Genesee at the time when the warriors of that tribe marched off to assist in laying the ambush at the Devil's Hole; and no one will doubt her having heard them rehearse the story of the event of that nefarious campaign, after they returned.

Chronology and history concur in stating that Fort Niagara was taken from the French, by the British, and that Gen. Prideaux was killed on the 25th of July, 1759.

Having obtained from Mrs. Jemison a kind of introduction to the story, I concluded that if it yet remained possible to procure a correct account of the circumstances which led to and attended that transaction, it would be highly gratifying to the American public, I accordingly directed a letter to Mr. Linus S. Everett, of Buffalo, whose ministerial labor, I well knew, frequently called him to Lewiston, requesting him to furnish me with a particular account of the destruction of the British, at the time and place before mentioned. He obligingly complied with my request, and gave me the result of his inquiries on that subject, in the following letter:—

Copy of a letter from Mr. Linus S. Everett, dated Fort Sclusser, 29th December, 1823.

Respected and dear friend,

I hasten, with much pleasure, to comply with your request, in regard to the affair at the Devil's Hole. I have often wondered that no authentic account has ever been given of that bloody and tragical scene.

I have made all the inquiries that appear to be of any use, and proceed to give you the result.

At this place, (Fort Sclusser,) an old gentleman now resides, to whom I am indebted for the best account of the affair that can be easily obtained. His name is Jesse Ware—his age about 74. Although he was not a resident of this part of the country at the time of the event, yet from his intimate acquaintance with one of the survivors, he is able to give much information, which otherwise could not be obtained.

The account that he gives is as follows:—In July, 1759, the British, under Sir William Johnston, took possession of Forts Niagara and Sclusser, which had before been in the hands of the French. At this time, the Seneca Indians, (which were a numerous and powerful nation,) were hostile to the British, and warmly allied to the French. These two posts, (viz.) Niagara and Sclusser, were of great importance to the British, on the account of affording the means of communication with the posts above, or on the upper lakes. In 1760, a contract was made between Sir William Johnston and a Mr. Stedman, to construct a portage road from Queenston landing to Fort Sclusser, a distance of eight miles, in order to facilitate the transportation of provision, ammunition, &c. from one place to the other. In conformity to this agreement, on the 20th of June, 1763, Stedman had completed his road, and appeared at Queenston Landing, (now Lewiston,) with twenty-five portage wagons, and one hundred horses and oxen, to transport to Fort Sclusser the king's stores.

At this time Sir William Johnston was suspicious of the intentions of the Senecas; for after the surrender of the forts by the French, they had appeared uneasy and hostile. In order to prevent the teams, drivers and goods, receiving injury, he detached 300 troops to guard them across the portage. The teams, under this escort, started from Queenston landing—Stedman, who had the charge of the whole, was on horse back, and rode between the troops and teams; all the troops being in front. On a small hill near the Devil's Hole, at that time, was a redoubt of twelve men, which served as a kind of guard on ordinary occasions, against the depredations of the savages. "On the arrival of the troops and teams at the Devil's Hole," says a manuscript in the hands of my informant, "the sachems, chiefs and warriors of the Seneca Indians, sallied from the adjoining woods, by thousands, (where they had been concealed for some time before, for that nefarious purpose,) and falling upon the troops, teams and drivers, and the guard of twelve men before mentioned, they killed all the men but three on the spot, or by driving them, together with the teams, down the precipice, which was about seventy or eighty feet! The Indians seized Stedman's horse by the bridle, while he was on him, designing, no doubt, to make his sufferings more lasting than that of his companions: but while the bloody scene was acting, the attention of the Indian who held the horse of Stedman being arrested, he cut the reins of his bridle—clapped spurs to his horse, and rode over the dead and dying, into the adjacent woods, without receiving injury from the enemy's firing. Thus he escaped; and besides him two others—one a drummer, who fell among the trees, was caught by his drum strap, and escaped unhurt; the other, one who fell down the precipice and broke his thigh, but crawled to the landing or garrison down the river." The following September, the Indians gave Stedman a piece of land, as a reward for his bravery.

With sentiments of respect, I remain, sir, your sincere friend, L. S. EVERETT.

Mr. J. E. Seaver.

A particular account of General Sullivan's Expedition against the Indians, in the western part of the State of New-York, in 1779.

It has been thought expedient to publish in this volume, the following account of Gen. Sullivan's expedition, in addition to the facts related by Mrs. Jemison, of the barbarities which were perpetrated upon Lieut. Boyd, and two others, who were taken, and who formed a part of his army, etc. A detailed account of this expedition has never been in the hands of the public; and as it is now produced from a source deserving implicit credit, it is presumed that it will be received with satisfaction.

John Salmon, Esq. to whom we are happy to acknowledge our indebtedness for the subjoined account, is an old gentleman of respectability and good standing in society; and is at this time a resident in the town of Groveland, Livingston county, New-York. He was a hero in the American war for independence; fought in the battles of his country under the celebrated Morgan; survived the blast of British oppression; and now, in the decline of life, sits under his own well earned vine and fig-tree, near the grave of his unfortunate countrymen, who fell gloriously, while fighting the ruthless savages, under the command of the gallant Boyd.

In the autumn after the battle at Monmouth, (1778,) Morgan's riflemen, to which corps I belonged, marched to Schoharie, in this state of New-York, and there went into winter quarters. The company to which I was attached, was commanded by Capt. Michael Simpson; and Thomas Boyd, of Northumberland county, Pennsylvania, was our Lieutenant.

In the following spring, our corps, together with the whole body of troops under the command of Gen. Clinton, to the amount of about 1500, embarked in boats at Schenectady, and ascended the Mohawk as far as German Flats. Thence we took a direction to Otsego lake, descended the Susquehanna, and without any remarkable occurrence, arrived at Tioga Point, where our troops united with an army of 1500 men under the command of Gen. Sullivan, who had marched through a part of New-Jersey, and had reached that place by the way of Wyoming, some days before us.

That part of the army under Gen. Sullivan, had, on their arrival at Tioga Point, found the Indians in some force there, with whom they had had some unimportant skirmishes before our arrival. Upon the junction of these two bodies of troops, Gen. Sullivan assumed the command of the whole, and proceeded up the Tioga. When within a few miles of the place now called Newtown, we were met by a body of Indians, and a number of troops well known in those times by the name of Butler's Rangers, who had thrown up, hastily, a breastwork of logs, trees, &c. They were, however, easily driven from their works, with considerable loss on their part, and without any injury to our troops. The enemy fled with so much precipitation, that they left behind them some stores and camp equippage. They retreated but a short distance before they made a stand, and built another breastwork of considerable length, in the woods, near a small opening. Sullivan was soon apprized of their situation, divided his army, and attempted to surround, by sending one half to the right and the other to the left, with directions to meet on the opposite side of the enemies. In order to prevent their retreating, he directed bomb-shells to be thrown over them, which was done: but on the shells bursting, the Indians suspected that a powerful army had opened a heavy fire upon them on that side, and fled with the utmost precipitation through one wing of the surrounding army. A great number of the enemy were killed, and our army suffered considerably.

The Indians having, in this manner, escaped, they went up the river to a place called the Narrows, where they were attacked by our men, who killed them in great numbers, so that the sides of the rocks next the river appeared as though blood had been poured on them by pailfulls. The Indians threw their dead into the river, and escaped the best way they could.

From Newtown our army went directly to the head of the Seneca lake; thence down that lake to its mouth, where we found the Indian village at that place evacuated, except by a single inhabitant—a male child about seven or eight years of age, who was found asleep in one of the Indian huts. Its fate I have never ascertained. It was taken into the care of an officer of the army, who, on account of ill health, was not on duty, and who took the child with him, as I have since understood, to his residence on or near the North river.

From the mouth of Seneca lake we proceeded, without the occurrence of any thing of importance, by the outlets of the Canandaigua, Honeoye, and Hemlock lakes, to the head of Connissius lake, where the army encamped on the ground that is now called Henderson's Flats.

Soon after the army had encamped, at the dusk of the evening, a party of twenty-one men, under the command of Lieut. Boyd, was detached from the rifle corps, and sent out for the purpose of reconnoitering the ground near the Genesee river, at a place now called Williamsburg, at a distance from the camp of about seven miles, under the guidance of a faithful Indian pilot. That place was then the site of an Indian village, and it was apprehended that the Indians and Rangers might be there or in that vicinity in considerable force.

On the arrival of the party at Williamsburg, they found that the Indian village had been recently deserted, as the fires in the huts were still burning. The night was so far spent when they got to their place of destination, that Lieutenant Boyd, considering the fatigue of his men, concluded to remain during the night near the village, and to send two men messengers with a report to the camp in the morning. Accordingly, a little before daybreak, he despatched two men to the main body of the army, with information that the enemy had not been discovered.

After day-light, Lieut. Boyd cautiously crept from the place of his concealment, and upon getting a view of the village, discovered two

Indians hovering about the settlement: one of whom was immediately shot and scalped by one of the riflemen, whose name was Murphy. Supposing that if there were Indians in that vicinity, or near the village, they would be instantly alarmed by this occurrence, Lieut. Boyd thought it most prudent to retire, and make the best of his way to the general encampment of our army. They accordingly set out and retraced the steps which they had taken the day before, till they were intercepted by the enemy.

On their arriving within about one mile and a half of the main army, they were surprized by the sudden appearance of a body of Indians, to the amount of five hundred, under the command of the celebrated Brandt, and the same number of Rangers, commanded by the infamous Butler, who had secreted themselves in a ravine of considerable extent, which lay across the track that Lieut. Boyd had pursued.

Upon discovering the enemy, and knowing that the only chance for escape was by breaking through their line, (one of the most desperate enterprizes ever undertaken,) Lieut. Boyd, after a few words of encouragement, led his men to the attempt. As extraordinary as it may seem, the first onset, though unsuccessful, was made without the loss of a man on the part of the heroic band, though several of the enemy were killed. Two attempts more were made, which were equally unsuccessful, and in which the whole party fell, except Lieut. Boyd, and eight others. Lieut. Boyd and a soldier by the name of Parker, were taken prisoners on the spot, a part of the remainder fled, and a part fell on the ground, apparently dead, and were overlooked by the Indians, who were too much engaged in pursuing the fugitives to notice those who fell.

When Lieut. Boyd found himself a prisoner, he solicited an interview with Brandt, whom he well knew commanded the Indians. This Chief, who was at that moment near, immediately presented himself, when Lieut. Boyd, by one of those appeals which are known only by those who have been initiated and instructed in certain mysteries, and which never fail to bring succor to a "distressed brother," addressed him as the only source from which he could expect a respite from cruel punishment or death. The appeal was recognized, and Brandt immediately, and in the strongest language, assured him that his life should be spared.

Lieut. Boyd, and his fellow-prisoner, Parker, were immediately conducted by a party of the Indians to the Indian village called Beard's Town, on the west side of Genesee river, in what is now called Leicester. After their arrival at Beard's Town, Brandt, their generous preserver, being called on service which required a few hours absence, left them in the care of the British Col. Butler, of the Rangers; who, as soon as Brandt had left them, commenced an interrogation, to obtain from the prisoners a statement of the number, situation and intentions of the army under Gen. Sullivan; and threatened them, in case they hesitated or prevaricated in their answers, to deliver them up immediately to be massacred by the Indians, who, in Brandt's absence, and with the encouragement of their more savage commander, Butler, were ready to commit the greatest cruelties. Relying, probably, on the promises which Brandt had made them, and which he undoubtedly meant to fulfil, they refused to give Butler the desired information. Butler, upon this, hastened to put his threat into execution. They were delivered to some of their most ferocious enemies, who, after having put them to very severe torture, killed them by severing their heads from their bodies.

The main army, immediately after hearing of the situation of Lieut. Boyd's detachment, moved on towards Genesee river, and finding the bodies of those who were slain in Boyd's heroic attempt to penetrate through the enemy's line, buried them in what is now the town of Groveland, where the grave is to be seen at this day.

Upon their arrival at the Genesee river, they crossed over, scoured the country for some distance on the river, burnt the Indian villages on the Genesee flats, and destroyed all their corn and other means of subsistence.

The bodies of Lieut. Boyd and Parker were found and buried near the bank of Beard's creek, under a bunch of wild plum-trees, on the road, as it now runs, from Moscow to Geneseo. I was one of those who committed to the earth the remains of my friend and companion in arms, the gallant Boyd.

Immediately after these events the army commenced its march back, by the same route that it came, to Tioga Point; thence down the Susquehanna to Wyoming; and thence across the country to Morristown, New-Jersey, where we went into winter quarters.

Gen. Sullivan's bravery is unimpeachable. He was unacquainted, however, with fighting the Indians, and made use of the best means to keep them at such a distance that they could not be brought into an engagement. It was his practice, morning and evening, to have cannon fired in or near the camp, by which the Indians were notified of their speed in marching, and of his situation, and were enabled to make a seasonable retreat.

The foregoing account, according to the best of my recollection is strictly correct.

JOHN SALMON.

Groveland, January 24, 1824.

Esq. Salmon was formerly from Northumberland county, Pennsylvania, and was first Serjeant in Capt. Simpson's and Lieut. Boyd's company.

Tradition of the Origin of the Seneca Nation.—Their Preservation from utter extinction.—The Means by which the People who preceded the Senecas were destroyed—and the Cause of the different Indian Languages.

The tradition of the Seneca Indians, in regard to their origin, as we are assured by Capt. Horatio Jones, who was a prisoner five years amongst them, and for many years since has been an interpreter, and agent for the payment of their annuities, is that they broke out of the earth from a large mountain at the head of Canandaigua Lake, and that mountain they still venerate as the place of their birth; thence they derive their name, "Ge-nun-de-wah," [Footnote: This by some is spoken Ge-nun-de-wah-gauh.] or Great Hill, and are called "The Great Hill People," which is the true definition of the word Seneca.

The great hill at the head of Canandaigua lake, from whence they sprung, is called Genundewah, and has for a long time past been the place where the Indians of that nation have met in council, to hold great talks, and to offer up prayers to the Great Spirit, on account of its having been their birth place; and also in consequence of the destruction of a serpent at that place, in ancient time, in a most miraculous manner, which threatened the destruction of the whole of the Senecas, and barely spared enough to commence replenishing the earth.

The Indians say, says Capt. Jones, that the fort on the big hill, or Genundewah, near the head of Canandaigua lake, was surrounded by a monstrous serpent, whose head and tail came together at the gate. A long time it lay there, confounding the people with its breath. At length they attempted to make their escape, some with their hommany-blocks, and others with different implements of household furniture; and in marching out of the fort walked down the throat of the serpent. Two orphan children, who had escaped this general destruction by being left some time before on the outside of the fort, were informed by an oracle of the means by which they could get rid of their formidable enemy—which was, to take a small bow and a poisoned arrow, made of a kind of willow, and with that shoot the serpent under its scales. This they did, and the arrow proved effectual; for on its penetrating the skin, the serpent became sick, and extending itself rolled down the hill, destroying all the timber that was in its way, disgorging itself and breaking wind greatly as it went. At every motion, a human head was discharged, and rolled down the hill into the lake, where they lie at this day, in a petrified state, having the hardness and appearance of stones.

To this day the Indians visit that sacred place, to mourn the loss of their friends, and to celebrate some rites that are peculiar to themselves. To the knowledge of white people there has been no timber on the great hill since it was first discovered by them, though it lay apparently in a state of nature for a great number of years, without cultivation. Stones in the shape of Indians' heads may be seen lying in the lake in great plenty, which are said to be the same that were deposited there at the death of the serpent.

The Senecas have a tradition, that previous to, and for some time after, their origin at Genundewah, this country, especially about the lakes, was thickly inhabited by a race of civil, enterprizing and industrious people, who were totally destroyed by the great serpent, that afterwards surrounded the great hill fort, with the assistance of others of the same species; and that they (the Senecas) went into possession of the improvements that were left.

In those days the Indians throughout the whole country, as the Senecas say, spoke one language; but having become considerably numerous, the before mentioned great serpent, by an unknown influence, confounded their language, so that they could not understand each other; which was the cause of their division into nations, as the Mohawks, Oneidas, &c. At that time, however, the Senecas retained their original language, and continued to occupy their mother hill, on which they fortified themselves against their enemies, and lived peaceably, till having offended the serpent, [Footnote: The pagans of the Senecas believe that all the little snakes were made of the blood of the great serpent, after it rolled into the lake.] they were cut off as before stated.

OF THEIR RELIGION—FEASTS—AND GREAT SACRIFICE

Perhaps no people are more exact observers of religious duties than those Indians among the Senecas, who are denominated pagans, in contradistinction from those, who, having renounced some of their former superstitious notions, have obtained the name of Christians. The traditionary faith of their fathers, having been orally transmitted to them from time immemorial, is implicitly believed, scrupulously adhered to, and rigidly practised. They are agreed in their sentiments—are all of one order, and have individual and public good, especially among themselves, for the great motive which excites them to attend to those moral virtues that are directed and explained by all their rules, and in all their ceremonies.

Many years have elapsed since the introduction of Christian Missionaries among them, whom they have heard, and very generally understand the purport of the message they were sent to deliver. They say that it is highly probable that Jesus Christ came into the world in old times, to establish a religion that would promote the happiness of the white people, on the other side of the great water, (meaning the sea,) and that he died for the sins of his people, as the missionaries have informed them: But, they say that Jesus Christ had nothing to do with them, and that the Christian religion was not designed for their benefit; but rather, should they embrace it, they are confident it would make them worse, and consequently do them an injury. They say, also, that the Great Good Spirit gave them their religion; and that it is better adapted to their circumstances, situation and habits, and to the promotion of their present comfort and ultimate happiness, than any system that ever has or can be devised. They, however, believe, that the Christian religion is better calculated for the good of white people than theirs is; and wonder that those who have embraced it, do not attend more strictly to its precepts, and feel more engaged for its support and diffusion among themselves. At the present time, they are opposed to preachers or schoolmasters being sent or coming among them; and appear determined by all means to adhere to their ancient customs.

They believe in a Great Good Spirit, (whom they call in the Seneca language Nau-wan-e-u,) as the Creator of the world, and of every good thing—that he made men, and all inoffensive animals; that he supplies men with all the comforts of life; and that he is particularly partial to the Indians, whom they say are his peculiar people. They also believe that he is pleased in giving them (the Indians) good gifts; and that he is highly gratified with their good conduct—that he abhors their vices, and that he is willing to punish them for their bad conduct, not only in this world, but in a future state of existence. His residence, they suppose, lies at a great distance from them, in a country that is perfectly pleasant, where plenty abounds, even to profusion. That there the soil is completely fertile, and the seasons so mild that the corn never fails to be good—that the deer, elk, buffalo, turkies, and other useful animals, are numerous, and that the forests are well calculated to facilitate their hunting them with success—that the streams are pure, and abound with fish: and that nothing is wanting, to render fruition complete. Over this territory they say Nauwaneu presides as an all-powerful king; and that without counsel he admits to his pleasures all whom he considers to be worthy of enjoying so great a state of blessedness.

To this being they address prayers, offer sacrifices, give thanks for favors, and perform many acts of devotion and reverence.

They likewise believe that Nauwaneu has a brother that is less powerful than himself, and who is opposed to him, and to every one that is or wishes to be good: that this bad Spirit made all evil things, snakes, wolves, catamounts, and all other poisonous or noxious animals and beasts of prey, except the bear, which, on the account of the excellence of its meat for food, and skin for clothing, they say was made by Nauwaneu. Besides all this they say he makes and sends them their diseases, bad weather and bad crops, and that he makes and supports witches. He owns a large country adjoining that of his brother, with whom he is continually at variance. His fields are unproductive; thick clouds intercept the rays of the sun, and consequently destructive frosts are frequent; game is very scarce, and not easily taken; ravenous beasts are numerous; reptiles of every poisoned tooth lie in the path of the traveller; streams are muddy, and hunger, nakedness and general misery, are severely felt by those who unfortunately become his tenants. He takes pleasure in afflicting the Indians here, and after their death receives all those into his dreary dominions, who in their life time have been so vile as to be rejected by Nauwaneu, under whose eye they are continued in an uncomfortable state forever. To this source of evil they offer some oblations to abate his vengeance, and render him propitious. They, however, believe him to be, in a degree, under subjection to his brother, and incapable of executing his plans only by his high permission.

Public religious duties are attended to in the celebration of particular festivals and sacrifices, which are observed with circumspection and attended with decorum.

In each year they have five feasts, or stated times for assembling in their tribes, and giving thanks to Nauwaneu, for the blessings which they have received from his kind and liberal and provident hand; and also to converse upon the best means of meriting a continuance of his favors. The first of these feasts is immediately after they have finished sugaring, at which time they give thanks for the favorable weather and great quantity of sap they have had, and for the sugar that they have been allowed to make for the benefit of their families. At this, as at all the succeeding feasts, the Chiefs arise singly, and address the audience in a kind of exhortation, in which they express their own thankfulness, urge the necessity and propriety of general gratitude, and point out the course which ought to be pursued by each individual, in order that Nauwaneu may continue to bless them, and that the evil spirit may be defeated.

On these occasions the Chiefs describe a perfectly straight line, half an inch wide, and perhaps ten miles long, which they direct their people to travel upon by placing one foot before the other, with the heel of one foot to the toe of the other, and so on till they arrive at the end. The meaning of which is, that they must not turn aside to the right hand or to the left into the paths of vice, but keep straight ahead in the way of well doing, that will lead them to the paradise of Nauwaneu.

The second feast is after planting; when they render thanks for the pleasantness of the season—for the good time they have had for preparing their ground and planting their corn; and are instructed by their Chiefs, by what means to merit a good harvest.

When the green corn becomes fit for use, they hold their third, or green corn feast. Their fourth is celebrated after corn harvest; and the fifth at the close of their year, and is always celebrated at the time of the old moon in the last of January or first of February. This last deserves a particular description.

The Indians having returned, from hunting, and having brought in all the venison and skins that they have taken, a committee is appointed, says Mrs. Jemison, consisting of from ten to twenty active men, to superintend the festivities of the great sacrifice and thanksgiving that is to be immediately celebrated. This being done, preparations are made at the council-house, or place of meeting, for the reception and accommodation of the whole tribe; and then the ceremonies are commenced, and the whole is conducted with a great degree of order and harmony, under the direction of the committee.

Two white dogs, [Footnote: This was the practice in former times; but at present I am informed that only one dog is sacrificed.] without spot or blemish, are selected (if such can be found, and if not, two that have the fewest spots) from those belonging to the tribe, and killed near the door of the council-house, by being strangled. A wound on the animal or an effusion of blood, would spoil the victim, and render the sacrifice useless. The dogs are then painted red on their faces, edges of their ears, and on various parts of their bodies, and are curiously decorated with ribbons of different colors, and fine feathers, which are tied and fastened on in such a manner as to make the most elegant appearance. They are then hung on a post near the door of the council-house, at the height of twenty feet from the ground.

This being done, the frolic is commenced by those who are present, while the committee run through the tribe or town, and hurry the people to assemble, by knocking on their houses. At this time the committee are naked, (wearing only a breech-clout,) and each carries a paddle, with which he takes up ashes and scatters them about the house in every direction. In the course of the ceremonies, all the fire is extinguished in every hut throughout the tribe, and new fire, struck from the flint on each hearth, is kindled, after having removed the whole of the ashes, old coals, &c. Having done this, and discharged one or two guns, they go on, and in this manner they proceed till they have visited every house in the tribe. This finishes the business of the first day.

On the second day the committee dance, go through the town with bear-skin on their legs, and at every time they start they fire a gun. They also beg through the tribe, each carrying a basket in which to receive whatever may be bestowed. The alms consist of Indian tobacco, and other articles that are used for incense at the sacrifice. Each manager at this time carries a dried tortoise or turtle shell, containing a few beans, which he frequently rubs on the walls of the houses, both inside and out. This kind of manoeuvering by the committee continues two or three days, during which time the people at the council-house recreate themselves by dancing.

On the fourth or fifth day the committee make false faces of husks, in which they run about, making a frightful but ludicrous appearance. In this dress, (still wearing the bear-skin,) they run to the council-house, smearing themselves with dirt, and bedaub every one who refuses to contribute something towards filling the baskets of incense, which they continue to carry, soliciting alms. During all this time they collect the evil spirit, or drive it off entirely, for the present, and also concentrate within themselves all the sins of their tribe, however numerous or heinous.

On the eighth or ninth day, the committee having received all the sin, as before observed, into their own bodies, they take down the dogs, and after having transfused the whole of it into one of their own number, he, by a peculiar slight of hand, or kind of magic, works it all out of himself into the dogs. The dogs, thus loaded with all the sins of the people, are placed upon a pile of wood that is directly set on fire. Here they are burnt, together with the sins with which they were loaded, surrounded by the multitude, who throw incense of tobacco or the like into the fire, the scent of which they say, goes up to Nauwaneu, to whom it is pleasant and acceptable.

This feast continues nine days, [Footnote: At present, as I have been informed, this feast is not commonly held more than from five to seven days. In former times, and till within a few years, nine days were particularly observed.] and during that time the Chiefs review the national affairs of the year past; agree upon the best plan to be pursued through the next year, and attend to all internal regulations.

On the last day, the whole company partake of an elegant dinner, consisting of meat, corn and beans, boiled together in large kettles, and stirred till the whole is completely mixed and soft. This mess is devoured without much ceremony—some eat with a spoon, by dipping out of the kettles; others serve themselves in small dippers; some in one way, and some in another, till the whole is consumed. After this they perform the war dance, the peace dance, and smoke the pipe of peace; and then, free from iniquity, each repairs to his place of abode, prepared to commence the business of a new year. In this feast, temperance is observed, and commonly, order prevails in a greater degree than would naturally be expected.

They are fond of the company of spectators who are disposed to be decent, and treat them politely in their way; but having been frequently imposed upon by the whites, they treat them generally with indifference.

OF THEIR DANCES

Of these, two only will be noticed. The war dance is said to have originated about the time that the Six Nations, or Northern Indians, commenced the old war with the Cherokees and other Southern Indian Nations, about one hundred years ago.

When a tribe, or number of tribes of the Six Nations, had assembled for the purpose of going to battle with their enemies, the Chiefs sung this song, and accompanied the music with dancing, and gestures that corresponded with the sentiments expressed, as a kind of stimulant to increase their courage, and anxiety to march forward to the place of carnage.

Those days having passed away, the Indians at this day sing the 'war song,' to commemorate the achievements of their fathers, and as a kind of amusement. When they perform it, they arm themselves with a war-club, tomahawk and knife, and commence singing with firm voice, and a stern, resolute countenance: but before they get through they exhibit in their features and actions the most shocking appearance of anger, fury and vengeance, that can be imagined: No exhibition of the kind can be more terrifying to a stranger.

The song requires a number of repetitions in the tune, and has a chorus that is sung at the end of each verse. I have not presumed to arrange it in metre; but the following is the substance: "We are assembled in the habiliments of war, and will go in quest of our enemies. We will march to their land and spoil their possessions. We will take their women and children, and lead them into captivity. The warriors shall fall by our war-clubs—we will give them no quarter. Our tomahawks we will dip in their brains! with our scalping knives we will scalp them." At each period comes on the chorus, which consists of one monosyllable only, that is sounded a number of times, and articulated like a faint, stifled groan. This word is "eh," and signifies "we will," or "we will go," or "we will do." While singing, they perform the ceremony of killing and scalping, with a great degree of dexterity.

The peace dance is performed to a tune without words, by both sexes. The Indians stand erect in one place, and strike the floor with the heel and toes of one foot, and then of the other, (the heels and toes all the while nearly level,) without changing their position in the least. The squaws at the same time perform it by keeping the feet close together, and without raising them from the ground, move a short distance to the right, and then to the left, by first moving their toes and then their heels. This dance is beautiful, and is generally attended with decency.

OF THEIR GOVERNMENT

Their government is an oligarchy of a mixed nature; and is administered by Chiefs, a part of whose offices are hereditary, and a part elective. The nation is divided into tribes, and each tribe commonly has two Chiefs. One of these inherits his office from his father. He superintends all civil affairs in the tribe; attends the national council, of which he is a member; assents to all conveyances of land, and is consulted on every subject of importance. The other is elected by the tribe, and can be removed at the pleasure of his constituents for malconduct. He also is a member of the national council: but his principal business is to superintend the military concerns of his tribe, and in war to lead his warriors to battle. He acts in concert with the other Chief, and their word is implicitly relied on, as the law by which they must be governed. That which they prohibit, is not meddled with. The Indian laws are few, and easily expounded. Their business of a public nature is transacted in council, where every decision is final. They meet in general council once a year, and sometimes oftener. The administration of their government is not attended with expense. They have no national revenue, and consequently have no taxes.

THE EXTENT AND NUMBER OF THE SIX NATIONS

The Six Nations in the state of New-York are located upon several reservations, from the Oneida Lake to the Cattaraugus and Allegany rivers.

A part of those nations live on the Sandusky, in the state of Ohio, viz— 380 Cayugas, 300 Senecas, 64 Mohawks, 64 Oneidas, and 80 Onondagas. The bulk of the Mohawks are on Grand River, Upper Canada, together with some Senecas, Tuscaroras, Cayugas, Oneidas, and Onondagas.

In the state of New-York there are 5000, and in the state of Ohio 688, as we are assured by Capt. Horatio Jones, agent for paying their annuities, making in the whole, in both states, 5688.

OF THEIR COURTSHIPS, &c

When an Indian sees a squaw whom he fancies, he sends a present to her mother or parents, who on receiving it consult with his parents, his friends, and each other, on the propriety and expediency of the proposed connexion. If it is not agreeable, the present is returned; but if it is, the lover is informed of his good fortune, and immediately goes to live with her, or takes her to a hut of his own preparing.

Polygamy is practised in a few instances, and is not prohibited.

Divorces are frequent. If a difficulty of importance arises between a married couple, they agree to separate. They divide their property and children; the squaw takes the girls, the Indian the boys, and both are at liberty to marry again.

They have no marriage ceremony, nor form of divorcement, other than what has been mentioned.

OF FAMILY GOVERNMENT

In their families, parents are very mild, and the mother superintends the children. The word of the Indian father, however, is law, and must be obeyed by the whole that are under his authority.

One thing respecting the Indian women is worthy of attention, and perhaps of imitation, although it is now a days considered beneath the dignity of the ladies, especially those who are the most refined; and that is, they are under a becoming subjection to their husbands. It is a rule, inculcated in all the Indian tribes, and practised throughout their generations, that a squaw shall not walk before her Indian, nor pretend to take the lead in his business. And for this reason we never can see a party on the march to or from hunting and the like, in which the squaws are not directly in the rear of their partners.

OF THEIR FUNERALS

The deceased having been laid out in his best clothing, is put into a coffin of boards or bark, and with him is deposited, in every instance, a small cup and a cake. Generally two or three candles are also put into the coffin, and in a few instances, at the burial of a great man, all his implements of war are buried by the side of the body. The coffin is then closed and carried to the grave. On its being let down, the person who takes the lead of the solemn transaction, or a Chief, addresses the dead in a short speech, in which he charges him not to be troubled about himself in his new situation, nor on his journey, and not to trouble his friends, wife or children, whom he has left. Tells him that if he meets with strangers on his way, he must inform them what tribe he belongs to, who his relatives are, the situation in which he left them, and that having done this, he must keep on till he arrives at the good fields in the country of Nauwaneu. That when he arrives there he will see all his ancestors and personal friends that have gone before him;

who, together with all the Chiefs of celebrity, will receive him joyfully, and furnish him with every article of perpetual happiness.

The grave is now filled and left till evening, when some of the nearest relatives of the dead build a fire at the head of it, near which they set till morning. In this way they continue to practise nine successive nights, when, believing that their departed friend has arrived at the end of his journey, they discontinue their attention. During this time the relatives of the dead are not allowed to dance.

Formerly, frolics were held, after the expiration of nine days, for the dead, at which all the squaws got drunk, and those were the only occasions on which they were intoxicated: but lately those are discontinued, and squaws feel no delicacy in getting inebriated.

OF THEIR CREDULITY

As ignorance is the parent of credulity, it is not a thing to be wondered at that the Indians should possess it in a great degree, and even suffer themselves to be dictated and governed by it in many of the most important transactions of their lives.

They place great confidence in dreams, attach some sign to every uncommon circumstance, and believe in charms, spirits, and many supernatural things that never existed, only in minds enslaved to ignorance and tradition: but in no instance is their credulity so conspicuous, as in their unalterable belief in witches.

They believe there are many of these, and that next to the author of evil, they are the greatest scourge to their people. The term witch, by them, is used both in the masculine and feminine gender, and denotes a person to whom the evil deity has delegated power to inflict diseases, cause death, blast corn, bring bad weather, and in short to cause almost any calamity to which they are liable. With this impression, and believing that it is their actual duty to destroy, as far as lies in their power, every source of unhappiness, it has been a custom among them from time immemorial, to destroy every one that they could convict of so heinous a crime; and in fact there is no reprieve from the sentence.

Mrs. Jemison informed us that more or less who had been charged with being witches, had been executed in almost every year since she has lived on the Genesee. Many, on being suspected, made their escape: while others, before they were aware of being implicated, have been apprehended and brought to trial. She says that a number of years ago, an Indian chased a squaw, near Beard's Town, and caught her; but on the account of her great strength she got away. The Indian, vexed and disappointed, went home, and the next day reported that he saw her have fire in her mouth, and that she was a witch. Upon this she was apprehended and killed immediately. She was Big-tree's cousin, Mrs. Jemison says she was present at the execution. She also saw one other killed and thrown into the river.

Col. Jeremiah Smith, of Leicester, near Beard's Town, saw an Indian killed by his five brothers, who struck him on the head with their tomahawks at one time. He was charged with being a witch, because of his having been fortunate enough, when on a hunting party, to kill a number of deer, while his comrades failed of taking any.

Col. Smith also saw a squaw, who had been convicted of being a witch, killed by having small green whips burnt till they were red hot, but not quite coaled, and thrust down her throat. From such trifling causes thousands have lost their lives, and notwithstanding the means that are used for their reformation, the pagans will not suffer "a witch to live."

OF THE MANNER OF FARMING, AS PRACTISED BY THE INDIAN WOMEN

It is well known that the squaws have all the labor of the field to perform, and almost every other kind of hard service, which, in civil society, is performed by the men. In order to expedite their business, and at the same time enjoy each other's company, they all work together in one field, or at whatever job they may have on hand. In the spring they choose an old active squaw to be their driver and overseer when at labor, for the ensuing year. She accepts the honor, and they consider themselves bound to obey her.

When the time for planting arrives, and the soil is prepared, the squaws are assembled in the morning, and conducted into a field, where each plants one row. They then go into the next field, plant once across, and so on till they have gone through the tribe. If any remains to be planted, they again commence where they did at first, (in the same field,) and so keep on till the whole is finished. By this rule they perform their labor of every kind, and every jealousy of one having done more or less than another, is effectually avoided.

Each squaw cuts her own wood; but it is all brought to the house under the direction of the overseer—each bringing one back load.

OF THEIR METHOD OF COMPUTING TIME, AND KEEPING THEIR RECORDS

This is done by moons and winters: a moon is a month, and the time from the end of one winter to that of another, a year.

From sunset till sunrise, they say that the sun is asleep. In the old of the moon, when it does not shine in the night, they say it is dead. They rejoice greatly at the sight of the new moon.

In order to commemorate great events, and preserve the chronology of them, the war Chief in each tribe keeps a war post. This post is a peeled stick of timber, 10 or 12 feet high, that is erected in the town. For a campaign they make, or rather the Chief makes, a perpendicular red mark, about three inches long and half an inch wide; on the opposite side from this, for a scalp, they make a red cross, thus, ; on another side, for a prisoner taken, they make a red cross in this manner, X', with a head or dot, and by placing such significant hireoglyphics in so conspicuous a situation, they are enabled to ascertain with great certainty the time and circumstances of past events.

Hiokatoo had a war-post, on which was recorded his military exploits, and other things that he tho't worth preserving.

ANECDOTES

Hiokatoo used to say that when he was a young man, there lived in the same tribe with him an old Indian warrior, who was a great counsellor, by the name of Buck-in-je-hil-lish. Buckinjehillish having, with great fatigue, attended the council when it was deliberating upon war, declared that none but the ignorant made war, but that the wise men and the warriors had to do the fighting. This speech exasperated his countrymen to such a degree that he was apprehended and tried for being a witch, on the account of his having lived to so advanced an age; and because he could not show some reason why he had not died before, he was sentenced to be tomahawked by a boy on the spot, which was accordingly done.

In the last war, (1814,) an Indian who had been on fatigue, called at a commissary's and begged some bread. He was sent for a pail of water before he received it, and while he was absent an officer told the commissary to put a piece of money into the bread, and observe the event. He did so. The Indian took the bread and went off: but on the next day having ate his bread and found the money, he came to the commissary and gave him the same, as the officer had anticipated.

Little Beard, a celebrated Indian Chief, having arrived to a very advanced age, died at his town on the Genesee river about the first of June, 1806, and was buried after the manner of burying chiefs. In his life time he had been quite arbitrary, and had made some enemies whom he hated, probably, and was not loved by them. The grave, however, deprives envy of its malignity, and revenge of its keenness.

Little Beard had been dead but a few days when the great eclipse of the sun took place, on the sixteenth of June, which excited in the Indians a great degree of astonishment; for as they were ignorant of astronomy, they were totally unqualified to account for so extraordinary a phenomenon. The crisis was alarming, and something effectual must be done, without delay, to remove, if possible, the cause of such coldness and darkness, which it was expected would increase. They accordingly ran together in the three towns near the Genesee river, and after a short consultation agreed that Little Beard, on the account of some old grudge which he yet cherished towards them, had placed himself between them and the sun, in order that their corn might not grow, and so reduce them to a state of starvation. Having thus found the cause, the next thing was to remove it, which could only be done the use of powder and ball. Upon this, every gun and rifle was loaded, and a firing commenced, that continued without cessation till the old fellow left his seat, and the obscurity was entirely removed, to the great joy of the ingenious and fortunate Indians.

In the month of February, 1824, Corn Planter, a learned pagan Chief at Tonnewonta, died of common sickness. He had received a liberal education, and was held in high estimation in his town and tribe, by both parties; but the pagans more particularly mourned his loss deeply, and seemed entirely unreconciled. They imputed his death to witchcraft, and charged an Indian by the name of Prompit, with the crime.

Mr. Prompit is a Christian Indian, of the Tuscarora nation, who has lived at Tonnewonta a number of years, where he has built a saw-mill himself, which he owns, and is considered a decent, respectable man.

About two weeks after the death of Corn Planter, Mr. Prompit happened in company where the author was present, and immediately begun to converse upon that subject. He said that the old fashioned Indians called him a witch—believed that he had killed Corn Planter, and had said that they would kill him. But, said he, all good people know that I am not a witch, and that I am clear of the charge. Likely enough they will kill me; but if they do, my hands are clean, my conscience is clear, and I shall go up to God. I will not run nor hide from them, and they may kill me if they choose to—I am innocent. When Jesus Christ's enemies, said he, wanted to kill him, he did not run away from them, but let them kill him; and why should I run away from my enemies?

How the affair will terminate, we are unable to decide.

DESCRIPTION OF GENESEE RIVER AND ITS BANKS, FROM MOUNT MORRIS TO THE UPPER FALLS

From Mount Morris the banks of the Genesee are from two to four hundred feet in height, with narrow flats on one side of the river or the other, till you arrive at the tract called Gardow, or Cross Hills. Here you come to Mrs. Jemison's flats, which are two miles and a quarter long, and from eighty to one hundred and twenty rods wide, lying mostly on the west side of the river.

Near the upper end of these flats is the Great Slide. Directly above this, the banks (still retaining their before mentioned height) approach so near each other as to admit of but thirty acres of flat on one side of the river only, and above this the perpendicular rock comes down to the water.

From Gardow you ascend the river five miles to the lower falls, which are ninety-three feet perpendicular. These falls are twenty rods wide, and have the greatest channel on the east side. From Wolf creek to these falls the banks are covered with elegant white and Norway pine.

Above the lower falls the banks for about two miles are of perpendicular rock, and retain their height of between two and four hundred feet. Having travelled this distance you reach the middle falls, which are an uninterrupted sheet of water fifteen rods wide, and one hundred and ten feet in perpendicular height. This natural curiosity is not exceeded by any thing of the kind in the western country, except the cataract at Niagara.

From the middle falls the banks gradually rise, till you ascend the river half a mile, when you come to the upper falls, which are somewhat rolling, 66 feet, in the shape of a harrow. Above this the banks are of moderate height. The timber from the lower to the upper falls is principally pine. Just above the middle falls a saw-mill was erected this season (1823) by Messrs. Ziba Hurd and Alva Palmer.

HUNTING ANECDOTE

In November, 1822, Capt. Stephen Rolph and Mr. Alva Palmer drove a deer into Genesee river, a short distance above the middle falls, where the banks were so steep and the current so impetuous, that it could not regain the shore, and consequently was precipitated over the falls, one hundred and ten feet, into the gulph below. The hunters ran along the bank below the falls, to watch the fate of the animal, expecting it would be dashed in pieces. But to their great astonishment it came up alive, and by swimming across a small eddy, reached the bank almost under the falls; and as it stood in that situation, Capt. Ralph, who was on the top of the bank, shot it. This being done, the next thing to be considered was, how to get their prize. The rock being perpendicular, upwards of one hundred feet, would not admit of their climbing down to it, and there was no way, apparently, for them to get at it, short of going down the river two miles, to the lower falls, and then by creeping between the water and the precipice, they might possibly reach their game. This process would be too tedious. At length Mr. Palmer proposed to Capt. Rolph and Mr. Heman Merwin, who had joined them, that if they would make a windlas and fasten it to a couple of saplings that stood near, and then procure some ropes, he would be let down and get the deer. The apparatus was prepared; the rope was tied round Palmer's body, and he was let down. On arriving at the bottom he unloosed himself, fastened the rope round the deer, which they drew up, and then threw down the rope, in which he fastened himself, and was drawn up, without having sustained any injury. From the top to the bottom of the rock, where he was let down, was exactly one hundred and twenty feet.

Look Back on Happiness

by

Knut Hamsun

Look Back on Happiness
by Knut Hamsun

Copyright © 2024

All Rights reserved.

No part of this publication may be reproduced, stored in a retrieval system, or transmitted in any form or by any means, electronic, mechanical, photocopying or Otherwise, without the written permission of the publisher.
The author/editor asserts the moral right to be identified as the author/editor of this work.

ISBN: 978-93-63052-33-8

Published by

DOUBLE 9 BOOKS

2/13-B, Ansari Road
Daryaganj, New Delhi – 110002
info@double9books.com
www.double9books.com
Tel. 011-40042856

This book is under public domain

ABOUT THE AUTHOR

Knut Hamsun, a luminary of Scandinavian literature and Nobel laureate, showcases his unparalleled storytelling prowess in his masterpiece, "Look Back on Happiness." This timeless novel delves into the depths of human emotion and existential angst, capturing the essence of the human condition with Hamsun's trademark blend of lyricism and introspection. Set against the backdrop of early 20th-century Norway, "Look Back on Happiness" follows the journey of its protagonist as he navigates love, loss, and the search for meaning in a rapidly changing world. Hamsun's keen insights into the complexities of human relationships and the intricacies of the human psyche are on full display, as he delves into the innermost thoughts and desires of his characters with unparalleled depth and nuance. Through vivid prose and evocative imagery, Hamsun invites readers to ponder life's fundamental questions and confront the existential dilemmas that haunt us all. "Look Back on Happiness" stands as a testament to Hamsun's literary genius and enduring legacy, cementing his reputation as one of the greatest writers of the 20th century.

CONTENTS

I	7
II	10
III	17
IV	20
V	22
VI	26
VII	28
VIII	31
IX	34
X	38
XI	41
XII	44
XIII	47
XIV	53
XV	55
XVI	59
XVII	64
XVIII	67
XIX	73
XX	76
XXI	79
XXII	83
XXIII	87

XXIV	90
XXV	94
XXVI	98
XXVII	101
XXVIII	106
XXIX	109
XXX	112
XXXI	114
XXXII	121
XXXIII	132
XXXIV	141
XXXV	148
XXXVI	156
XXXVII	166
XXXVIII	175

I

I have gone to the forest.

Not because I am offended about anything, or very unhappy about men's evil ways; but since the forest will not come to me, I must go to it. That is all. I have not gone this time as a slave and a vagabond. I have money enough and am overfed, stupefied with success and good fortune, if you understand that. I have left the world as a sultan leaves rich food and harems and flowers, and clothes himself in a hair shirt.

Really, I could make quite a song and dance about it. For I mean to roam and think and make great irons red-hot. Nietzsche no doubt would have spoken thus: The last word I spake unto men achieved their praise, and they nodded. But it was my last word; and I went into the forest. For then did I comprehend the truth, that my speech must needs be dishonest or foolish.... But I said nothing of the kind; I simply went to the forest.

You must not believe that nothing ever happens here. The snowflakes drift down just as they do in the city, and the birds and beasts scurry about from morning till night, and from night till morning. I could send solemn stories from this place, but I do not. I have sought the forest for solitude and for the sake of my great irons; for I have great irons which lie within me and grow red-hot. So I deal with myself accordingly. Suppose I were to meet a buck reindeer one day, then I might say to myself:

"Great heavens, this is a buck reindeer, he's dangerous!"

But if then I should be too frightened, I might tell myself a comforting lie and say it was a calf or some feathered beast.

You say nothing happens here?

One day I saw two Lapps meet. A boy and a girl. At first they behaved as people do. "*Boris!*" they said to each other and smiled. But immediately after, both fell at full length in the snow and were gone from my sight. After a quarter of an hour had passed, I thought, "You'd better see to them; they may be smothered in the snow." But then they got up and went their separate ways.

In all my weatherbeaten days, I have never seen such a greeting as that.

Day and night I live in a deserted hut of peat into which I must crawl on my hands and knees. Someone must have built it long ago and used it, for lack of a better,--perhaps a man who was in hiding, a man who concealed himself here for a few autumn days. There are two of us in the hut, that is if you regard Madame as a person; otherwise there is only one. Madame is a mouse I live with, to whom I have given this honorary title. She eats everything I put aside for her in the nooks and corners, and sometimes she sits watching me.

When I first came, there was stale straw in the hut, which Madame by all means was allowed to keep; for my own bed I cut fresh pine twigs, as is fitting. I have an ax and a saw and the necessary crockery. And I have a sleeping bag of sheepskin with the wool inside. I keep a fire burning in the fireplace all night, and my shirt, which hangs by it, smells of fresh resin in the morning. When I want coffee, I go out, fill the kettle with clean snow, and hang it over the fire till the snow turns to water.

Is this a life worth living?

There you have betrayed yourself. This is a life you do not understand. Yes, your home is in the city, and you have furnished it with vanities, with pictures and books; but you have a wife and a servant and a hundred expenses. Asleep or awake you must keep pace with the world and are never at peace. I have peace. You are welcome to your intellectual pastimes and books and art and newspapers; welcome, too, to your bars and your whisky that only makes me ill. Here am I in the forest, quite content. If you ask me intellectual questions and try to trip me up, then I will reply, for example, that God is the origin of all things and that truly men are mere specks and atoms in the universe. You are no wiser than I. But if you should go so far as to ask me what is eternity, then I know quite as much in this matter, too, and reply thus: Eternity is merely unborn time, nothing but unborn time.

My friend, come here to me and I will take a mirror from my pocket and reflect the sun on your face, my friend.

You lie in bed till ten or eleven in the morning, yet you are weary, exhausted, when you get up. I see you in my mind's eye as you go out into the street; the morning has dawned too early on your blinking eyes. I rise at five quite refreshed. It is still dark outdoors, yet there is enough to look at--the moon, the stars, the clouds, and the weather portents for the day. I prophesy the weather for many hours ahead. In what key do the winds whistle? Is the crack of the ice in the Glimma light and dry, or deep and long? These are splendid portents, and as it grows lighter, I add the visible signs to the audible ones, and learn still more.

Then a narrow streak of daylight appears far down in the east, the stars fade from the sky, and soon light reigns over all. A crow flies over the woods, and I warn Madame not to go outside the hut or she will be devoured.

But if fresh snow has fallen, the trees and copses and the great rocks take on giant, unearthly shapes, as though they had come from another world in the night. A storm-felled pine with its root torn up looks like a witch petrified in the act of performing strange rites.

Here a hare has sprung by, and yonder are the tracks of a solitary reindeer. I shake out my sleeping bag and after hanging it high in a tree to escape Madame, who eats everything, I follow the tracks of the reindeer into the forest. It has jogged along without haste, but toward a definite goal--straight east to meet the day. By the banks of the Skiel, which is so rapid that its waters never freeze, the reindeer has stopped to drink, to scrape the hillside for moss, to rest a while, and then moved on.

And perhaps what this reindeer has done is all the knowledge and experience I gain that day. It seems much to me. The days are short; at two, I am already strolling homeward in the deep twilight, with the good, still night approaching. Then I begin to cook. I have a great deal of meat stored in three pure-white drifts of snow. In fact I have something even better: eight fat cheeses of reindeer milk, to eat with butter and crisp-bread.

While the pot is boiling I lie down, and gaze at the fire till I fall asleep. I take my midday nap before my meal. And when I waken, the food is cooked, filling the hut with an aroma of meat and resin. Madame darts back and forth across the floor and at length gets her share. I eat, and light my cutty-pipe.

The day is at an end. All has been well, and I have had no unpleasantness. In the great silence surrounding me, I am the only adult, roaming man; this makes me bigger and more important, God's kin. And I believe the red-hot irons within me are progressing well, for God does great things for his kin.

I lie thinking of the reindeer, the path it took, what it did by the river, and how it continued on its journey. There under the trees it has nibbled, and its horns have rubbed against the bark, leaving their marks; there an osier bed has forced it to turn aside; but just beyond, it has straightened its path and continued east once more. All this I think of.

And you? Have you read in a newspaper, which disagrees with another newspaper, what the public in Norway is thinking of old-age insurance?

II

On stormy days I sit indoors and find something to occupy my time. Perhaps I write letters to some acquaintance or other telling him I am well, and hope to hear the same from him. But I cannot post the letters, and they grow older every day. Not that it matters. I have tied the letters to a string that hangs from the ceiling to prevent Madame from gnawing at them.

One day a man came to the hut. He walked swiftly and stealthily; his clothes were ordinary and he wore no collar, for he was a laboring man. He carried a sack, and I wondered what could be in it.

"Good morning," we said to each other. "Fine weather in the woods."

"I didn't expect to find anybody in the hut," said the man. His manner was at once forceful and discontented; he flung down the sack without humility.

"He may know something about me," I thought, "since he is such a man."

"Have you lived here long?" he asked. "And are you leaving soon?"

"Is the hut yours, perhaps?" I asked in my turn.

Then he looked at me.

"Because if the hut is yours, that's another matter," I said. "But I don't intend like a pickpocket to take it with me when I leave."

I spoke gently and jestingly to avoid committing a blunder by my speech.

But I had said quite the right thing; the man at once lost his assurance. Somehow I had made him feel that I knew more about him than he knew about me.

When I asked him to come in, he was grateful and said:

"Thank you, but I'm afraid I'll get snow all over your floor."

Then he took special pains to wipe his boots clean, and bringing his sack with him, crawled in.

"I could give you some coffee," I said.

"You shouldn't trouble on my account," he replied, wiping his face and panting with the heat, "though I've been walking all night."

"Are you crossing the fjeld?"

"That depends. I don't suppose there's work to be got on a winter day on the other side, either."

I gave him coffee.

"Got anything to eat?" he said. "It's a shame to ask you. A round of crisp-bread? I had no chance to bring food with me."

"Yes, I've got bread, butter, and reindeer cheese. Help yourself."

"It's not so easy for a lot of people in the winter," said the man as he ate.

"Could you take some letters to the village for me?" I asked. "I'll pay you for it."

"Oh, no, I couldn't do that," the man replied. "I'm afraid that's impossible. I must cross the fjeld now. I've heard there's work in Hilling, in the Hilling Forest. So I can't."

"Must get his back up a bit again," I thought. "He just sits now there without any guts at all. In the end he'll start begging for a few coppers."

I felt his sack and said:

"What's this you're lugging about with you? Heavy things?"

"Mind your own business!" was his instant retort, as he drew the sack closer to him.

"I wasn't going to steal any of it; I'm no thief," I said, jesting again.

"I don't care what you are," he muttered.

The day wore on. Since I had a visitor, I had no desire to go to the woods, but wanted to sit and talk to him and ask him questions. He was a very ordinary man, of no great interest to the irons in my fire, with dirty hands, uneducated and uninteresting in his speech; probably he had stolen the things in his sack. Later I learned that he was quick in much small knowledge that life had taught him. He complained that his heels felt cold, and took off his boots. And no wonder he felt cold, for where the heels of his stockings should have been there were only great holes. He borrowed a knife to cut away the ragged edges, and then drew on the stockings again back to front, so that the torn soles came over his instep. When he had put on his boots again, he said, "There, now it's nice and warm."

He did no harm. If he took down the saw and the ax from their hooks to inspect them, he put them back again where he had found them. When he examined the letters, trying perhaps to read the addresses, he did not let them go carelessly, leaving them to swing back and forth, but held the string so that it hung motionless. I had no reason to complain about him.

He had his midday meal with me, and when he had eaten, he said:

"Do you mind if I cut myself some pine twigs to sit on?"

He went out to cut off some soft pine, and we had to move Madame's straw to make room for the man inside the hut. Then we lay on our twigs, burning resin and talking.

He was still there in the afternoon, still lying down as though to postpone the time of his leaving. When it began to grow dark, he went to the low doorway and looked out at the weather. Then, turning his head back, he asked:

"Do you think there'll be snow tonight?"

"You ask me questions and I ask you questions," I said, "but it looks like snow; the smoke is blowing down."

It made him uneasy to think it might snow, and he said he had better leave that night. Suddenly he flew into a rage. For as I lay there, I stretched, so that my hand accidentally touched his sack again.

"You leave me alone!" he shouted, tearing the sack from my grasp. "Don't you touch that sack, or I'll show you!"

I replied that I had meant nothing by it, and had no intention of stealing anything from him.

"Stealing, eh! What of it? I'm not afraid of you, and don't you go thinking I am! Look, here's what I've got in the bag," said the man, and began to rummage in it and to show me the contents: three pairs of new mittens, some sort of thick cloth for garments, a bag of barley, a side of bacon, sixteen rolls of tobacco, and a few large lumps of sugar candy. In the bottom of the bag was perhaps half a bushel of coffee beans.

No doubt it was all from the general stores, with the exception of a heap of broken crisp-bread, which might have been stolen elsewhere.

"So you've got crisp-bread after all," I said.

"If you knew anything about it, you wouldn't talk like that," the man replied. "When I'm crossing the fjeld on foot, walking and walking, don't I need food to put in my belly? It's blasphemy to listen to you!"

Neatly and carefully he put everything back into the sack, each article in its turn. He took pains to build up the rolls of tobacco round the bacon, to protect the cloth from grease stains.

"You might buy this cloth from me," he said. "I'll let you have it cheap. It's duffle. It only gets in my way."

"How much do you want for it?" I asked.

"There's enough for a whole suit of clothes, maybe more," he said to himself as he spread it out.

I said to the man:

"Truly you come here into the forest bringing with you life and the world and intellectual values and news. Let us talk a little. Tell me something: are you afraid your footprints will be visible tomorrow if there's fresh snow tonight?"

"That's my business. I've crossed the field before and I know many paths," he muttered. "I'll let you have the cloth for a few crowns."

I shook my head, so the man again neatly folded the cloth and put it back in the bag exactly as though it belonged to him.

"I'll cut it up into material for trousers; then the pieces won't be so large, and I'll be able to sell it."

"You'd better leave enough for a whole suit in one piece," I said, "and cut up the rest for trousers."

"You think so? Yes, maybe you're right."

We calculated how much would be necessary for a grown man's suit, and took down the string from which the letters hung to measure our own clothes, so as to be sure to get the measurements right. Then we cut into the edge of the cloth, and tore it across. In addition to one complete suit, there was enough left for two good-sized pairs of trousers.

Then the man offered to sell me other things out of his sack, and I bought some coffee and a few rolls of tobacco. He put the money away in a leather purse, and I saw how empty the purse was, and the circumstantial and poverty-stricken fashion in which he put the money away, afterward feeling the outside of his pocket.

"You haven't been able to sell me much," I said, "but I don't need any more than that."

"Business is business," said he. "I don't complain."

It was quite decent of him.

While he was making ready to depart and clearing his bed of pine needles out of the way, I thought pityingly of his sordid little theft. Stealing because he was needy--a side of bacon and a length of cloth which he was trying to sell in the forest! Theft has indeed ceased to be a matter of great moment. This is because legal punishment for misdemeanors of all kinds has also ceased to be of great moment. It is only a dull, human punishment; the religious element has been removed from the law, and a local magistrate is no longer a man of mystic power.

I well remember the last time I heard a judge explain the meaning of the oath as it should be explained. It chilled us all to the bone to hear him. We need some witchcraft again, and the Sixth Book of Moses, and the sin against the Holy Ghost, and signing your name in the blood of a newly baptized child! Steal a sack of money and silver treasure, if you like, and hide the sack in the hills where on autumn evenings a blue flame will hover over the spot. But don't come to me with three pairs of mittens and a side of household bacon!

The man no longer worried about the sack; leaving it behind, he crawled out of the hut to study the weather. The coffee and tobacco I had bought I put back into the sack, for I did not need them. When he returned, he said:

"I think after all I'd better stop the night here with you, if you don't mind."

In the evening he gave no indication of being prepared to contribute any of his own food. I cooked some coffee and gave him some dry bread to eat with it.

"You shouldn't have expenses for me," he said.

Then he began to rummage in his sack again, pushing the bacon well down so that the cloth might not be stained by it; after this he took off his leather belt and put it round the sack, with a loop to carry over one shoulder.

"Now if I take the neck of the sack over the other shoulder, I'll find it easier to carry," he said.

I gave him my letters to post on the other side of the fjeld and he stowed them away safely, slapping the outside of his pocket afterward; I also gave him a special envelope in which to keep the money for the stamps, and tied it to the neck of the sack.

"Where do you live?" I asked him.

"Where can a poor man live? Of course I live by the sea. I'm sorry to say I have a wife and children--no use denying it."

"How many children have you?"

"Four. One's got a crippled arm and the others--there's something wrong with all of them. It's not easy for a poor devil. My wife's ill, and a few days ago she thought she was dying and wanted Communion."

A sad note crept into his voice. But the note was false. He was telling me a pack of lies. When they came to look for him from the village, no Christian would have the heart to accuse a man with such a large and sick family. This, no doubt, was his meaning.

Man, oh man, thou art worse than a mouse!

I questioned him no further, but asked him to sing something, a ballad or a song, since we had nothing else to do.

"I've no heart to sing now," he replied. "Except possibly a hymn."

"All right; sing a hymn, then."

"Not now. I'd like to do you a favor, but--"

His uneasiness was rising. A little later he took his sack and went out.

"Well, he's gone," I thought, "but he hasn't said the customary peace-be-with-you. I'm glad I've come into the forest," I thought. "This is my home, and from this day forth, no mother's son shall come within my walls again."

I made an elaborate agreement with myself that I should have no more truck with men.

"Madame, come here," I said. "I esteem you highly, and herewith, Madame, I undertake to enter upon a union with you for life!"

Half an hour later, the man returned. He carried no sack.

"I thought you'd gone," I said.

"Gone? I'm not a dog," he replied. "I've met people before this, and I say good morning when I come and peace-be-with-you when I go. You shouldn't sneer at me, you know."

"What have you done with the sack?"

"I've carried it part of the way."

His concealing the sack in case anyone should come proved he had forethought, for it was easier to get away scot-free without a burden on one's back. To stop him from telling me any more lies about his poverty, I said:

"I expect you've raised plenty of dust in your day? Still do, for that matter?"

"Well, I do what I can," he replied cheerfully. "I can lift a barrel easier than most, and nobody was able to dance me off the floor last Christmas! Hush--is that someone coming?"

We listened. His eyes darted toward the entrance, and in a moment he had chosen to meet danger halfway. He was taut and splendid; I could see his jaw working.

"It's nothing," I said.

Resolute and strong as a bull, he crawled out of the hut and was gone for a few minutes. When he returned, breathing heavily, he said:

"It's nothing."

We lay down for the night.

"In God's name!" he said, as he settled himself on his pine bed. I fell asleep at once, and for some time slept deeply. But during the night restlessness seized on the man again. "Peace be with you!" I heard him mutter as he crawled out of the hut.

In the morning I burned the man's bed of pine needles; it made a lively fire of crackling pine in the hut.

Outside, the ground was covered with new-fallen snow.

III

There is nothing like being left alone again, to walk peacefully with oneself in the woods. To boil one's coffee and fill one's pipe, and to think idly and slowly as one does it.

There, now I'll fill the kettle with snow, I think, and now I'm crushing the coffee beans with a stone; later I must beat my sleeping bag well in the snow and get the wool white again. There is nothing in this of literature or great novels or public opinion; does it matter? But then I haven't been toiling just to get this coffee into my life. Literature? When Rome ruled the world, she was no more than Greece's apprentice in literature. Yet Rome ruled the world. Let us look too at another country we know: it fought a war of independence the glory of which still shines, and it brought forth the greatest school of painting in the world. Yet it had no literature, and has none today....

Day by day I grow more knowing in the ways of the trees and the moss and the snow on the ground, and all things are my friends. The stump of a fir tree stands thawing in the sun; I feel my familiarity with it grow, and sometimes I stand there loving it, for there is something in it that moves my soul. The bark is badly broken. One winter in the deep snow, the tree must have been crippled, and now it points upward long and naked. I put myself in its place, and look at it with pity. My eyes perhaps have the simple, animal expression that human eyes had in the age of the mastodons.

No doubt you will seize this opportunity to mock me, for there are many amusing things you can say about me and this stump of a fir. Yet in your heart, you know that I am superior to you in this as in everything else, with the single exception that I have not your conventional accomplishments, nor have I passed examinations. About the forest and the earth you can teach me nothing, for here I feel what no man else has felt.

Sometimes I take the wrong direction and lose my way. Yes, truly this may happen sometimes. But I do not begin to twist and lose myself outside my very door, like the children of the city. I am twelve miles out, far up the opposite bank of the Skjel River, before I begin to get lost, and then only on a sunless day, with perhaps thick, wild snow coming down, and no north or south in the sky. Then you must know the special marks of this kind of tree and that, the galipot of the pine, the bark of deciduous trees, the moss that grows at their roots, the angle of the south and north-pointing branches, the stones that are moss-covered and those that are bare, and the pattern of the network of veins in the leaves. From all these things while there is daylight I can find my way.

But if the dusk falls, I know it will be impossible for me to get home till the next day. "How shall I pass this night?" I say to myself. And I roam about till I find a sheltered spot; the best is a crag standing with its back to the wind. Here I collect a few armfuls of pine needles, button my jacket tight, and take a long time to settle. No one who has not tried it knows anything of the fine pleasure that streams through the soul as one sits in a snug shelter on such a night. I light my pipe to pass the time, but the tobacco doesn't agree with me because I haven't eaten, so I put some resin in my mouth to chew as I lie thinking of many things. The snow continues to fall outside; if I have been lucky enough to find a shelter facing the right way, the snowdrifts will close in over me and form a crest like a roof above my retreat. Then I am quite safe, and may sleep or wake as I please; there will be no danger of freezing my feet.

Two men came to my hut; they were in a great hurry, and one of them called to me:

"Good morning. Has a man passed this way?"

I didn't like his face. I was not his servant and his question was too stupid.

"Many people may have passed this way. Do you mean have I *seen* a man go by?"

So much for him!

"I meant what I said," the man replied surlily. "I'm asking you in the name of the law."

"Oh."

I had no desire for further conversation, and crawled into my hut.

The two men followed me. The constable grinned and said:

"Did you *see* a man pass by here yesterday?"

"No," I said.

They looked at each other, and took counsel together; then they left the hut and returned to the village.

I thought: What zeal this policeman showed in the execution of his duties, how he shone with public spirit! There will be bonuses for the capture and transport of the criminal; there will be honor in having carried out the deed. All mankind should adopt this man because he is its son, created in its image! Where are the irons? He would rattle the links a little and lift them on his arm like the train of a riding skirt, to make me feel his terrifying power to put people in irons ... I feel nothing.

And what tradesmen--what kings of trade--we have today! They instantly miss what a man can carry off in a sack, and notify the police.

From now on I begin to long for the spring. My peat hut lies still too near to mankind, and I will build myself another when the frost has gone out of the ground. On the other side of the Skjel, I have chosen a spot in the forest which I think I shall like. It is twenty-four miles from the village and eighteen across the fjeld.

IV

Have I said that I was too near men? Heaven help me, for some days in succession I have been taking strolls in the forest, saying good morning and pretending I was in human company. If it was a man I imagined beside me, we carried on a long, intelligent conversation, but if it was a woman, I was polite: "Let me carry your parcel, miss." Once it must have been the Lapp's daughter I seemed to meet, for I flattered her most lavishly and offered to carry her fur cloak if she would take it off and walk in her skin; tut, tut.

Heaven help me, I am no longer too near men. And probably I will not build that peat hut still further away from them.

The days grow longer, and I do not mind. The truth is that in the winter I suffered privation and learned much in order to master myself. It has taken time and sometimes a resolute will, so it cannot be denied that I am paying for my education rather dearly. Sometimes I have been needlessly stern with myself.

"There is a loaf of bread," I said. "It doesn't surprise me, it doesn't interest me; I am used to it. But if you see no bread for twelve hours, it will mean something to you," I said, and hid the bread away.

That was in the winter.

Were they dreary days? No, good days. My liberty was so great that I could do and think as I pleased; I was alone, the bear of the forest. But even in the heart of the forest no man dares speak aloud without looking round; rather, he walks in silence. For a time you console yourself that it's typically English to be silent, it's regal to be silent. But suddenly you find this has gone too far, your mouth begins to wake, to stretch, and suddenly to shout nonsense.

"Bricks for the palace! The calf is much stronger today!"

Perhaps if your voice is strong, the sound will carry for a quarter of a mile--but then you feel a sting as though after a slap. If only you had kept your regal silence! One day the postman who crosses the fjeld once a month came on me just as I had shouted.

"What?" he called from the wood.

"Careful below!" I called back to save my face. "I've put out a trap."

But with the longer days, my courage grows; it must be the spring that causes this mysterious revival within me, and I no longer fear a shout more or less. I needlessly rattle my pots and pans as I cook, and I sing at the top of my voice. It is spring.

Yesterday I stood on a hillock and looked out across the wintry woods. They have a different expression now; they have gone gray and bedraggled, and the midday sun has thawed down the snow and diminished it. There are catkins everywhere, drifts of them in the underbrush, looking like letters of the alphabet piled in a heap. The moon rises, the stars break forth. I am cold and shiver a little, but I have nothing to do in the hut, and prefer to shiver as long as possible. In the winter I did nothing so foolish, but went home if I was cold. Now I'm tired of that, too. It is the spring.

The sky is pure and cool, lying wide open to all the stars. There is a great flock of worlds up in that endless meadow, tiny, teeming worlds, so tiny that they are like the sound of a tinkling bell; as I look at them, I can hear thousands of tiny bells. Yes, certainly I am being drawn more and more toward the grassy slopes of spring.

V

I fill the fireplace with pine wood, hoist my belongings to my back, and leave the hut. "Farewell, Madame."

That was the end.

I feel no pleasure at leaving my shelter, but a touch of sadness--as I always do on leaving a place that has been my home for some time. But all the world stands outside calling to me. Indeed I am like all lovers of the woods and fields; wordlessly we had agreed to meet, and as I sat there last night, I felt my eyes being drawn to the door.

Several times I look back at the hut, with the smoke rising up from the chimney; the smoke billows and waves to me, and I wave back.

The silky pallor of the morning refreshes me; in a long blue haze over the forest, a slow dawn rises. It looks like a cheerful piratical coast in the sky before me. The mountains are all on my left.

After a few hours' march I am like new from top to toe, and I press on swiftly. I beat the air with my stick, and it says "hoo" as it swishes; whenever I think I deserve it, I sit down and give myself food.

No, you have not my pleasures in the town.

I beat my legs with my stick from the sheer exuberance of living, and nearly cry out. I behave as though the burden on my back had no weight, taking needless leaps, and overexerting myself a little; but an overexertion to which one is driven by inner content is easy to bear. In my solitude, many miles from men and houses, I am in a childishly happy and carefree state of mind, which you are incapable of understanding unless someone explains it to you. I play a little game with myself, pretending to have discovered a remarkable kind of tree. At first I pay little attention, then I stretch my neck and contract my eyelids and gaze.

"What!" I say to myself. "Surely it couldn't be--"

I throw down my burden and approach, inspect the tree and nod sagely, saying it is a strange, fabled tree that I have discovered. And I take out my notebook and describe it.

Merely jest and happiness, a queer little impulse to play. Children have done it before me. And here comes no postman to surprise me. As suddenly as I have begun the game, I end it again, as children do. But for a moment I was transported back to the dear, foolish bliss of childhood.

Perhaps it was the anticipation of soon seeing men again that made me playful and happy!

Next day, just as a raw mist descends on mountain and forest, I reach the Lapp's house. I enter. But though I meet with nothing but kindness, a Lapp hut contains little that is interesting. There are spoons and knives of bone on the peat wall, and a small paraffin lamp hangs from the roof. The Lapp himself is a dull nonentity who can neither tell fortunes nor conjure. His daughter has gone across the field; she has learned to read, but not to write, at the village school. The two old people, husband and wife, are fools. The whole family share a sort of animal dumbness; if I ask them a question, I may or may not get half a reply: "Mm-no, mm-yes." I am not a Lapp, and so they distrust me.

All the afternoon the mist lay white on the forest. I slept a while. In the evening, the sky was clear again, and there were a few degrees of frost. I left the hut. The moon stood full and silent above the earth.

Heigh-ho--what untuned strings!

> But where are the birds all gone away,
> and what kind of place is this?
> Here where I stand nothing moves or stirs,
> in this world that is dead, no event occurs;
> I stand in a silvermine.
> My eyes sweep round, but I sorely miss
> a homely, well-known outline.
>
> And so he came to a silver wood--
> thus ran an ancient tale.
> Here rests a song of shimmering fire
> as though it were sung by a starry choir.
> And swift in my youth, I leap
> to bind fast the troll, the cunning male,
> and awaken a maid from her sleep.

Today I smile at childish tales,
old age has made me wise.
Once proudly in prodigal youth I trod,
now by age my foot is heavily shod;
yet my heart--my heart would fly.
I am driven by fire and bound by ice,
no rest nor repose have I.

A shuddering chill falls on the night,
like a cloud from the lungs in the cold.
There passed a great gust through the silver lace
of the woods, like a lion's royal pace
on paws that are soundless and still.
It may be a god on his evening stroll.
The roots of the forest thrill.

When I returned to the hut, the daughter had also returned home, and sat eating after her long march. Olga the Lapp, tiny and queer, conceived in a snowdrift, in the course of a greeting. "*Boris!*" they said and fell on their noses.

She had bought red and blue pieces of cloth at the draper's shop in the village, and no sooner had she finished eating than she pushed the cups and plates away and began to embroider her Sunday jacket with pretty strips of the cloth. All the while she never spoke a word, because a stranger was in the room.

"You know me, Olga, don't you?"

"Mm."

"But you look so angry."

"M-no."

"How's the snow track across the fjeld?"

"All right."

I knew there was a deserted hut the family had once lived in, and asked:

"How far is it to your old hut?"

"Not far," said Olga.

Olga Lapp has someone to smile at surely, even if she will not smile at me. Here she sits in the great forest, pandering to her vanity and sewing wonderful scrolls on her jacket. On Sunday, no doubt, she will wear it to church and meet the man whose eyes it is meant to gladden.

I was not anxious to stay any longer with these small beings, these human grains of sand. As I had slept enough in the afternoon and the moon was bright, I prepared to leave. After laying in a further supply of reindeer cheese and whatever other food I could get, I left the hut. But what a surprise: the bright moonlight was gone, and the sky was overcast; there was no frost, only mild weather and wet woods. It was spring.

When Olga Lapp saw this, she advised me against leaving; but why should I listen to her chatter? She came with me a little way into the woods to direct me, then turned and went back, tiny and queer, her feathers ruffled like a hen's.

VI

It was difficult to advance. Never mind. A few hours later I found myself high up on the fjeld; I must have strayed from the path. What is that dark shape there? A mountain peak. And that over there? Another peak. Let us pitch camp on the spot, then.

There was a deep goodness and tenderness about this mild night. I sat in the dark recalling forgotten memories of my childhood, and many experiences in this place and that. And what a satisfaction it is, too, to have money in one's pocket, even if one sleeps in the open!

During the night I woke up; I found it growing too warm for me under my crag, and loosened my sleeping bag. It seemed to me, too, that a sound still hummed in my ear, as though I had called out or sung in my sleep. Suddenly I felt completely rested, and turned to look about me. It was dark and mild, a stone-still world. The sky was paler than the ring of mountains round me; I lay in the center of a city of peaks, at the foot of a great cliff, huge to the point of deformity. The wind began to blow, and suddenly there was a booming in the distance. Then came a streak of lightning, and immediately after the thunder rolled down like a gigantic avalanche between the most distant peaks. It was matchless to lie there listening, and a supernatural delight, a thrill of enjoyment, ran through me. A stranger madness filled me than I had ever felt before, and I gave it expression by laughing aloud in wanton and humorous abandon. Many a thought ran through my mind, witticisms alternating with moments of such great sorrow that I lay sighing deeply. The lightning and thunder came closer, and it began to rain--a torrential rain. The echoes were overpowering; all nature was an uproar, a hullabalooing. I tried to conquer the night by shouting at it, lest mysteriously it should rob me of my strength and leave me without a will. These mountains, I thought, are sheer incantations against my journey, great planted curses that block my path. Or perhaps I have only strayed into a mountains' trade union? But I nod my head repeatedly. That means I am brave and happy. Perhaps after all they are only stuffed mountains.

More lightning and thunder and torrential rain; it felt as though the near-by echo had slapped me, reverberating a hundred times through me. Never mind. I have read about many battles and been in a rain of bullets before this. Yet in a moment of sadness and humility in the presence of the powers about me, I weep and think:

"Who am I now among men? Or am I lost already? Am I nothing already?"

And I cry out and call my name to hear if it still lives.

A wheel of gold turned before my eyes, and the thunder clapped over my very head, on my own fjeld. Instantly I started out of the sleeping bag and left my shelter. The thunder rolled on, there was lightning and more thunder, worlds were uprooted. Why had I not listened to Olga's advice and remained in the hut? Is it the Lapps whose magic powers are doing this? The Lapps? Those human mites, those mountain dwarfs! What is all this noise to me? I made a feeble effort to walk against it, but stopped again, for I was among giants, and saw the foolishness of trying to battle with the thunder.

I leaned against the side of the mountain: no longer did I stand shouting and hurling challenges at my opponent, but looked at him with milk-blue eyes. And now that I have yielded, none but a mountain would be so hard. But I am not rhymes and rhythms alone; did you think I should waste my good brain chasing such rainbows? You lie. Here I lean against the whole world, and you, perhaps, believe the blue of my eyes....

At that, the lightning struck me. This was a miracle, and it happened to me. It ran down my left elbow, scorching the sleeve of my jacket. The lightning seemed like a ball of wool that dropped to the ground. I felt a sensation of heat, and saw that the ground farther down the mountain was struck a loud blow and then split. A great oppression held me down; a spear of darkness shot through me. And then it thundered beyond all measure, not long and rumbling, but firm and clear and rattling.

The storm passed on.

VII

Next day I arrived at the deserted hut, drenched to the skin, struck by lightning, but in a strangely gentle and yielding mood, as after a punishment. My good fortune in the midst of my ill-luck made me overfriendly to everything; I tramped on without hurting the ground, and I avoided sinful thoughts, though it was spring. I was not even out of temper when I had to retrace my steps across the fjeld to find my way again to the hut. I had time; there was no hurry. I was the first tourist of the spring season, and far too early.

So I remained at my ease in the hut for a few days. Sometimes at night verses and small poems blossomed in my mind as though I had become a real poet. At any rate there were signs that great changes had taken place within me since the winter, when I had desired nothing but to lie blinking my eyes and be left in peace.

One day when everything was thawing in the sun, I left the hut and walked about the mountains for some hours. I had lately been thinking of writing some children's verses, addressed to a certain little girl, but nothing had come of it. Now as I walked on the mountainside, I felt again a desire for this pastime, and worked at it on several occasions, but could not get it into shape. The night, when one has slept an hour or two, is the time when such things come to one.

So I went straight on to the village and bought myself a good store of food. There were many people in this district, and it did me good to hear human speech and laughter again; but there was no place here where I could stay, and in any case I had come too early. I had much to carry on my way home to my hut again. About halfway I met a man, a casual laborer, a vagabond, whose name was Solem. Later I heard that he was the bastard son of a telegraph operator who had been in Rosenlund nearly a generation before.

That this man should have stepped off the path to let me pass with my burden was a good trait in him, and I thanked him and said, "I shouldn't have run over you in any case, ha, ha!"

He asked me if there was much snow on the way to the village. I told him it was much the same as here. "I see," he said, and turned away. I thought that perhaps he had come a long way, and since he carried nothing that looked like provisions, I offered him some of mine in order to make him talk a little. He thanked me and accepted.

He was above middle height, and quite young, not more than in his twenties, possibly just on thirty--a fine fellow. After the swaggering fashion of wanderers, he had a lock of hair escaping from under the peak of his cap; but he wore no beard. This full-grown man still shaved without growing tired of doing so, and this, together with his fringe of hair and his general manner, gave me the impression that he wished to seem younger than he was.

We talked while he ate; he laughed readily and was in a cheerful mood, and since his face was beardless and hard, it looked like a laughing iron mask. But he was sensible and pleasant. There was only one thing: I had been silent for so long that I talked now perhaps too readily; and if it happened that both this boy Solem and I spoke at once, he would stop immediately to let me have my say. When this had happened several times, I grew tired of winning, and stopped too. But that merely made him nod and say: "Go ahead."

I explained to him that I idled in solitude, studying strange trees, and writing a thing or two about them, that I lived in a hut, but that today I had finished my stock of provisions and had had to go to the village. When he heard about the hut, he stopped chewing, and sat as though he were listening; then he said hastily: "Yes, in a way I know these telegraph poles across the mountains very well. Not these particular poles, but others. I was a linesman till not long ago."

"Were you?" I said. "Haven't you passed my hut today?" I added.

He hesitated a moment, but when he saw that I was not trying to put him in the wrong, he admitted that he had been in the hut and rested, and found my crisp-bread there.

"It wasn't easy to sit there without taking some of it," he said.

We spoke of many things. His language was hardly coarse at all, nor did he dawdle over his food. My own manners had run wild to such an extent that I valued his good behavior.

He offered to help me carry my pack as a mark of his gratitude for the food, and I accepted his offer. It was in this way that the stranger returned to the hut with me. As soon as I came in I saw a note on the table, a sort of thanks for the bread; it was an extremely ill-mannered epistle, full of obscene expressions. When Solem saw what I was reading, his iron face broke into a smile. I pretended not to understand the note and threw it back on the table; he picked it up and tore it to shreds.

"I'm sorry you've seen it," he said. "We linesmen have a way of doing that sort of thing, and I'd forgotten I'd left it here."

Soon after this he went out.

He stayed that night and next day, and found a means of repaying me by washing some of my clothes and making himself useful in other ways. There was a large tub outside the hut--had been since the Lapps lived there--which was cracked and leaked abundantly, but Solem stopped the cracks with bacon fat and boiled my clothes in it. It was very funny to watch him imperturbably skimming off the fat that floated up.

He seemed to want to stay till we had finished the provisions again, and then to go with me to the village; but when he heard I was going the other way, to the mountain farm somewhere under the great peaks of the Tore, where summer visitors stayed and many travelers passed, he wanted to go there, too. He was a bird of passage.

"Can't I come with you and help you carry?" he asked me. "I'm used to farm work, too, and perhaps I can get a job there."

VIII

The bustle of spring season had already started at the great farm; men and animals were awake, the barn re-echoed with lowing the whole day long, and the goats had long since been let out to pasture.

It was a long way between neighbors here; one or two cotters had cleared an area in the forest, which they had then bought; apart from that, all the land in sight belonged to the farm. Many new houses had been built here as the traffic over the fjelds increased, and gargoyles, homelike and Norwegian, sat on the gable ends, while the sound of a piano came from the living-room. Do you know the place? You have been here, and the people of the farm have asked after you.

Good days, nothing but good days: a suitable transition from solitude. I speak to the young people who own the homestead now, and to the husband's old father and young sister Josephine. The old man leaves his room to look at me. He is terrifyingly old, perhaps ninety; his eyes are worn and half-crazed, and his figure has shrunk to nothing. He toils with both hands to drag himself into the day, and each time it is as though he left his mother's womb anew and found a world before him:

"Look, how strange, there are houses on the farm," he thinks as he gazes at them. And when the barn doors stand open, he looks at them, too, and thinks:

"Just like a doorway; what can it be? Looks exactly like a doorway...."

And he stands still a long time staring at it.

But Josephine, the daughter of his latest marriage, is young and plays the piano for me. Ah, Josephine! As she runs through the garden, her feet are like a breeze under her skirt. How kind she is to the visitors! Surely she has seen us coming a long way off, Solem and myself, and sat down to play the piano. She has gray, pathetic, young girl's hands--hands which confirm an old observation of mine that one's hands reveal one's sexual character, showing chastity, indifference, or passion.

It is pleasant to watch Josephine crouch down to milk the goat. But she is only doing this now to charm and please the stranger. Ordinarily she has no time for such work, for she is too busy at her indoor tasks, waiting at table and watering the flowers and chatting with me about who climbed the Tore Peak last summer, and who did it the summer before that. These are Josephine's tasks.

Refreshed and rejuvenated, I idle about, stand for a while watching Solem, who has been put to carting manure, then drift on down through the wood to the cotters' houses. Neat, compact houses, barns with room for two cows and a couple of goats in each, half-naked children playing homemade games outside the barns, quarrels and laughter and tears. The men at both places cart manure on sleighs, seeking a path where the snow and ice still lie on the ground, and doing very well with it. I do not descend to the houses, but watch the work from my point of vantage. Well do I know the life of labor, and well do I like it.

It was no small area these cotters had broken up; the homesteads were tiny but the fences surrounding the land included a good section of forest. When the ground was cleared all the way to the fence, this would be a farm with five cows and a horse. Good luck!

The days pass, the windowpanes have thawed, the snow is melting away, green things grow against south walls, and the leaves break out in the woods. My original intention to make great irons hot within me is unchanged; but if I ever thought this an easy task I must be an incredible fool. I do not even know with any certainty if there are irons in me still, or whether I can shape them if there are. Since the winter, life has made me lonely and small; I idle and loiter here, remembering that once things were different. Now that I have reached daylight and men again, I begin to understand all this. I was a different person once. The wave has its feathered crest, and so had I; wine has its fire, and so had I. Neurasthenia, the ape of all the diseases, pursues me.

What then? No, I do not mourn this. Mourn? It is for women to mourn. Life is only a loan, and I am grateful for the loan. At times I have had gold and silver and copper and iron and other small metals; it was a great delight to live in the world, much greater than an endless life away from the world; but pleasure cannot last. I know of no one who has not been through the same thing; but I know of no one who will admit it. How they have declined! But they themselves have said:

"See how everything is better!"

At their first jubilee, they left life behind and began a vegetating existence; once one is fifty, the seventies begin. And the irons were no longer red-hot; there were no irons. But by heaven, how stubbornly Simplicity insisted the irons were there, insisted that they were red.

"See the irons!" Simplicity said. "See how red they are!"

As though it mattered that death can be kept off for another twenty years from one who has already begun to perish! I have no use for such a way of thinking; but you have, no doubt, you with your cheerful mediocrity and school education. A one-armed man can still walk; a one-legged man can lie down. Has the forest taught you nothing, then? What have I learned in the forest? *That young trees grow there.*

In my footsteps walks youth, youth that is shamelessly, barbarously scorned, merely because it is young, scorned by stupidity and degeneration. I have seen this for many years. I know nothing more despicable than your school education and your school-education standards. Whether you have a catechism or a compass by which to guide your life is all the same; come here, my friend, and I will give you a compass made of my latest iron.

IX

A tourist arrived at the farm: the first tourist. And the master of the house himself went with him across the fjeld, and as for Solem, why, he, too, went with him so that he might know the way for later tourists. We found the fat, short, and thin-haired stranger standing in the yard, an elderly, well-to-do man who walked for the sake of his health and the last twenty years of his life. Josephine, the dear girl, made her feet a breeze beneath her skirts, and got him into the living room, with its piano and its earthenware bowls with beaded edges. When he was leaving, he brought out his small change, which Josephine received in her gray, young-girl's fingers. On the other side of the fjeld, Solem was given two crowns for acting as guide, and that was good pay. All went so well that the master himself was content.

"Now they'll be coming," he said. "If only they would leave us in peace," he added.

By this he meant he regretted the good, carefree days that he and his household had enjoyed till now; but in a few weeks a motor road would be opened in the neighboring valley, and then it was a question whether the tourist traffic might not be deflected there. His wife and Josephine were a little afraid it would be; but he himself had held as long as possible to the opinion that all their regular visitors who had come again year after year would remain faithful. No matter how many roads and motor cars they might have in other places, they could not get the peaks of the Tore range anywhere but here.

The master of the house had felt so confident that once more he had much timber lying by the wall of the barn, ready to be built into new cottages, with six new guestrooms, a great hall with reindeer horns and log chairs, and a bathroom. But what was the matter with him today; was he beginning to doubt? "If only they would leave us in peace," he said.

A week later Mrs. Brede arrived with her children; she had a cottage to herself, as in previous summers. So she must be rich and fashionable, this Mrs. Brede, since she had a cottage to herself. She was a charming lady, and her little daughters were well-grown, handsome children. They curtsied to me, making me feel, I don't know why, as though they were giving me flowers. A strange feeling.

Then came Miss Torsen and Mrs. Molie, who were both to stay for the summer. They were followed by Schoolmaster Staur, who would stay a week. Later came two schoolmistresses, the Misses Johnsen and Palm, and still later Associate Schoolmaster Höy and several others--tradesmen, telephone operators, a few people from Bergen, one or two Danes. There were many of us at table now, and the talk was lively. When Schoolmaster Staur was asked if he wanted more soup, he replied: "No, thank you; I require no more!" and then rolled his eyes at us to show that this was the correct thing to say. Between meals we made up small parties, going this way and that on the sides of the fjeld and in the woods. But of transient guests there were few or none at all, and it was really on these that the house would earn well--on rooms for a night, on single meals, on cups of coffee. Josephine seemed to be worrying lately, and her young fingers grew more greedy as they counted silver coins.

Lean brook trout, goat's-meat stew, and tinned foods. Some of the guests were dissatisfied people who spoke of leaving; others praised both the food and the wild mountain scenery. Schoolmistress Torsen wanted to leave. She was tall and handsome and wore a red hat on her dark hair; but there were no suitable young men here, and in the long run it was a bore to waste her holidays so completely. Tradesman Batt, who had been in both Africa and America, was the only possibility, for even the Bergensians amounted to nothing.

"Where's Miss Torsen?" Batt would ask us.

"Here I am; I'm coming," the lady answered.

They did not care for walks up the fjeld, but preferred to go to the woods together, where they talked for hours. But Tradesman Batt did not amount to much either; he was short and freckled, and talked of nothing but money and trade. Besides, he had only a small shop in the town, and dealt in tobacco and fruit. No, he did not amount to much.

One day, during a long spell of rain, I sat talking with Miss Torsen. She was an extraordinary girl, ordinarily proud and reserved, but sometimes talkative, lively, and perhaps a little inconsiderate, too. We sat in the living room, with people coming and going continually, but she did not let that disturb her, and talked in high, clear tones; in her eagerness she sometimes clasped her hands, and then dragged them apart again. After we had been sitting there for some time, Tradesman Batt came in, listened to her for a moment, and then said:

"I'm going out now, Miss Torsen; are you coming?"

She swept him once with her eyes from head to foot; then she turned away and went on talking, looking very proud and determined as she did so. No doubt she had many good qualities; she was twenty-seven, she said, and sick and tired of a teacher's life.

But why had she ever entered on such a life in the first place?

"Oh, just doing what everybody else did," she replied. "The girls next door were also going to walk the road of scholarship; to study languages, as they called it, study grammar; it all sounded so fine. We were going to be independent and earn a lot of money. That's what I thought! Have a home, however small, that was quite my own. How we slogged away all through school! Some of the girls had money, but those of us who were poor couldn't dress like them, and we hadn't well-kept hands like theirs. And so we came to avoid all work at home for the sake of our hands.

"And we played up to the boys at school, too. We thought them such fine gentlemen; one of them had a riding horse, bit of a fool, of course, but he was a millionaire's son and awfully decent, gave us banknotes--me, anyhow--and he kissed me many times. His name was Flaten; his father was a merchant. Of course, he being so handsome and dashing, we wanted to be nice to him too. I should have done anything he asked; I used to pray to God for him.

"I'm sure I wasn't the only one who wanted to be smart and pretty. That was how we passed the time. Washing and cooking and mending fell to the lot of my mother and sisters; we students wouldn't do anything but sit round being very learned and getting seraphic hands. We were quite mad, as I don't mind admitting. It was in the course of those years that we acquired all the distorted ideas we've been burdened with since; we grew dull with school wisdom, anaemic, unbalanced: sometimes terribly unhappy about our sad lot, sometimes hysterically happy, and pluming ourselves on our examinations and our importance. We were the pride of the family.

"And of course we were independent. We got jobs in offices, at forty *kroner* a month. Because now there was no longer anything in the least extraordinary about us students--we were no rarity, there were hundreds of us--forty *kroner* was the most they gave us. Thirty went to Father and Mother for our keep, and ten for ourselves. It wasn't enough. We had to have pretty clothes for the office, and we were young, we liked to walk out; but everything was too dear for us, we went into debt, and some of us got engaged to poor devils like ourselves. The narrow school life during our years of development did more than hurt our intelligence; we wanted to show spirit, too, and not recoil before any experience, so some of us went to the bad, others married--and with such antecedents, of course, there was first-rate mismanagement in the home; others disappeared to America. But probably all of them are still boasting their languages and their examinations. It's all they have left--not happiness or health or innocence, but their matriculation. Good God!"

"But surely some of you have become schoolmistresses with good salaries?"

"Good salaries! Anyhow, first we had to start studying all over again. As though Father and Mother and brothers and sisters hadn't sacrificed enough for our sakes already! There was cramming again for long periods, and then we began life in the schoolroom--to give to others the same unnatural upbringing we had had ourselves. Oh, yes, ours was a noble vocation; it was almost like being missionaries. But now if you'll excuse me, I'd like to talk about something besides this exalted position. Anything else you please."

Tradesman Batt opened the door and said:

"Are you coming, Miss Torsen? It's stopped raining now."

"Oh, leave me alone," she replied.

Tradesman Batt withdrew.

"Why do you turn him away like that?" I asked.

"Because ... well, the weather is bad," she said, looking out of the window. "Besides, he's such a fool. And he takes such liberties."

How sure of herself she looked, and how right she seemed!

Poor Miss Torsen! True or not, the news gradually spread that Miss Torsen had recently lost her post at the school, where indulgence had been exercised for a long time toward her eccentric methods of teaching.

So that was it.

But certainly what she had told me was nonetheless true.

X

The news has leaked out that the master of the homestead here owes a huge debt, and that because he needs cash he has sold new, valuable plots of land to his cotters. I am finding out many things now. Mrs. Brede with the handsome, well-modeled head knows something about everything, for her many summers at the farm have given her knowledge. When she talks about conditions here, she need not grope for words.

The master has taken a large mortgage.

No one would believe that all is not well here; the many new buildings and flagpoles, the curtains at the windows and the red-painted well house--all give an impression of great prosperity. The rooms, too, make a good impression. I shall not speak of the piano, but here are pictures on the walls and photographs of the farm seen from all angles; good newspapers are kept and there is a selection of novels on the tables; though guests sometimes take books away with them, the books are never missed. Or take a thing like this: you get your bill on a handsomely printed paper, with a picture at the top of the farm and the Tore range in the background. In short, no one would doubt for a moment that there is a fortune here. And why not, after twenty years as a kind of resort for tourists and pensioners?

Nevertheless, the truth is that this homestead with all its interior and exterior furnishings costs more than the business is worth. Manufacturer Brede, too, has put money into it, and that is why Mrs. Brede comes here every year with her children, to get their dividends in board and lodging.

No wonder she has a house to herself; after all, it's her own house.

"It was a good place in the old days," says Mrs. Brede. "Travelers stopped here and had a meal and a bed for the night; it cost nothing to run the place then. But the tourist traffic has forced him to make improvements and enlargements. You have to keep pace with development, and be as good as other such places in the country; they're all competing. And probably the master here is not the right man to carry on such an irregular and capricious business; he has learned to like idleness too much, and lets the farm take care of itself. But the two cotters are hard-working fellows. They're nephews of his, and bit by bit they're buying the farm from him and cultivating it. My husband often says it will end with the cotters or their children buying this whole place of his, Paul's."

"How can the cotters get power to do that?"

"They work hard; they're peasants. They started in the forest with three or four goats each, first one of them, then the other one, working down in the village and coming home with food and money, and all the time clearing their own ground. The goats grew more numerous, a cow was added, they bought more virgin land, and they acquired still more livestock. They sowed grain and planted potatoes and cultivated pasture land; the owner here buys root vegetables from his cotters; he hasn't time to toil with such things himself; there's a great deal of work in it. Oh, no, they don't sow anything but green fodder for the stock here; Paul says it's not worth-while. And in a way he's right. He's tried hiring enough men to run the farm too, but it won't work. It's just in the spring season that the tourists start coming, and then the men are constantly being interrupted in their work on the farm to pilot tourists across the fjeld, or to do this or that for the guests. And this goes on all through the short summer months; for several years, they haven't even found the time to spread all their manure. But the worst time is really the autumn, when the tourists are all rushing to get home again, and it's quite impossible to do the harvesting undisturbed. It's almost become a custom here now, my husband says, for the cotters to get half the harvest of the farm's outlying fields."

On my wondering at Mrs. Brede's knowledge of farming, she told me with a shake of the head that she herself knew very little about it, and had all her information from her husband. The fact was that every time these cotters wanted to buy a fresh piece of land from Paul, her husband had to give his consent. This was because of the mortgage, and this, too, was how they had learned of these matters. Manufacturer Brede, as a matter of fact, was most anxious to be released from his undertaking, but this was by no means easy. It was with great apprehensions that he now regarded the new automobile route.

Mrs. Brede was full of a maternal gentleness; she played with her little girls, and seemed to enjoy an admirable balance of mind. One day, for example, a goat came home with one of its hind legs broken, and all the guests hurried out with brandy and lanolin and bandages for the wound; but Mrs. Brede remained quietly where she was, experienced, wise, and a little surprised at all the excitement.

"All you can do with such a goat," she said, "is to slaughter it."

The lady, I understood, must have married early, for her two little girls were twelve and ten. Her husband seemed to deal in important business, for he spent a large part of the year in Iceland, and traveled a good deal elsewhere as well. This, too, the lady bore quietly. And yet she was still young and handsome, a little plump, perhaps, for her height, but with a lovely, unwrinkled skin. She was quite unlike Miss Torsen, the only other good-looking lady at the farm; Miss Torsen was tall and dark.

But perhaps Mrs. Brede was not always so calm as she seemed. One evening when she went down to the men's hut and asked Solem to do her a service, I saw that her face was strange and covered with blushes. Would Solem come to her room and repair a window-blind that had fallen down? It was late in the evening, and the lady seemed to have been in bed already, and to have risen again. Solem did not appear very willing. Suddenly their eyes met, and clung for a moment. Yes, certainly, of course he would come....

What an iron face he had, and what a rogue he was!

Mrs. Brede departed.

But a moment later she returned to say that she had changed her mind. Never mind, thank you, she would fix the blind in position herself.

XI

An occasional tourist came or went, Solem accompanied him across the fjeld, and he was gone. But where were all the foreigners this year? Bennett's and Cook's conducted tours, the hordes that would "do" the mountain peaks of Norway--where were they?

At last two solitary Englishmen turned up. They were middle-aged, unshaven and ill-groomed altogether, two engineers or something of that sort, but quite as speechless and uncivil as the grandest of the traveling British clowns. "Guide! Guide!" they called. "You the guide?" Nothing about them was any different from what we had grown to expect; these two traveled brainlessly and solemnly to the mountain tops, were in a hurry, had a purpose, behaved as though they were running to catch a doctor. Solem went with them to the top and down the other side, and they offered him a fifty-*öre* bit. Solem held out the palm of his hand, he told me afterwards, for he thought they would put more in it, but nothing came of that. So he created a disturbance--Solem has grown spoiled and insolent from all his idling with tourists.

"*Mehr*, more," said he.

No, they would not. Solem flung the coin on the ground and struck his hands together repeatedly. This had the required effect, and one *krone* made its appearance. But on Solem's taking the noble lord by the shoulder and exerting a little pressure, two *kroner* were at last forthcoming.

At length a conducted party arrived. Many tongues, both sexes, huntsmen, fishermen, dogs, mountaineers, porters. There was a tremendous commotion at the farm; the flag was run up, Paul bent double under all the orders he received, and Josephine ran, flew at every call. Mrs. Brede had to give up her sitting room to three English ladies, and the rest of us were crowded together as close as possible. I, for my part, was to be allowed to keep my bed because of my settled age; but I said, "By no means, let this English solicitor or whatever he is have my bed; what does it matter for a night!"

Then I went out.

If one keeps one's eyes open, one may see a great deal at such a resort in the daytime. And one may see much at night, too. What is the meaning of all this bleating of goats in the shed? Why are the animals not at rest? The door is closed; none of the visiting dogs has got in. Or--*have* some of the visiting dogs got in? Vice, like virtue, walks in rings and circles; nothing is new, all returns to its beginnings and repeats itself. The Romans ruled the world, yes. They were so mighty, the Romans, so invincible, that they could permit themselves a vice or two, they could afford to live at the arena, they had their fun with young boys and animals. Then one day retribution overtook them, their children's children lost battles everywhere, and their children's children again only sat--sat and looked backward. The ring was closed; none were less rulers of the world than the Romans.

They paid no attention to me, the two Englishmen in the goats' shed; I was merely one of the natives, a Norwegian, who had but to accept the ways of the mighty tourists. But they themselves belonged to that nation of gamblers, coachmen, and vice which one day the wholesome Gothic soul will castigate to death....

The disturbance continued all night, and very early, the dogs began to bark. The caravan awoke; it was six in the morning, and doors began to bang in all the houses. They were in a great hurry, these travelers; they were running to catch the doctor. They had breakfast in two sessions, but though the household was bent double before them and gave of its best, they were not satisfied. "If we had only known a little earlier," said Paul. But they muttered that we should just wait; there were motor cars in other places. Then Paul spoke--Paul, the master of the farm, the man who lived under the Tore peaks:

"But I'm going to enlarge; don't you see all the timber outside? And I'm planning to get a telephone...."

The caravan paid the exact amount of their small bill and departed, accompanied by the master and Solem, both carrying trunks.

Peace descended on us again.

Schoolmaster Staur left now, too. He had been busy collecting plants round the Tore peaks, and talked about his plants at table in a very learned fashion, giving the Latin names, and pointing out their peculiarities. Yes, indeed, he had learned a great deal at school.

"Here you see an *Artemis cotula*," he said.

Miss Torsen, who had also imbibed much learning, recognized the name and said:

"Yes, take plenty of it with you."

"What for?"

"It's insect powder."

Schoolmaster Staur knew nothing of that, and there was a good deal of discussion in which Associate Master Höy had to take a hand.

No, Schoolmaster Staur knew nothing of that. But he could classify plants and learn their names by heart. He enjoyed that. The peasant children in his neighborhood were ignorant of these classes and names, and he could teach them. He enjoyed that so much.

But was the spirit of the soil his friend? The plant that is cut down one year, yet grows again the next--did this miracle make him religious and silent? The stones, and the heather, and the branches of trees, and the grass, and the woods, and the wind, and the great heaven of all the universe--were these his friends?

Artemis cotula....

XII

When I get tired of Associate Master Höy and the ladies.... Sometimes I think of Mrs. Molie. She sits sewing while the Associate Master gravely keeps her company; they talk about the servants at home whose only desire is to stay out all night. Mrs. Molie is a thin, flat-chested lady, but probably she has at one time been less plain; her bluish teeth look as though they were cold, as though they were made of ice, but perhaps a few years ago, her full lips and the dark down at the corners of her mouth seemed to her husband the most beautiful thing he knew. Her husband--well, he was a seafaring man, a ship's captain; he only came home on rare occasions, just often enough to increase the family; usually he was in Australia, China, or Mexico. It was hail and farewell with him. And here is his wife now for the sake of her health. I wonder--is it only for her health, or are she and the Associate Master possibly children of the same provincial town?

When I get tired of Associate Master Höy and the ladies, I leave them and go out. And then I stay out all day long and nobody knows where I keep myself. It is fitting that a settled man should be different from the Associate Master, who is very far from being so settled. So I go out. It is a bright day with just the right amount of warmth, and my summer woods are filled with the fragrance of plants. I rest frequently, not because I need to, but because the ground is full of caresses. I go so far that no one can find me; only then am I released. No sound reaches me from farms or men, no one is in sight; only this overgrown little goat track, which is green at the edges and lovely. Only a bit of a goat track which looks as though it had fallen asleep in the woods, lying there so thin and lonely.

You who read this feel nothing, but I who sit here writing feel a kind of sweetness at the memory of a mere track in the woods. It was like meeting a child.

With my hands under my neck and my nose in the air, my eyes flit across the sky. High up above the peaks of Tore, a clustering mist sways in slow rhythm, breaks apart and presses close again, fluctuates and strains to give birth to something. But when I rise to walk on, the end is not yet in sight.

I meet a line of ants, a procession of ants, busy travelers. They neither toil nor carry anything; they simply move. I retrace my steps to see if I can find their leader, but it is useless: farther and farther I retreat, I begin to run, but the procession is endless before and behind me. Perhaps they started a week ago. So I go on my way, and the other insects go on theirs.

Surely this is not a mountainside I walk on; this is a bosom, an embrace, in its softness. I tread gently, for I do not wish to stamp or weigh it down, and I marvel: a mountain so tender and defenseless, indulgent like a mother. To think of an ant walking on this! Here and there lie stones, half-covered with moss, not because they have fallen there, but because this is their home, and they have lived here long. This is peerless.

When I reach the top and look back, it is high noon. Far away on another peak walks one of the cows of the cotters, a strange little cow with red and white flanks. A crow sits on a high cliff above me and caws down at me in a voice like an iron rasp scraping against the stone. A warm thrill runs through me, and I feel, as I have done in the woods so many times before, that someone has just been here, and has stepped to one side. Someone is with me here, and a moment later I see his back disappearing into the woods. "It is God," I think. There I stand, neither speaking nor singing. I only see. I feel all my face being filled with the sight. "It was God," I think.

"A vision," you say. "No, a little insight into things," I reply. "Am I making a god of nature? Do not you? Have not the Mohammedans their god, the Jews theirs, the Hindus theirs? No one knows God, my friend; man knows only gods. And sometimes I meet mine."

I go home by a different route, which forms a vast arc with the one I came by. The sun is warmer now and the ground less smooth. I reach a great ruin, the remnant of a landslide, and here, to amuse myself, I pretend to be tired, flinging myself on the ground exactly as though someone were watching me and saw how exhausted I am. It is only for my amusement, because my brain has been idle so long. The sky is clear everywhere; the clusters of mist over the Tore peaks are gone, heaven knows where, but they have stolen away. In their place, an eagle swings in great circles over the valley. Huge, black, and inaccessible, he traces ring after ring as though held on a rail in the air, moving with voluptuous languor, a thick-necked male, a winged stallion exulting. It is like music to watch him. At length he disappears behind the peaks.

And here are only myself and the ruin and the little juniper trees. What miracles all things are! These stones in the ruin perhaps hold some meaning; they have lain here for thousands of years, but perhaps they, too, roam, and make an inexpressible journey. The glaciers move, the land rises, and the land falls; there is no hurry here. But since my consciousness cannot associate fact with such a conception, it grows blind with fury and revolts: The ruin cannot move; these are mere words, a game!

This ruin is a town; here and there lie scattered buildings of stone. It's a peaceable gathering, without sensations or suicides, and perhaps a well-shaped soul sits in each of these stones. But heaven protect me just the same from the inhabitants of these towns! Rolling stones cannot bark, neither do they attract thieves; they are mere ballast. Quiet behavior: that is what I hold against them, that they make no fiery gestures; it would become them to roll a little, but there they lie, with even their sex unknown. But you saw the eagle instead! Be still....

A gentle wind begins to blow, swaying the bracken a little, the flowers and the straw; but the straw cannot sway, it only trembles.

I walk on along my great arc and come down by the first cotter's house.

"Well, I expect you'll end up by building a summer resort too," I tell him in the course of our conversation.

"Oh, no; we couldn't venture on anything like that," he replies cunningly. In his heart I daresay he has no desire to, for he has seen what it leads to.

I didn't like him; his eyes were fawning and rested on the ground. He thought of nothing but land; he was land-greedy, like an animal that sought to escape its padlock. The other cotter had bought a slightly larger piece of land than he, a marsh that would feed one cow more; but he himself had only got this bit of a field. Still, this would amount to something, too, as long as he kept his health to work it.

He gripped his spade again.

XIII

Solem was being discussed at dinner; I don't know who began it, but some of the ladies thought he was good-looking, and they nodded and said, Yes, he was the right sort.

"What do you mean by the right sort?" Associate Master Höy asked, looking up from his plate.

No one answered.

Then Associate Master Höy could not help smiling broadly, and said:

"Well, well! I must have a look at this Solem some time. I've never paid any attention to him."

Associate Master Höy might look at Solem all he pleased; he would grow no bigger for that, nor Solem smaller. The good Mr. Höy was annoyed, and that was the truth. It is catching for a woman to discover that a man is "the right sort"; the other women grow curious, and stick their noses into it: "So-o-o, is he?" And a few days later the whole flock of them are of one opinion: "Yes, indeed, he's the right sort!"

Pity the poor, left-over associate masters then!

Poor Mr. Höy; there was Mrs. Molie, too, nodding her head for Solem. To tell the truth, she had no appearance of knowing much about the matter, but she could not lag behind the others.

"So, Mrs. Molie is nodding, too!" said Mr. Höy, and smiled again. He was intensely annoyed. Mrs. Molie turned pink and pretty.

At the next meal, Mr. Höy could contain himself no longer.

"Ladies," he said, "mine eyes have now beheld Master Solem."

"Well?"

"Common sneak-thief!"

"Oh, shame!"

"You must admit he has a brazen look on his face. No beard. Blue chin, a perfect horse-face...."

"There's no harm in that," said Mrs. Molie.

Mrs. Molie doesn't seem to have gone quite out of circulation after all, I thought. In fact, she had lately been developing quite a little cushion over her chest, and no longer looked so hunched up. She had eaten well and slept well, and improved at this resort. Mrs. Molie, I suspect, still has plenty of life left in her.

This proved true a few days later. Once again: poor Associate Master Höy! For now we had a new visitor at the farm, a gay dog of a lawyer, and he talked more to Mrs. Molie than to anyone else. Had there been anything between her and Mr. Höy? True, he was not much to look at, but then neither was she.

The young lawyer was a sportsman, yet he was learned in the social sciences, too, had been in Switzerland and studied the principle of the referendum. At first he had worked a few years in an architect's office, he told us, but then he had changed to the law instead, which in its turn had led him into social problems. No doubt he was a rich and unselfish man to be able to change his vocation and to travel in this way. "Ah, Switzerland!" he said, and his eyes watered. None of us could understand his fervor.

"Yes, it must be a wonderful country," Mrs. Molie said.

The Associate Master looked ready to burst, and was quite incapable of restraining himself.

Speaking of Solem, he said suddenly, "I've changed my mind about him lately. He's ten times better than many another."

"There, you see!"

"Yes, he is. And he doesn't pretend to be anything more than he is. And what he is, is of some use. I saw him slaughter the lame goat."

"Did you stop to watch that?"

"I happened to be passing. It was the work of a moment for him. And later I saw him in the woodshed. He knows his job, that fellow. I can well understand that the ladies see something in him."

How the Associate Master clowned! He finished by imploring the wife of the captain who was sailing the China seas to be sure and remain faithful to her Chinaman.

"Do be quiet and let the lawyer tell us about Switzerland," said Mrs. Molie.

Witch! Did she want to drive her fellow-being the Associate Master into jumping off the highest peak of the Tore tonight?

But then Mrs. Brede took a hand. She understood Mr. Höy's torment and wanted to help him. Had not this same Mr. Höy just expressed himself kindly about Solem, and was not Solem the lad who one fine evening had caused her to tear down her window blind? There is cause and effect in all things.

"Switzerland," said Mrs. Brede in her gentle fashion, and then she reddened and laughed a little. "I don't know anything about Switzerland; but once I bought some dress material that was Swiss, and I've never in my life been so cheated."

The lawyer only smiled at this.

Schoolmistress Johnsen talked about what she had learned, watchmakers and the Alps and Calvin--

"Yes, those are the only three things in a thousand years," said the Associate Master, his face quite altered and pale with suppressed rage.

"Really, really, Associate Höy!" exclaimed Schoolmistress Palm with a smile.

But the lawyer focused everyone's admiration on himself by telling them all about Switzerland, that wonderful country, that model for all small countries of the world. What social conditions, what a referendum, what planning in the exploitation of the country's natural wonders! There they had sanatoriums; there they knew how to deal with tourists! Tremendous!

"Yes, and what Swiss cheese," said the Associate Master. "It smells like tourists' feet."

Dead silence. So Associate Master Höy was prepared to go to such lengths!

"Well, what about Norwegian old-milk cheese?" said a Danish voice mildly.

"Yes, that's filthy stuff, too," Mr. Höy replied. "Just the thing for Schoolmaster Staur pontificating in his armchair."

Laughter.

Since matters were now smoothed over again, the lawyer could safely continue:

"If we could only make such Swiss cheese here," he said, "we should not be so poor. Generally speaking, I found after my modest investigations in that country that they are ahead of us in every respect. We have everything to learn from them: their frugality, their diligence, their long working hours, the small home industries--"

"And so on," interrupted Associate Master Höy. "All trifles, nothingness, negativity! A country that exists thanks only to the mercy of its neighbors ought not to be a model for any other country on earth. We must try to rise above the wretched stench of it, which only makes us ill. The big countries and big circumstances should be our model. Everything grows, even the small things, unless they're predestined to a Lilliput existence. A child can learn from another child, of course, but the model is the adult. Some day the child will be an adult itself. A pretty state of affairs it would be if an eternal child, a born pygmy, were to be its model! But that's what all this rubbish about Switzerland really amounts to. Why on earth should we, of all people, take the smallest and meanest country as our model? Things are small enough here anyhow. Switzerland is the serf of Europe. Have you ever heard of a young South American country of Norway's size trying to be on a level with Switzerland? Why do you think Sweden is taking such great strides forward now? Not because it looks to Switzerland, or to Norway, but to Germany! Honor to Sweden for that! But what about us? We don't want to be a piddling little nation stuck up in our mountains, a nation that brings forth peace conferences, ski-runners, and an Ibsen once every thousand years; we have potentialities for a thousand times more--"

The lawyer had for some time been holding up his hand to indicate that he wanted to reply; now he shouted at the top of his voice:

"Just a moment!"

The Associate Master stopped.

"Just one question--a small, trifling question," said the lawyer, preparing his ground well. "Have you ever once set foot in the country you speak of?"

"I should think I have," replied the Associate Master.

There! The lawyer got nothing for his trifling question. And then it all came out what a heartless jilt Mrs. Molie was. She had known all the time that Mr. Höy had been on a traveling scholarship in Switzerland, but she had never mentioned it. What a snake in the grass! She had even encouraged the lawyer, but no one else, to talk about Switzerland.

"Oh, yes, of course Associate Master Höy has been in Switzerland" she said, as though to clinch the matter.

"In that case, the Associate Master and I have looked on the country with different eyes; that's all," said the lawyer, suddenly anxious to end the controversy.

"They haven't even folk tales there," said the Associate Master, who seemed unable to stop. "There they sit, generation after generation, filing watch springs and piloting Englishmen up their mountains. But it's a country without folk music or folk tales. I suppose you think we ought to work hard to resemble the Swiss in that, too?"

"What about William Tell?" asked Miss Johnsen.

Several of the ladies nodded, or at any rate Miss Palm did.

At this point Mrs. Molie turned her head and looked out of the window as she said:

"You really had a very different opinion about Switzerland before, Mr. Associate Master."

This was a hit below the belt. He wanted to reply, wanted to annihilate her, but he restrained himself and remained silent.

"Don't you remember?" she asked, goading him.

"No," he replied. "You mistook my meaning. Really, I can't understand it, I usually make myself quite clear; after all, I'm accustomed to explaining to children."

Another foul. Mrs. Molie said no more, merely smiling patiently.

"I can only say that my opinion is diametrically opposed to yours," the lawyer repeated. "But I did think," he went on, "that this was one thing I knew something about, however...."

Mrs. Molie got up and went out with her head bent, seemingly on the point of bursting into tears. The Associate Master sat still for a moment, and then followed her, whistling and putting on as brave a manner as though he felt quite easy in his mind.

"What's your opinion?" asked Mrs. Brede, turning to the doyen of the company, namely myself.

And as becomes a man of settled years, I replied:

"Probably there has been a little exaggeration on both sides."

Everybody agreed with this. But I could never have acted as a mediator, for I thought the Associate Master was right. In one's early seventies, one still has many pathetically young ideas.

The lawyer rounded off the discussion thus:

"Well, when all's said and done we have Switzerland to thank for being able to sit here at our ease in this comfortable mountain resort. We get tourists into the country on the Swiss model, and earn money and pay off our debts. Ask this man if he would have been willing to do without all we have learned from Switzerland...."

That evening Mrs. Brede asked,

"Why did you make Mr. Höy look so unreasonable today, Mrs. Molie?"

"I?" said Mrs., Molie innocently. "Well, really--!"

As a matter of fact, it seemed as though Mrs. Molie had really been innocent, for the very next morning she and the Associate Master set off up the fjeld together in a very gay mood, and remained away till midday. If they had the matter out between them, then no doubt the lady spoke to her much-tried friend as follows:

"Surely you can see I'm not interested in that lawyer-person! What an idea! I only drew him out so you'd have the chance to give him a good dressing down--don't you understand that? Really, you're the silliest, sweetest--come here, let me kiss you...."

XIV

Since the departure of the great caravan, there have been no other visitors. Some of us cannot understand it; others have in a manner of speaking got a whiff of what is wrong; but all of us still believe there will be more visitors, because after all we're the only ones that have the Tore peaks!

But no one appears.

The women of the house do their daily work for the inmates and do not complain, but they are not happy. Paul still takes things quietly; he sleeps a great deal in his room behind the kitchen, but once or twice I have seen him walking away from the house at night, walking in deep thought toward the woods.

From the neighboring valley comes the rumor that the motor traffic has started there now. So this is the explanation of the quiet in our valley! Then one day a Dane came down to us from the fjeld. He had climbed the Tore peaks from the other side, something that had been thought impossible till now. He had simply driven in a car to the foot of the mountains and walked across!

So we no longer had the Tore peaks to ourselves, either.

I wonder whether, after all, Paul is not going to try to sow green-fodder in the long strip of land down by the river. That, at any rate, had been his original intention, but then came the great caravan, and he neglected it. Now, of course, the season is too far advanced for sowing, and there will be nothing but docks and chickweed. Could not the field be turfed, at least, and sown? Why didn't Paul think of such things instead of walking the woods at night?

But Paul has many thoughts. At an early age, his interest in farming was diverted to the tourist traffic, and there it has remained. He hears that our lawyer is also an architect and asks him to draw a plan for the big new house with the six rooms, the hall and the bathroom. Paul has already ordered the log chairs and the reindeer horns for the hall.

"If you weren't alone up here, you might have got some of the cars coming here too," said the lawyer.

"I've thought of that," Paul replied. "It's not impossible I can do something about it. But I must have the house first. And I must have a road."

The lawyer promised to draw a plan of the house, and went round to look at the site. The house was to cost such and such a sum. Paul was already quite convinced that three or four good tourist summers would pay it off.

Paul was not worrying. As we looked over the site together, I discovered that he smelled of brandy.

Finally a small party of Norwegians and foreigners arrived, travelers who were out to walk, and not to drive in cars. Everyone's spirits rose; the strangers stayed a few days and nights, and were guided across the fjeld by Solem, who earned a fair penny. Paul, too, was visibly cheered, and strolled about the farm in his Sunday clothes. He had a few things to discuss with the lawyer about the house.

"If there's anything to consult about, we had better do it now," he said. "I shall be away for a couple of days."

So they attended to a few minor matters.

"Are you going to town?" asked the lawyer.

"No," Paul replied; "only down to the village. I want to see if I can get the people there to co-operate on a few ideas of mine: a telephone and automobile service and so on."

"Good luck!" said the lawyer.

So the lawyer sat drafting plans while the rest of us went about our own affairs. Josephine went to Solem and said:

"Will you go and sow the field by the river?"

"Has Paul said so?" he asked.

"Yes," she replied.

Solem went very unwillingly. While he was drawing the harrow, Josephine went down to him and said:

"Harrow it once more."

What a brisk little thing she was, with far more forethought than the men! She looked bewitching, for all her hard work. I have seen her many times with her hair tumbled, but it didn't matter. And when she pretended that none but the maids milked the goats and did outside work, it was for the good name of the house. She had learned to play the piano for the same reason. The mistress of the house helped her nobly, for both women were thoughtful and industrious, but Josephine was everywhere, for she was light as a feather. And the chaste little hands she had!

"Josephine, Joséfriendly!" I called her wittily.

XV

Our dark beauty, Miss Torsen, was now seriously considering taking her departure. She was healthy enough in any case, so she did not need a stay in the mountains on that account, and if she was bored, why should she stay?

But a minor event caused her to stay.

In their lack of occupation, the ladies at the resort began to cultivate Solem. They ate so much and grew so fat and healthy that they felt a need to busy themselves with something, and to find someone to make a fuss over. And here was the lad Solem. They got into the habit of telling one another what Solem had said and what Solem believed, and they all listened with great interest. Solem himself had grown spoiled, and joked disrespectfully with the ladies; he called himself a great chap, and once he had even bragged in a most improper way, saying:

"Look, here's a sinful devil for you!"

"Do you know what Solem said to me?" asked Miss Palm. "He's chopping wood and he's got a bandage on his finger, and it keeps getting caught in the wood and bothers him, poor fellow. So he said: 'I wish I had time to stop so I could chop this blasted finger right off my hand!'"

"Tough, isn't he?" said the other ladies. "He's quite capable of doing it, too!"

A little later I passed the woodshed and saw Mrs. Brede there, tying a fresh bandage on Solem's finger.... Poor lady! She was chaste, but young.

The days have been oppressively warm for some time now, with the heat coming down in waves from the mountain and robbing us of all our strength. But in the evenings we recovered somewhat, and busied ourselves in various ways: some of us wrote letters or played forfeit games in the garden, while others were so far restored that they went for a walk "to look at nature."

Last Sunday evening I stood talking to Solem outside his room. He had on his Sunday clothes, and seemed to have no intention of going to bed.

Miss Torsen came by, stopped, and said:

"I hear you're going for a walk with Mrs. Brede?"

Solem removed his cap, which left a red ring round his forehead.

"Who, me?" he said. "Well, maybe she said something about it. There was a path through the woods she wanted me to show her, she said."

Miss Torsen was filled with madness now; handsome and desperate, she paced back and forth; you could almost see the sparks flying. Her red felt hat was held on the back of her head by a pin, the brim turned up high in front. Her throat was bare, her frock thin, her shoes light.

It was extraordinary to watch her behavior; she had opened a window onto her secret desires. What cared she for Tradesman Batt! Had she not toiled through her youth and gained school knowledge? But no reality! Poor Miss Torsen. Solem must not show a path to any other lady tonight.

As nothing more was said, and Solem was preparing to depart, Miss Torsen cleared her throat.

"Come with me instead!" she said.

Solem looked round quickly and said, "All right."

So I left them; I whistled as I walked away with exaggerated indifference, as though nothing on earth were any concern of mine.

"Come with me instead," she said. And he went. They were already behind the outhouses, then behind the two great rowan trees; they hurried lest Mrs. Brede should see them. Then they were gone.

A door wide open, but where did it lead? I saw no sweetness in her, nothing but excitement. She had learned grammar, but no language; her soul was undernourished. A true woman would have married; she would have been a man's wife, she would have been a mother, she would have been a benediction to herself. Why pounce on a pleasure merely to prevent others from having it? And she so tall and handsome!

The dog stands growling over a bone. He waits till another dog approaches. Then suddenly he is overcome with gluttony, pounces on the bone and crushes it between his teeth. Because the other dog is approaching.

It seemed as though this small event had to happen before my mind was ready for the night. I awoke in the dark and felt within me the nursery rhyme I had dawdled over so long: four rollicking verses about the juniper tree.

> To the top of the steepest mountains,
> where the little juniper stands,
> no other tree can follow

from all the forest lands.
Halfway to the hilltop
the shivering pine catches hold;
the birch has actually passed him,
though sneezing with a cold.
But a little shrub outstrips them,
a sturdy fellow he,
and stands quite close to the summit,
though he measures barely a yard.
They look like a train from the valley below
with the shortest one for the guard.
Or else perhaps he's a coachman now--
why, it's only a juniper tree.

Down dale there's summer lightning,
green leaves and St. John's feast,
with songs and games of children,
and a dozen dances at least.
But high on the empty mountain
stands a shrub in lonely glory,
with only the trolls that prowl about,
just like in a story.
The wind with the juniper's forelock
is making very free;
it sweeps across the world beneath
that lies there helpless and bare,
but the air on the heights is fresher
than you'll ever find it elsewhere.
None can see so far around
as such a juniper tree.

There hovers over the mountain
for a moment summer's breath;
at once eternal winter
brings back his companion, death.
Yet sturdy stands the juniper
with needles ever green.
I wonder how the little chap
can bear a life so lean.
He's hard as bone and gristle,
as anyone can see;
when every other tree is stripped,
his berries are scarlet and sleek,

and every berry's plainly marked
with a cross upon its cheek.
So now we know what he looks like too,
this jolly juniper tree.

At times I think he sings to himself
a cheerful little song:
"I've got a bright blue heaven
to look at all day long!"
Sometimes to his juniper brothers
he calls that they need not fear
the trolls that are prowling and peering
about them far and near.
Gently the winter evening
falls over the copse on the height,
and a thousand stars and candles
are lit in the plains of the sky.
The juniper trees grow weary
and nod their heads on the sly;
before we know it they're fast asleep,
so we say: "Good night, good night!"

I got up and wrote out these rhymes on a sheet of paper, which I sent to a little girl, a child with whom I had walked much in the country, and she learned them at once. Then I read them to Mrs. Brede's little girls, who stood still like two bluebells, listening. Then they tore the paper out of my hand and ran to their mother with it. They loved their mother very much. And she loved them too; they had the most delightful fun together at bedtime.

Brave Mrs. Brede with her children! She might have committed a madness, but could not find it in her heart to do so. Yet did anyone prize her for that? Who? Her husband?

A man should take his wife to Iceland with him. Or risk the consequences of her being left behind for endless days.

XVI

Miss Torsen no longer talks about leaving. Not that she looks very happy about staying, either; but Miss Torsen is altogether too restless and strange to be contented with anything.

Naturally she caught cold after that evening in the woods with Solem, and stayed in bed with a headache next day; when she got up again, she was quite all right.

Was she? Why was her throat so blue under the chin, as though someone had seized her by it?

She never went near Solem any more, and behaved as though he were nonexistent. Apparently there had been a struggle in the woods that had made her blue under the chin, and they were friends no longer! It was like her to want nothing real, nothing but the sensation, nothing but the triumph. Solem had not understood that, and had flown into a passion. Had it been thus?

Yes, there was no doubt that Solem had been cheated. He was more direct and lacked subtlety; he made allusions, and said things like "Oh, yes, that Miss Torsen, she's a fine one; I'll bet she's as strong as a man!"

And then he laughed, but with repressed fury. He followed her with gross eyes wherever she went, and in order to assert himself and seem indifferent, he would sing a song of the linesman's life whenever she was about. But he might have saved himself the trouble. Miss Torsen was stone-deaf to his songs.

And now it seemed she was going to stay at the resort out of sheer defiance. We enjoyed her company no more than we had done before, but she began to make herself agreeable to the lawyer, sitting by his work table in the living room as he drew plans of houses. Such is the perverse idleness of summer resorts.

So the days pass; they hold no further novelty for me, and I begin to weary of them. Now and then comes a stranger who is going across the fjeld, but things are no longer, I am told, as they were in other years, when visitors came in droves. And things will not improve until we, too, get roads and cars.

I have not troubled to mention it before this, but the neighboring valley is called Stordalen (Great Valley), while ours is only called Reisa after the river: the whole of the Reisa district is no more than an appendage. Stordalen has all the advantages, even the name. But Paul, our host, calls the neighboring valley Little Valley, because, says Paul, the people there are so petty and avaricious.

Poor Paul! He has returned from his tour to the village as hopeless as he went, and hopelessly drunk besides. For more than a day, he stayed in his room without once emerging. When he reappeared at last, he was aloof and reserved, pretending he had been very successful during his absence; he should manage about the cars, never fear! In the evening, after he had had a few more drinks, he became self-important in a different way: oh, those fools in the village had no sense of any kind, and had refused to give their consent to a road to his place. He was the only one with any sense. Would not such a bit of a road be a blessing to the whole appendage? Because then the caravans would come, scattering money over the valley. They understood nothing, those fools!

"But sooner or later there will have to be a road here," said the lawyer.

"Of course," replied Paul with finality.

Then he went to his room and lay down again.

On another day, a small flock of strangers came again; they had toiled up themselves, carrying their luggage in the hot sun, and now they wanted some help. Solem was ready at once, but he could not possibly carry all the bags and knapsacks; Paul was lying down in his room. I had seen Paul again during the night go out to the woods, talking loudly and flinging his arms about as though he had company.

And here were all the strangers.

Paul's wife and Josephine came out of the house and sent Solem across to Einar, the first cotter, to ask if he would come and help them carry. In the meantime the travelers grew impatient and kept looking at their watches, for if they could not cross the Tore fjeld before nightfall, they would have to spend the night outdoors. One of them suggested to the others that perhaps this delay was intentional. The owner of the place probably wanted them to spend the night there; they began to grumble among themselves, and at last they asked:

"Where is the master, the host?"

"He's ill," said Josephine.

Solem returned and said:

"Einar hasn't time to come; he's lifting his potatoes."

A pause.

Then Josephine said:

"I've got to go across the fjeld anyhow--wait a minute!"

She was gone for a moment, then returned, loaded the bags and knapsacks on her little back, and trotted off. The others followed.

I caught up with Josephine and took her burden from her. But I would not allow her to turn back, for this little tour away from the house would do her good. We walked together and talked on the way: she had really no complaints, she said, for she had a tidy sum of money saved up.

When we reached the top of the fjeld, Josephine wanted to turn back. She thought it a waste of time to walk by my side, with nothing to do but walk.

"I thought you had to cross the fjeld anyhow?" I said.

She was too shrewd to deny it outright, for in that case she, the daughter of the old man at the Tore Peak farm, would have been going with the tourists solely to carry their luggage.

"Yes, but there's no hurry. I was to have visited someone, but that can wait till the winter."

We stood arguing about this, and I was so stubborn that I threatened to throw all the luggage down the mountainside, and then she would see!

"Then I'll just take them and carry them myself," replied Josephine, "and then *you'll* see!"

By this time the others had caught up with us, and before I knew what had happened, one of the strangers had come forward and lifted the burden from my back, taken off his cap with a great deal of ceremony, and told me his own and his companions' names. I must excuse them, I really must forgive them; this was too bad, he had been so unobserving....

I told him I could easily have carried him as well as the bags. It is not strength I lack; but day and night I carry about with me the ape of all the diseases, who is heavy as lead. Ah, well, many another groans under a burden of stupidity, which is little better. We all have our cross to bear....

Then Josephine and I turned homeward again.

Yes, indeed, people treat me with uncontrollable politeness; this is because of my age. People are indulgent toward me when I am troublesome to others, when I am eccentric, when I have a screw loose; people forgive me because my hair is gray. You who live by your compass will say that I am respected for the writing I have been doing all these years. But if that were so, I should have had respect in my young days when I deserved it, not now when I no longer deserve it so well. No one--no one in the world--can be expected to write after fifty nearly so well as before, and only the fools or the self-interested pretend to improve after that age.

Now it is a fact that I have been practicing a most distinctive authorship, better than most; I know that very well. But this is due, not so much to my endeavors, as to the fact that I was born with this ability.

I have made a test of this, and I know it is true. I have thought to myself: "Suppose someone else had said this!" Well, no doubt others have said it sometimes, but that has not hurt me. I have gone even further than this: I have intentionally exposed myself to direct contempt from other literary men, and this has not hurt me either. So I am sure of my ground. On the other hand, my way of life has lent me an inner distinction for which I have a right to demand respect, because it is the fruit of my own endeavors. You cannot make me out a small man without lying. Yet one can endure even such a lie if one has character.

You may quote Carlyle against me--how authors are misjudged!-- *"Considering what book-writers do in the world, and what the world does with book-writers, I should say it is the most anomalous thing the world at present has to show."* You may quote many others as well; they will assert that a great to-do is made over me for my authorship as well as my native ability, and my struggle to hammer this ability into a useful shape. And I say only what is the truth, that most of the fuss is made because I have reached an age in which my years are revered.

And that is what seems to me so wrong; it is a custom which makes it easy to hold down the gifted young in a most hostile and arrogant fashion. Old age should not be honored for its own sake; it does nothing but halt and delay the march of man. The primitive races, indeed, have no respect for old age, and rid themselves unhesitatingly of it and of its defects. A long time ago I deserved honor much more, and valued it; now, in more than one sense, I am a richer man and can afford to do without.

Yet now I have it. If I enter a room, respectful silence falls. "How old he's grown!" everyone present thinks. And they all remain silent so that I may speak memorable words in that room. Amazing nonsense!

The noise should raise the roof when I enter: "Welcome, old fellow and old companion; for pity's sake don't say anything memorable to us--you should have done that when you were better able to. Sit down, old chap, and keep us company. But don't let your old age cast a shadow on us, and don't restrain us; you have had your day--now it's our turn...."

This is honest speech.

In peasant homes they still have the right instinct: the mothers preserve their daughters, the fathers their sons, from the rough, unpleasant labors. A proper mother lets her daughter sew while she herself works among the cattle. And the daughter will do the same with her own daughter. It is her instinct.

XVII

Dear me, these human beings grow duller every day, and I see nothing in them that I have not known before. So I sink to the level of watching Solem's increasing passion for Miss Torsen. But that too is familiar and dull.

Solem, after all the attention the ladies have paid him, has a delusion of greatness; he buys clothes and gilt watch chains for the money he earns, and on Sundays wears a white woolen pullover, though it is very warm; round his neck and over his chest lies a costly silk tie tied in a sailor's knot. No one else is so smart as he, as he well knows; he sings as he crosses the farmyard, and considers no one too good for him now. Josephine objects to his loud singing, but Solem lad has grown so indispensable at the resort that he no longer obeys all orders. He has his own will in many things, and sometimes Paul himself takes a glass in his company.

Miss Torsen appears to have settled down. She is very busy with the lawyer, and makes him explain each and every angle he draws in his plans. Quite right of her, too, for undeniably the lawyer is the right man for her, a wit and a sportsman, well-to-do, rather simple-minded, strong-necked. At first Mrs. Molie seemed unable to reconcile herself to the constant companionship of these two in the living room, and she frequently had some errand that took her there; what was she after, Mrs. Molie, of the ice-blue teeth?

At last the lawyer finished his plans and was able to deliver them. He began to speak again about a certain peak of the Tore range which no one had yet climbed, and was therefore waiting to be conquered by him. Miss Torsen objected to this plan, and as she grew to know him better, begged him most earnestly not to undertake such a mad climb. So he promised with a smile to obey her wishes. They were in such tender agreement, these two!

But the blue peak still haunted the lawyer's mind; he pointed it out to his lady, and smacked his lips, his eyes watering again.

"Gracious, it makes me dizzy just to look at it!" she said.

So the lawyer put his arm round her to steady her.

The sight was painful to Solem, whose eyes were continually on the pair. One day as we left the luncheon table, he approached Miss Torsen and said:

"I know another path; would you like to see it tonight?"

The lady was confused and a little embarrassed, and said at length:

"A path? No, thank you."

She turned to the lawyer, and as they walked away together, she said:

"I never heard of such brazenness!"

"What got into him?" said the lawyer.

Solem went away, his teeth gleaming in a sneer.

That evening, Solem repeated the performance. He went up to Miss Torsen again and said:

"What about that path? Shall we go now?"

As soon as she saw him coming, she turned quickly and tried to elude him. But Solem did not hesitate to follow her.

"Now I've just got one thing to say," she said, stopping. "If you're insolent to me again, I'll see that you're driven off the farm...."

But it was not easy to drive Solem off the farm. After all, he was guide and porter to the tourists, and the only permanent laborer on the farm as well. And soon the hay would have to be brought in, and casual laborers would be engaged to work under him. No, Solem could not be driven off. Besides, the other ladies were on his side; the mighty Mrs. Brede alone could save him by a word. She held the Tore Peak resort in the palm of her hand.

Solem was not discharged; but he held himself in check and became a little more civil. He seemed to suffer as much as ever. Once at midday, as he was standing in the woodshed, I saw him make a scratch with the ax across the nail of his thumb.

"What on earth are you doing?" I asked.

"Oh, I'm just marking myself," he replied, laughing gloomily. "When this scratch grows out--"

He stopped.

"What then?"

"Oh, I'll be away from here then," he said.

But I had the impression that he meant to say something different, so I probed further.

"Let me look. Well, it's not a deep scratch; you won't be here long then, will you?"

"Nails grow slowly," he muttered.

Then he strolled away whistling, and I set about chopping wood.

A little later Solem returned across the farmyard with a cackling hen under his arm. He went to the kitchen window and called:

"This the kind of hen you want me to kill?"

"Yes," was the reply.

Solem came back to the woodshed and asked me for the ax, as he wanted to behead a few hens. It was easy to see that he did everything on the farm; he was, hand and brain, indispensable.

He laid the hen on a block and took aim, but it was not easy, for she twisted her head like a snake and would not lie still. She had stopped cackling now.

"I can feel her heart jumping inside her," said Solem.

Suddenly he saw his chance and struck. There lay the head; Solem still held the body, which jerked under his hand. The thing was done so quickly that the two sections of the bird were still one in my eyes; I could not grasp a separation so sudden and unbelievable, and it took my sight a second or two to overtake the event. Bewilderment was in the expression of this detached head, which looked as though it could not believe what had happened, and raised itself a little as if to show there was nothing the least bit wrong. Solem let the body go. It lay still for a moment, then kicked its legs, leaped to the ground and began to hop, the headless body reeling on one wing till it struck the wall and spattered blood in wide arcs before it fell at last.

"I let her go too soon after all," said Solem.

Then he went off to fetch another hen.

XVIII

I return to the mad idea of Solem's being discharged. This would, to be sure, have averted a certain disaster here at the farm: but who would fetch and carry then? Paul? But I've told you he just lounges all day in his room, and has been doing so lately more than ever; the guests never see him except through an unsuccessful maneuver on his part.

One evening he came walking across the lawn. He must, in his disregard of time, have thought the guests had already retired, but we all sat outside in the mild darkness. When Paul saw us, he drew himself up and saluted as he passed; then, calling Solem to him, he said:

"You mustn't cross the field again without letting me know. I was right there in my room, writing. The idea of Josephine carrying luggage!"

Paul strode on. But even yet he felt he had not appeared important enough, so he turned round and asked:

"Why didn't you take one of my cotters with you to act as porter?"

"They wouldn't go," Solem replied. "They were busy lifting potatoes."

"Wouldn't go?"

"That's what Einar said."

Paul thought this over.

"What insolence! They'd better not go too far or I'll drive them off the place."

Then the law awoke in the lawyer's bosom, and he asked:

"Haven't they bought their land?"

"Yes," said Paul. "But I'm the master of this farm. I have a say in things too. I'm not without power up here in Reisa, believe me...."

Then he said sternly to Solem:

"You come to me next time."

Whereupon he stalked off to the woods again.

"He's a bit tight again, our good Paul," said the lawyer.

Nobody replied.

"Can you imagine an innkeeper in Switzerland behaving like that?" the lawyer remarked.

Mrs. Brede said gently:

"What a pity! He never drank before."

And at once the lawyer was charitable again:

"I'll have a good talk with him," he said.

There followed a period in which Paul was sober from morning till night, when Manufacturer Brede paid us a visit. The flag was hoisted, and there was great commotion at the farm; Josephine's feet said *whrr* under her skirt. The manufacturer arrived with a porter; his wife and children went far down the road to meet him, and the visitors at the resort sallied forth too.

"Good morning!" he greeted us with a great flourish of his hat. He won us all over. He was big and friendly, fat and cheerful, with the broad good cheer that plenty of money gives. He became good friends with us at once.

"How long are you staying, Daddy?" his little girls asked, as they clung to him.

"Three days."

"Is that all!" said his wife.

"Is that all?" he replied, laughing. "That's not such a short time, my dear; three days is a lot for me."

"But not for me and the children," she said.

"Three whole days," he repeated. "I can tell you I've had to do some moving to be able to stay as quiet as this, ha, ha!"

They all went in. The manufacturer had been here before and knew the way to his wife's cottage. He ordered soda water at once.

In the evening, when the children had gone to bed, the manufacturer and his wife joined us in the living room; he had brought whisky with him for the gentlemen, and ordered soda water; for the ladies he had wine. It was quite a little party, the manufacturer playing the host with skill, and we were all well satisfied. When Miss Palm played folk melodies on the piano, this heavy-built man grew quiet and sentimental; but he didn't think only of himself, for suddenly he went out and lowered the flag. Flags should be lowered at sunset, he said. Once or twice he went across to the cottage, too, to see if the children were sleeping well. Generally speaking, he seemed fond of the children. Though he owned factories and hotels and many other things, yet he seemed to take the greatest pride of all in possessing a couple of children.

One of the men from Bergen struck his glass for silence, and began to make a speech.

The Bergensians had all long been very quiet and retiring, but here was a perfect occasion for making speeches. Was not here a man from the great world outside, from the heart of life, who had brought them wine and good cheer and festivity? Strange wares up here in this world of blue mountains ... and so on.

He talked for about five minutes, and became very animated.

The manufacturer told us a little about Iceland--a neutral country that neither the Associate Master nor the lawyer had visited, and therefore could not disagree about. One of the Danes had been there and was able to confirm the justness of the manufacturer's impressions.

But most of the time he told cheerful anecdotes:

"I have a servant, a young lad, who said to me one day, when I was in a bad temper: 'You've become a great hand at swearing in Icelandic!' Ha, ha, ha--he appreciated me: 'a great hand at swearing in Icelandic,' he said!"

Everybody laughed, and his wife asked:

"And what did you say?"

"What did I say? Why, I couldn't say anything, could I, ha, ha, ha!"

Then another man from Bergen took the floor: we must not forget we had the family of a real man of the world with us here--his wife, "this peerless lady, scattering charm and delight about her," and the children, dancing butterflies! And a few minutes later, "Hip, hip, hurrah!" followed by a flourish on the piano.

The manufacturer drank a toast with his wife.

"Well, that's that!" was all he said.

Mrs. Molie sat off in a corner talking in a loud voice with the Dane who had come over the top of the Tore from the wrong end; she seemed purposely to be talking so audibly. The manufacturer's attention was attracted, and he asked for further information about the motor cars in the neighboring valley: how many there were, and how fast they could go. The Dane told him.

"But just imagine coming across the fjeld from the other side!" said Mrs. Molie. "It hasn't been done before."

In response to the manufacturer's questions, the Dane told him about this adventurous journey also.

"Isn't there a blue peak somewhere in the mountains about here?" said Mrs. Molie. "I suppose you'll be going up that next. Where ever will you stop?"

Yes, the Dane felt quite tempted by this peak, but said he believed it was unconquerable.

"I should have climbed that peak long ago if you, Miss Torsen, hadn't forbidden me," said the lawyer.

"You'd never have made it," said Mrs. Molie in an indifferent tone. This was probably her revenge. She turned to the Dane again as though ready to believe him capable of anything.

"I shouldn't want anyone to think of climbing that peak," said Miss Torsen. "It's as bare as a ship's mast."

"What if I tried it, Gerda?" the manufacturer asked his wife with a smile. "After all, I'm an old sailor."

"Nonsense," she said, smiling a little.

"Well, I climbed the mast of a schooner last spring."

"Where?"

"In Iceland."

"What for?"

"I don't know, though--all this mountain climbing--I haven't much use for it," said the manufacturer.

"What did you do it for? What did you climb the mast for?" his wife repeated nervously.

The manufacturer laughed.

"The curiosity of the female sex--!"

"How can you do a thing like that! And what about me and the children if you--"

She broke off. Her husband grew serious and took her hand.

"It was stormy, my dear; the sails were flapping, and it was a question of life and death. But I shouldn't have told you. Well--we'd better say good night now, Gerda."

The manufacturer and his wife got up.

Then the first man from Bergen made another speech.

The manufacturer stayed with us for the promised three days, and then made ready to travel again. His mood never changed; he was contented and entertaining the whole time. Every evening one whisky and soda was brought him--no more. Before their bedtime, his little girls had a wildly hilarious half-hour with him. At night a tremendous snoring could be heard from his cottage. Before his arrival, the little girls had spent a good deal of time with me, but now they no longer knew I existed, so taken up with their father were they. He hung a swing for them between the two rowan trees in the field, taking care to pack plenty of rag under the rope so as not to injure the tree.

He also had a talk with Paul; there were rumors that he was intending to take his money out of the Tore Peak resort. Paul's head was bent now, but he seemed even more hurt that the manufacturer should have paid a visit to the cotters to see how they were getting on.

"So that's where he's gone?" he said. "Well, let him stay there, for all I care!"

The manufacturer cracked jokes to the very end. Of course he was a little depressed by the farewells, too, but he had to keep his family's courage up. His wife stood holding one of his arms with both hands, and the children clung to his other arm.

"I can't salute you," the manufacturer said to us, smiling. "I'm not allowed to say good-bye."

The children rejoiced at this and cried, "No, he can't have his arm back; Mummy, you hold him tight, too!"

"Come, come!" the father said. "I've got to go to Scotland, just a short trip. And when you come home from the mountains, I'll be there, too."

"Scotland? What are you going to Scotland for?" the children asked.

He twisted round and nodded to us.

"These women! All curiosity!" he said.

But none of his family laughed.

He continued to us:

"I was telling my wife a story about a rich man who was curious, too. He shot himself just to find out what comes after death. Ha, ha, ha! That's the height of curiosity, isn't it? Shooting yourself to find out what comes after death!"

But he could not make his family laugh at this tale, either. His wife stood still; her face was beautiful.

"So you're leaving now," was all she said.

Mr. Brede's porter came out with his luggage; he had stayed at the farm for these three days in order to be at hand.

Then the manufacturer walked down through the field, accompanied by his wife and children.

I don't know--this man with his good humor and kindliness and money and everything, fond of his children, all in all to his wife--

Was he really everything to his wife?

The first evening he wasted time on a party, and every night he wasted time in snoring. And so the three days and nights went by....

XIX

It is very pleasant here at harvest time. Scythes are being sharpened in the field, men and women are at work; they go thinly clad and bareheaded, and call to one another and laugh; sometimes they drink from a bucket of whey, then set to work again. There is the familiar fragrance of hay, which penetrates my senses like a song of home, drawing me home, home, though I am not abroad. But perhaps I am abroad after all, far away from the soil where I have my roots.

Why, indeed, do I stay here any longer, at a resort full of schoolmistresses, with a host who has once more said farewell to sobriety? Nothing is happening to me; I do not grow here. The others go out and lie on their backs; I steal off and find relish in myself, and feel poetry within me for the night. The world wants no, poetry; it wants only verses that have not been sung before.

And Norway wants no red-hot irons; only village smiths forge irons now, for the needs of the mob and the honor of the country.

No one came; the stream of tourists went up and down Stordalen and left our little Reisa valley deserted. If only the Northern Railway could have come to Reisa with Cook's and Bennett's tours--then Stordalen in its turn would have lain deserted. Meanwhile, the cotters who are cultivating the soil will probably go on harvesting half the crop of the outlying fields for the rest of time. There is every reason to think so--unless our descendants are more intelligent than we, and refuse to be smitten with the demoralizing effects of the tourist traffic.

Now, my friend, you mustn't believe me; this is the point where you must shake your head. There is a professor scuttling about the country, a born mediocrity with a little school knowledge about history; you had better ask him. He'll give you just as much mediocre information, my friend, as your vision can grasp and your brain endure.

Hardly had Manufacturer Brede left when Paul began to live a most irregular life again. More and more all roads were closed to him; he saw no way out and therefore preferred to make himself blind, which gave him an excuse for not seeing. Seven of our permanent guests now left together: the telephone operators, Tradesman Batt, Schoolmistresses Johnsen and Palm, and two men who were in some sort of business, I don't quite know what. This whole party went across the fjeld to Stordalen to be driven about in cars.

Cases of various kinds of foodstuffs arrived for Paul; they were carried up one evening by a man from the village. He had to make several journeys with the side of his cart let down, and bring the cases over the roughest spots one by one. That was the kind of road it was. Josephine received the consignment, and noticed that one of the cases gave forth the sound of a liquid splashing inside. That had come to the wrong place, she said, and writing another address on it, she told the man to take it back. It was sirup that had come too late, she said; she had got sirup elsewhere in the meantime.

Later in the evening we heard them discussing it in the kitchen; the sirup had not come too late, Paul said angrily.

"And I've told you to clear these newspapers away!" he cried. We heard the sound of paper and glass being swept to the floor.

Well, things were not too easy for Paul; the days went by dull and empty, nor had he any children to give him pleasant thoughts at times. Though he wanted to build still more houses, he could not use half those he had already. There was Mrs. Brede living alone with her children in one of them, and since seven of the guests had left, Miss Torsen was also alone in the south wing. Paul wanted at all costs to build roads and share in the development of the tourist traffic; he even wanted to run a fleet of motor cars. But since he had not the power to do this alone and could get no assistance, nothing was left him but to resign himself. And now to make matters worse Manufacturer Brede had said he would withdraw his money....

Paul's careworn face looked out of the kitchen door. Before going out himself he wanted to make sure there was no one about, but he was disappointed in this, for the lawyer at once greeted him loudly: "Good evening, Paul!" and drew him outside.

They strolled down the field in the dusk.

Assuredly there is little to be gained by "having a good talk" with a man about his drinking; such matters are too vital to be settled by talking. But Paul seems to have admitted that the lawyer was right in all he said, and probably left him with good resolutions.

Paul went down to the village again. He was going to the post office; the money he had from the seven departed guests would be scattered to all quarters of the globe. And yet it was not enough to cover everything--in fact not enough for anything, for interest, repayments, taxes, and repairs. It paid only for a few cases of food from the city. And of course he stopped the case of sirup from going back.

Paul returned blind-drunk because he no longer wished to see. It was the same thing all over again. But his brain seemed in its own way to go on searching for a solution, and one day he asked the lawyer:

"What do you call those square glass jars for keeping small fish in--goldfish?"

"Do you mean an aquarium?"

"That's it," said Paul. "Are they dear?"

"I don't know. Why?"

"I wonder if I could get one."

"What do you want it for?"

"Don't you think it might attract people to the place? Oh, well, perhaps it wouldn't."

And Paul withdrew.

Madder than ever. Some people see flies. Paul saw goldfish.

XX

The lawyer is constantly in Miss Torsen's company; he even swings her in the children's swing, and puts his arm around her to steady her when the swing stops. Solem watches all this from the field where he is working, and begins to sing a ribald song. Certainly these two have so ill-used him that if he is going to sing improper songs in self-defense, this is the time to do it; no one will gainsay that. So he sang his song very loud, and then began to yodel.

But Miss Torsen went on swinging, and the lawyer went on putting his arm round her and stopping her....

It was a Saturday evening. I stood talking to the lawyer in the garden; he didn't like the place, and wanted to leave, but Miss Torsen would not go with him, and going alone was such a bore. He did not conceal that the young woman meant something to him.

Solem approached, and lifted his cap in greeting. Then he looked round quickly and began to talk to the lawyer--politely, as became his position of a servant:

"The Danish gentleman is going to climb the peak tomorrow. I'm to take a rope and go with him."

The lawyer was startled.

"Is he--?"

The blankness of the lawyer's face was a remarkable sight. His small, athletic brain failed him. A moment passed in silence.

"Yes, early tomorrow morning," said Solem. "I thought I'd tell you. Because after all it was your idea first."

"Yes, so it was," said the lawyer. "You're quite right. But now he'll be ahead of me."

Solem knew how to get round that.

"No, I didn't promise to go," he said. "I told him I had to go to the village tomorrow."

"But we can't deceive him. I don't want to do that."

"Pity," said Solem. "Everybody says the first one to climb the Blue Peak will be in all the papers."

"He'll take offense," the lawyer murmured, considering the matter.

But Solem urged him on:

"I don't think so. Anyhow, you were the first one to talk about it."

"Everybody here will know, and I'll be prevented," said the lawyer.

"We can go at dawn," said Solem.

In the end they came to an agreement.

"You won't tell anyone?" the lawyer said to me.

The lawyer was missed in the course of the morning; he was not in his room, and not in the garden.

"Perhaps the Danish mountaineer can tell us where he is," I said. But it transpired that the Dane had not even thought of climbing the Blue Peak that day, and knew nothing whatever about the expedition.

This surprised me greatly.

I looked at the clock; it was eleven. I had been watching the peak through my field glasses from the moment I got up, but there was nothing to be seen. It was five hours since the two men had left.

At half-past eleven Solem came running back; he was drenched in sweat and exhausted.

"Come and help us!" he called excitedly to the group of guests.

"What's happened?" somebody asked.

"He fell off."

How tired Solem was and drenched to the skin! But what could we do? Rush up the mountainside and look at the accident too?

"Can't he walk?" somebody asked.

"No, he's dead," said Solem, looking from one to another of us as though to read in our faces whether his message seemed credible. "He fell off; he didn't want me to help him."

A few more questions and answers. Josephine was already halfway across the field; she was going to the village to telephone for the doctor.

"We shall have to get him down," said the Danish mountaineer.

So he and I improvised a stretcher; Solem was instructed to take brandy and bandages to the site of the accident, and the Bergensians, the Associate Master, Miss Torsen, and Mrs. Molie went with him.

"Did you really say nothing to Solem about climbing the peak today?" I asked the Dane.

"No," he replied. "I never said a word about it. If I had meant to go, I should certainly not have wanted company...."

Later that afternoon we returned with the lawyer on the stretcher. Solem kept explaining all the way home how the accident had happened, what he had said and what the lawyer had said, pointing to objects on the way as though this stone represented the lawyer and that the abyss into which he had plunged.... Solem still carried the rope he had not had a chance to use. Miss Torsen asked no more than anyone else, and made purely conventional comments: "I advised him against it, I begged him not to go...."

But however much we talked, we could not bring the lawyer back to life. Strange--his watch was still going, but he himself was dead. The doctor could do nothing here, and returned to his village.

There followed a depressing evening. Solem went to the village to send a telegram to the lawyer's family, and the rest of us did what we thought decent under the circumstances: we all sat in the living room with books in our hands. Now and again, some reference would be made to the accident: it was a reminder, we said, how small we mortals were! And the Associate Master, who had not the soul of a tourist, greatly feared that this disaster would injure the resort and make things still more difficult for Paul; people would shun a place where they were likely to fall off and be killed.

No, the Associate Master was no tourist, and did not understand the Anglo-Saxon mind.

Paul himself seemed to sense that the accident might benefit him rather than do him harm. He brought out a bottle of brandy to console us on this mournful evening.

And since it was a death to which we owed this attention, one of the men from Bergen made a speech.

XXI

The accident became widely known. Newspapermen came from the city, and Solem had to pilot them up the mountain and show them the spot where it had taken place. If the body had not been removed at once, they would have written about that, too.

Children and ignoramuses might be inclined to think it foolish that Solem should be taken from the work in the fields at harvest time, but must not the business of the tourist resort go before all else?

"Solem, tourists!" someone called to him. And Solem left his work. A flock of reporters surrounded him, asked him questions, made him take them to the mountains, to the river. A phrase was coined at the farm for Solem's absences:

"Solem's with death."

But Solem was by no means with death; on the contrary, he was in the very midst of life, enjoying himself, thriving. Once again he was an important personage, listened to by strangers, doling out information. Nor did his audience now consist of ladies only--indeed, no; this was something new, a change; these were keen, alert gentlemen from the city.

To me, Solem said:

"Funny the accident should have happened just when the scratch on my nail has grown out, isn't it?"

He showed me his thumbnail; there was no mark on it.

The newspaper reporters wrote articles and sent telegrams, not only about the Blue Peak and the dreadful death, but about the locality, and about the Tore Peak resort, that haven for the weary, with its wonderful buildings set like jewels in the mountains. What a surprise to come here: gargoyles, living room, piano, all the latest books, timber outside ready for new jewels in their setting, altogether a magnificent picture of Norway's modern farming.

Yes, indeed, the newspapermen appreciated it. And they did their advertising.

The English arrived.

"Where is Solem?" they asked, and "Where is the Blue Peak?" they asked.

"We ought to get the hay in," said Josephine and the wife at the farm. "There'll be rain, and fifty cartloads are still out!"

That was all very well, but "Where is Solem?" asked the English. So Solem had to go with them. The two casual laborers began to cart away the hay, but then the women had no one to help them rake. Confusion was rife. Everyone rushed wildly hither and thither because there was no one to lead them.

The weather stayed fine overnight; it was patient, slow-moving weather. As soon as the dew dried up, more hay would be brought in, perhaps all the hay. Oh, we should manage all right.

More English appeared; and "Solem--the Blue Peak?" they said. Their perverse, sportsmen's brains tingled and thrilled; they had successfully eluded all the resorts on the way, and arrived here without being caught. There was the Blue Peak, like a mast against the sky! They hurried up so fast that Solem was hardly able to keep pace with them. They would have felt for ever disgraced if they had neglected to stand on this admirable site of a disaster, this most excellent abyss. Some said it would be a lifelong source of regret to them if they did not climb the Blue Peak forthwith; others had no desire but to gloat over the lawyer's death fall, and to shout down the abyss, gaping at the echo, and advancing so far out on the ledge that they stood with their toes on death.

But it's an ill wind that blows good to none, and the resort earned a great deal of money. Paul began to revive again, and the furrows in his face were smoothed out. A man of worth grows strong and active with good fortune; in adversity he is defiant. One who is not defiant in adversity is worth nothing; let him be destroyed! Paul stopped drinking; he even began to take an interest in the harvesting, and worked in the field in Solem's place. If only he had begun when the weather was still slow and patient!

But at least Paul began to tackle things in the right spirit again; he only regretted that he had set aside for the cotters those outlying fields from which they were used to getting half the hay; this year he would have liked to keep it himself. But he had given his word, and there was nothing to be done about it.

Besides, it was raining now. Haymaking had to stop; they could not even stack what had already been gathered. Outside, three cartloads of fodder were going to waste.

Before long the novelty of the Tore Peak resort wore off again. The newspapermen wrote and sent telegrams about other gratifying misfortunes, the death on the Blue Peak having lost its news value. It had been an intoxication; now came the morning after.

The Danish mountaineer quite simply deserted. He strapped on his knapsack and walked across the field like one of the villagers, caring no more for the Blue Peak. The commotion he had witnessed in the last week had taught him a lesson.

And the tourists swarmed on to other places.

"What harm have I done them," Paul probably thought, "that they should be going again? Have I been too much in the fields and too little with them? But I greeted them humbly and took my man out of the harvesting work to help them...."

Then two young men arrived, sprouts off the Norwegian tree, sportsmen to their finger tips, who talked of nothing but sailing, cycling, and football; they were going to be civil engineers--the young Norway. They, too, wanted to see the Blue Peak to the best of their ability; after all, one must keep pace with modern life. But they were so young that when they looked up at the peak, they were afraid. Solem had learned more than one trick in tourist company; craftily he led them on, and then extorted money from them in return for a promise not to expose their foolishness. So all was well; the young sprouts came down the mountain again, bragging and showing off their sportsmanship. One of them brought down a bloodstained rag which he flung on the ground, saying,

"There's what's left of your lawyer that fell off."

"Ha, ha, ha, ha!" laughed the other sprout.

Yes, truly, they had acquired dashing ways among their sporting acquaintances.

It rained for three weeks; then came two fine days, and then rain again for a fortnight. The sun was not to be seen, the sky was invisible, the mountain tops had disappeared; we saw nothing but rain. The roofs at the Tore Peak resort began to leak more and more.

The hay that still lay spread on the ground was black and rotting, and the stacks had gone moldy.

The cotters had got their hay indoors during the patient spell. They had carried it, man, woman, and child, on their backs.

The men from Bergen and Mrs. Brede with her children have left for home. The little girls curtsied and thanked me for taking them walking in the hills and telling them stories. The house is empty now. Associate Master Höy and Mrs. Molie were the last to go; they left last week, traveling separately, though both were going to the same small town.

He went by way of the village--a very roundabout route--while she crossed the field. It is very quiet now, but Miss Torsen is still here.

Why do I not leave? Don't know. Why ask? I'm here. Have you ever heard anyone ask: "How much is a northern light?" Hold your tongue.

Where should I go if I did leave? Do you imagine I want to go to the town again? Or do you think I'm longing for my old hut and the winter, and Madame? I'm not longing for any specific place; I am simply longing.

Of course I ought to be old enough to understand what all sensible Norwegians know, that our country is once more on the right road. The papers are all writing about the splendid progress the tourist traffic has made in Stordalen since the motor road was opened--ought I not to go there and feel gratified?

From old habit, I still take an interest in the few of us who are left; Miss Torsen is still here.

Miss Torsen--what more is there to be said about her? Well, she does not leave; she stays here to complete the picture of the woman Torsen, child of the middle class who has read schoolbooks all through her formative years, who has learned all about *Artemis cotula*, but undernourished her soul. That is what she is doing here.

I remember a few weeks ago, when we were infested with Englishmen, a young sprout coming down from the mountain top with a bloodstained rag which he threw on the ground, saying, "Here's what's left of your lawyer that fell off!" Miss Torsen heard it, and never moved a muscle. No, she never mourned the death of the lawyer very keenly; on the contrary, she wrote off at once to ask another friend to come. When he came, he turned out to be a swaggering scatterbrain--a "free lance," he called himself in the visitors' book. I have not mentioned him before because he was less important than she; less important, in fact, than any of us. He was beardless and wore his collar open; heaven knows if he wasn't employed at a theater or in the films. Miss Torsen went to meet him when he came, and said, "Welcome to our mountains," and "Thanks for coming." So evidently she had sent for him. But why did she not leave? Why did she seem to strike root in the place, and even ask others to come here? Yet she had been the first to want to leave last summer! There was something behind this.

XXII

I muse on all this, and understand that her staying here is somehow connected with her carnal desires, with the fact that Solem is still here. How muddled it all is, and how this handsome girl has been spoiled! I saw her not long ago, tall and proud, upright, untouched, walking intentionally close to Solem, yet not replying to his greeting. Did she suspect him of complicity in the death of the lawyer and avoid him for that reason? Not in the least; she avoided him less than before, even letting him take her letters to the post office, which she had not done previously. But she was unbalanced, a poor thing that had lost her bearings. Whenever she could, she secretly defiled herself with pitch, with dung; she sniffed at foulness and was not repelled.

One day, when Solem swore a needlessly strong oath at a horse that was restless, she looked at him, shivered, and went a deep red. But she mastered herself at once, and asked Josephine:

"Isn't that man leaving soon?"

"Yes," Josephine replied, "in a few days."

Though she had seized this opportunity to ask her question with a great show of indifference, I am certain it was an important one to her. She went away in silence.

Yes, Miss Torsen stayed, for she was sexually bound to Solem. Solem's despair, Solem's rough passion that she herself had inflamed, his brutality, his masculinity, his greedy hands, his looks--she sniffed at all this and was excited by it. She had grown so unnatural that her sexual needs were satisfied by keeping this man at a distance. The Torsen type no doubt lies in her solitary bed at night, reveling in the sensation that in another house a man lies writhing for her.

But her friend, the actor? He was in no sense the other's equal. There was nothing of the bull in him, nothing of action, only the braggadocio of the theater....

Here am I, growing small and petty with this life. I question Solem about the accident. We are alone together in the woodshed.

Why had he lied and said the Dane wanted to climb the Blue Peak that unfortunate Sunday morning?

Solem looked at me, pretending not to understand.

I repeated my question.

Solem denied he had said any such thing.

"I heard you," I said.

"No, you didn't," he said.

A pause.

Suddenly he dropped to the floor of the shed, convulsed, without shape, an outline merely; a few minutes passed before he got up again. When he was on his feet once more, pulling his clothes to rights, we looked at each other. I had no wish to speak to him further, and left him. Besides, he was going away soon.

After this, everything was dull and empty again. I went out alone, aping myself and shouting: "Bricks for the palace! The calf is much stronger today!" And when this was done, I did other nothings, and when my money began to run out, I wrote to my publisher, pretending I would soon send him an unbelievably remarkable manuscript. In short, I behaved like a man in love. These were the typical symptoms.

And to take the bull by the horns: no doubt you suspect me of dwelling on the subject of Miss Torsen out of self-interest? In that case I must have concealed well in these pages that I never think of her except as an object, as a theme; turn back the pages and you will see! At my age, one does not fall in love without becoming grotesque, without making even the Pharaohs laugh.

Finis.

But there is one thing I cannot finish doing, and that is withdrawing to my room, and sitting alone with the good darkness round me. This, after all, is the last pleasure.

An interlude:

Miss Torsen and her actor are walking this way; I hear their footsteps and their voices; but since I am sitting in the dark of the evening, I cannot see them. They stop outside my open window, leaning against it, and the actor says something, asks her to do something she does not want to do, tries to draw her with him; but she resists.

Then he grows angry.

"What the devil did you send for me for?" he asks roughly.

And she begins to weep and says:

"So that's all you've come for! Oh, oh! But I'm not like that at all. Why can't you leave me alone? I'm not hurting you."

Am I one who understands women? Self-deception. Vain boasting. I made my presence known then because her weeping sounded so wretched; I moved a chair and cleared my throat.

The sound caught his attention at once, and he hushed her, trying to listen; but she said:

"No, it was nothing...."

But she knew very well this was not true; she knew what the sound was. It was not the first time Miss Torsen used this trick with me; she had often pretended that she thought I was not within hearing, and then created some such delicate situation. Each time I had promised myself not to intervene; but she had not wept before; now she wept.

Why did she use these wiles? To clear herself in my eyes--mine, the eyes of a settled man--to make me believe how good she was, how well-behaved! But, dear child, I knew that before; I could see it from your hands! You are so unnatural that in your seven and twentieth year, you walk unmarried, barren and unopen!

The pair drifted away.

And there is something else I cannot finish doing: withdrawing into solitude in the woods, alone with the good darkness round me. This is the last pleasure.

One needs solitude and darkness, not because one flees the company of others and can endure only one's own, but because of their quality of loftiness and religion. Strange how all things pass distantly, yet all is near; we sit in an omnipresence. It must be God. It must be ourselves as a part of all things.

> What would my heart, where would I stray?
> Shall I leave the forest behind me?
> It was my home but yesterday;
> now toward the city I wend my way;
> to the darkness of night I've resigned me.
>
> The world round me sleeps as I tarry, alone,
> soothing my ear with its quiet.

How large and gray is the city of stone
in which the many all hopes enthrone!
Shall I, too, accept their fiat?

Hark! Do the bells ring on the hillside?

Back to the peace of the forest I turn
in the nightly hour that's hoarest.
There's a sweet-smelling hedgerow to which I yearn;
I shall rest my head on heather and fern,
and sleep in the depths of the forest.

  Hark, how the bells ring on the hillside!

Romantic? Yes. Mere sentimentality, mood, rhyme--nothing? Yes. It is the last happiness.

XXIII

The sun has returned. Not darkly glowing and regal--more than that: imperial, because it is flaming. This you do not understand, my friend, whatever the language in which it is dished up for you. But I say there is an imperial sun in the sky.

It's a good day for going to the woods; it is sweeping time, for the woods are full of yellow things that have come suddenly into being. A short time ago they were not there, or I did not see them, or they had the earth's own complexion. There is something unborn about them, like embryos in an early stage. But if I whirl them about, they are miracles of fulfillment.

Here are fungi of every sort, mushrooms and puffballs. How close is the poisonous mushroom to the happy family of the edible mushroom, and how innocently it stands there! Yet it is deadly. What magnificent cunning! A spurious fruit, a criminal, habitual vice itself, but preening in splendor and brilliance, a very cardinal of fungi. I break off a morsel to chew; it is good and soft on the tongue, but I am a coward and spit it out again. Was it not the poisonous mushroom that drove men berserker? But in the dawn of our own day, we die of a hair in the throat.

The sun is already setting. Far up the mountainside are the cattle, but they are moving homeward now; I can hear by their bells that they are moving. Tinkling bells and deep-mouthed bells, sometimes sounding together as though there were a meaning in it, a pattern of tones, a rapture.

And rapture, too, to see all the blades of grass and the tiny flowers and plants. Beside me where I lie is a small pod plant, wonderfully meek, with tiny seeds pushing out of the pod--God bless it, it's becoming a mother! It has got caught in a dry twig and I liberate it. Life quivers within it; the sun has warmed it today and called it to its destiny. A tiny, gigantic miracle.

Now it is sunset, and the woods bend under a rustling that passes through them sweet and heavy; it is the evening.

I lie for another hour or two; the birds have long since gone to rest, and darkness falls thick and soft.... As I walk homeward, my feet feel their way and I hold my hands before me till I reach the field, where it is a little lighter. I walk on the hay that has been left outdoors; it is tough and black, and I slip on it because it is already rotting. As I approach the houses, bats fly noiselessly past me, as though on wings of foam. A slight shudder convulses me whenever they pass.

Suddenly I stop.

A man is walking here. I can see him against the wall of the new house. He has on a coat that looks like the actor's raincoat, but it is not the little comedian himself. There he goes, into the house, right into the house. It is Solem.

"Why, that's where she sleeps!" I think. "Ah, well. Alone in the building, in the south wing, Miss Torsen alone--yes, quite alone. And Solem has just gone in."

I stand there waiting to be at hand, to rush in to the rescue, for after all I am a human being, not a brute. Several minutes pass. He has not even bothered to be very quiet, for I hear him clicking the key in the lock. Surely I ought to hear a cry now? I hear nothing, nothing; a chair scraping across the floor, that is all.

"But good heavens, he may do her some harm! He may injure her; he may overpower her with rape! Ought I not to tap on the window? I--what for? But at the very first cry, I shall be on the spot, take my word for it."

Not a single cry.

The hours pass; I have settled down to wait. Of course I cannot go my way and desert a helpless woman. But the hours wear on. A very thorough business in there, nothing niggardly about this; it is almost dawn. It occurs to me that he may be killing her, perhaps has killed her already; I am alarmed and about to get up--when the key clicks in the lock again and Solem emerges. He does not run, but walks back the way he came, down to the veranda of my own house. There he hangs the actor's raincoat where it hung before, and emerges again. But this time he is naked. He has been naked under the coat all this time. Is it possible? Why not? No inhibitions, no restraint, no covering; Solem has thought it all out. Now, stark naked, he stalks to his room.

What a man!

I sit thinking and collecting myself and regaining my wits. What has happened? The south wing is still wrapped in silence, but the lady is not dead; I can see that from Solem's fearless manner as he goes to his room, lights the lamp, and goes to bed.

It relieves me to know she is alive, revives me, and makes me superlatively brave: if he has dared to kill her, I will report it at once. I shall not spare him. I shall accuse him of both her death and the lawyer's. I shall go further: I shall accuse others--the thief of last winter, the man that stole the sides of bacon from a tradesman and sold me rolls of tobacco out of his bag. No, I shall not keep silence about anything then....

XXIV

When it grew light, Solem went to the kitchen, had his breakfast, settled his business with Paul and the women, and returned to his room. He was in no hurry; though it was no longer early in the day, he took his time about tying his bundles, preparatory to leaving. Lingeringly he looked into the windows of the south wing as he passed.

Then Solem was gone.

A little later Miss Torsen came in to breakfast. She asked at once about Solem. And why might she be so interested in Solem? She had certainly stopped in her room intentionally so as to give him time to leave; if she wanted to see him she could have been here long ago. But was it not safest to seem a little angry? Supposing, night owl that I was, that I had seen something!

"Where is Solem?" she asked indignantly.

"Solem has gone now," Josephine replied.

"Lucky for him!"

"Why?" asked Josephine.

"Oh, he's a dreadful creature!"

How agitated she was! But in the course of the day she calmed down. Her anger dissolved, and there was neither weeping nor a scene; only she did not walk proudly, as was her habit, but preferred to sit in silence.

That passed too; she roused herself briskly soon after Solem's departure, and in a few days she was the same as ever. She took walks, she talked and laughed with us, she made the actor swing her in the children's swing, as in the lawyer's day....

I went out one evening, for there was good weather and darkness for walking; there was neither a moon nor stars. The gentle ripple of the little Reisa river was all the sound I heard; there were God and Goethe and *über allen Gipfeln ist Ruh'* that night. On my return, I was in the mood to walk softly and on tiptoe, so I undressed and went to bed in the dark.

Then they came again to my window, those two lunatics, the lady and the actor. What next? But it was not he that chose this spot; of that I was sure. She chose it because she was convinced I had returned. There was something she *wanted* me to hear.

Why should I listen to him still pleading with her?

"I've had enough of this," he said. "I'm leaving tomorrow."

"Oh, well...." she said. "No, let's not tonight," she added suddenly; "some other time. Yes? In a few days? We'll talk about it tomorrow. Good night."

For the first time it struck me: she wants to rouse you, too, settled man though you are; she wants to make you as mad as the others! That's what she's after!

And now I remember, before the lawyer arrived, when there was Tradesman Batt--I remember how during his first few days here, she would give me a kind word or a look that was quite out of the picture, and as unmistakable as her pride would permit. No, she had no objections to seeing old age wriggle. And listen to this: before this she had been intent to show a well-behaved indifference to sex, but that was finished; was she not at this moment resisting only faintly, and raising definite hopes? "Not tonight, but some other time," she had said. Yes, a half-refusal, a mere postponement, that I was meant to hear. She was corrupt, but she was also cunning, with the cunning of a madman. So corrupt.

Dear child, Pharaoh laughs before his pyramids; standing before his pyramids he laughs. He would laugh at me, too.

Next day we three remaining guests were sitting in the living room. The lady and the actor read one book; I read another.

"Will you," she says to him, "do me a great favor?"

"With pleasure."

"Would you go out in the grounds where we sat yesterday and fetch my galoshes?"

So he went out to do her this great favor. He sang a well-known popular song as he crossed the yard, cheerful in his own peculiar way.

She turned to me.

"You seem silent."

"Do I?"

"Yes, you're very silent."

"Listen to this," I said, and began to read to her from the book I held in my hands. I read a longish bit.

She tried to interrupt me several times, and at length said impatiently:

"What is this you want me to listen to?"

"The *Musketeers*. You must admit it's entertaining."

"I've read it," she said. And then she began to clasp her hands and drag them apart again.

"Then you must hear something you haven't read before," I replied, and went across to my room to fetch a few pages I had written. They were only a few poems--nothing special, just a few small verses. Not that I am in the habit of reading such things aloud, but I seized on this for the moment because I wanted to prevent her from humbling herself, and telling me anything more.

While I was reading the poems to her, the actor returned.

"I couldn't find any galoshes there," he said.

"No?" she replied absently.

"No, I really looked everywhere, but...."

She got up and left the room.

He looked after her in some surprise, and sat still for a moment. Then it occurred to him.

"I believe her galoshes are in the passage outside her door," he said, and hurried after her.

I sat back, thinking it over. There had been a sweetness in her face as she said, "Yes, you're very silent." Had she seen through me and my pretext for reading to her? Of course she had. She was no fool. I was the fool, nobody else. I should have driven a sportsman to despair. Some practice the sport of making conquests and the sport of making love, because they find it so agreeable; I have never practiced sport of any kind. I have loved and raged and suffered and stormed according to my nature--that is all; I am an old-fashioned man. And here I sit in the shadow of evening, the shadow of the half-century. Let me have done!

The actor returned to the living room confused and dejected. She had turned him out; she had wept.

I was not surprised, for it was the mode of expression of her type.

"Have you ever heard the like of it? She told me to get out! I shall leave tomorrow."

"Have you found the galoshes?" I asked.

"Of course," he replied. "They were right in the passage. 'Here they are,' I said to her. 'Yes, yes,' she said. 'Right under your nose,' I said. 'Yes, yes, go away,' she said, and began to cry. So I went away."

"She'll get over it."

"Do you think so? Yes, I expect she will. Oh, well, it's my opinion nobody can understand women, anyhow. But they're a mighty sex, the women, a mighty sex. They certainly are."

He sat on a while, but he had no peace of mind, and soon went out again.

That evening the lady was in the dining room before us; she was there when we came in, and we all nodded slightly in greeting. To the actor she was very kind, quite making up for her petulance of the afternoon.

When he sat down he found a letter in his table napkin: a written note folded into the napkin. He was so surprised that he dropped everything he was doing to unfold and read it. With an exclamation and a smile, his blue, delighted eyes splashed over her; but she was looking down into her lap with her forehead wrinkled, so he put the note away in his vest pocket.

Then it probably dawned on him that he had betrayed her, and he tried to cover it up somehow.

"Well, here goes for food!" he said, as though he were going to require all his energy for the task of eating.

Why had she written? There was nothing to prevent her speaking to him. He had, after all, been sitting on the doorstep when she emerged from her room and passed him. Had she foreseen that the good comedian could not contain himself, but would surely let a third person into the secret?

Why probe or question further? The actor did not eat much, but he looked very happy. So the note must have said yes, must have been a promise; perhaps she would not tantalize him further.

XXV

A few days later, they were going to leave. They would travel together, and that would be the end.

I might have pitied them both, for though life is good, life is stern. One result at any rate was accomplished. She had not sent for him in vain, nor had he come in vain.

That was the end of the act. But there were more acts to come--many more.

She had lost much: having been ravished, she gave herself away; why be niggardly now? And this is the destiny of her type, that they lose increasingly much, retaining ever less; what need to hold back now? The ground has been completely shifted: from half-measures to the immolation of all virtue. The type is well-known, and can be found at resorts and boarding-houses, where it grows and flourishes.

In spite of her wasted adolescence, her examination and her "independence," she has been coming home from her office stool or her teacher's desk more or less exhausted; suddenly she finds herself in the midst of a sweet and unlimited idleness, with quantities of tinned food for her meals. The company round her is continually changing, tourists come and go, and she passes from hand to hand for walks and talks; the tone is "country informality." This is sheer loose living; this is a life stripped of all purpose. She does not even sleep enough because she hears through the thin wall every sound made by her neighbor in the next room, while arriving or departing Englishmen bang doors all night. In a short time she has become a neurotic, sated with company, surfeited with herself and the place. She is ready to go off with the next halfway respectable organ grinder that happens along. And so she pairs off with the most casual visitors, flirts with the guide, hovering about him and making bandages for his fingers, and at last throws herself into the arms of a nameless nobody who has arrived at the house today.

This is the Torsen type.

And now, at this very moment, she retires to her room to collect the fragments of herself, in preparation for her departure--at the end of the summer. It takes time; there are so many fragments, one in every corner. But perhaps it consoles her to think that she knows the genitive of *mensa*.

Things are not quite so bad for the actor. He has staked nothing, is committed to nothing. No part of his life is destroyed, nor anything within him. As he came, so he goes, cheerful, empty, nice. In fact he is even something more of a man because he has really made a conquest. He has no wish but to spend some pleasant hours with the Torsen type.

He strolled about the garden waiting for her to get ready. Once she was visible through the doorway, and he called to her:

"Aren't you coming soon? Don't forget we've got to cross the mountain!"

"Well, I can't go bareheaded," she replied.

He was impatient.

"No, you've got to put your hat on, and what a lot of time that takes! Ugh!"

She measured him coldly and said:

"You're very--familiar."

If he had paid her back in the same coin there would have been weeping and gnashing of teeth and cries of "Go away! Go alone!" and an hour's delay, and reconciliation and embraces. But the actor's manner changed at once, and he replied docilely, as his nature was,

"Familiar? Well--perhaps. Sorry!"

Then he strolled about the garden again, humming occasionally and swinging his stick. I took note of the oddly feminine shape of his knees, and the unusual plumpness of his thighs; there was something unnatural about this plumpness, as though it did not belong to his sex.

His shoes were down at the heel, and his collar was open. His raincoat hung regally from his shoulders and flapped in the wind, though it was not raining. He was a proud and comical sight. But why speak harsh words about a raincoat? It was not he, the owner, that had abused it, and it hung from his shoulders as innocently as a bridal veil.

Why speak harsh words about anyone? Life is good, but life is stern. Perhaps when she comes out, I think to myself, the following scene will take place: I stand here waiting only for this departure. So she gives me her hand and says good-bye.

"Why don't you say something?" she asks in order to seem bright and easy in her mind.

"Because I don't want to hurt you in the great error of your ways."

"Ha, ha, ha," she laughs, too loudly and in a forced tone; "the great error of my ways! Well, really!"

And her anger grows, while I am assured and fatherly, standing on the firm ground of conscious virtue. Yet I say an unworthy thing like this:

"Don't throw yourself away, Miss Torsen!"

She raises her head then; yes, the Torsen type would raise her head and reply, pale and offended:

"Throw myself away?--I don't understand you."

But it is possible, too, that Miss Torsen, at heart a fine, proud girl, would have a lucid moment and see things in their true light:

"Why not, why shouldn't I throw myself away? What is there to keep? I am thrown away, wasted ever since my school days, and now I am seven and twenty...."

My own thoughts run away with me as I stand there wishing I were somewhere else. Perhaps she, too, in her room wishes me far away.

"Good-bye," I say to the actor. "Will you remember me to Miss Torsen? I must go now."

"Good-bye," says he, shaking hands in some surprise. "Can't you wait a few minutes? Well, all right, I'll give her your greeting. Good-bye, good-bye."

I take a short cut to get out of the way, and as I know every nook and corner, I am soon outside the farm, and find a good shelter. From here I shall see when these two leave. She has only to say good-bye now to the people of the farm.

It struck me that yesterday was the last time I spoke to her. We spoke only a few insignificant words that I have forgotten, and today I have not spoken to her....

Here they come.

Curious--they seemed somehow to have become welded together; though they walked separately up the mountain track, yet they belonged together. They did not speak; the essential things had probably already been said. Life had grown ordinary for them; it still remained to them to be of use to each other. He walked first, while she followed many paces behind; it was lonely to look at against the rugged background of the mountain. Where had her tall figure gone to? She seemed to have grown shorter because she had hitched up her skirt and was carrying her knapsack on her back. They each carried one, but he carried hers and she his, probably because, owing to the greater number of her clothes, hers was the heavier sack. Thus had they shifted their burdens; what burdens would they carry in the future? She was, after all, no longer a schoolmistress, and perhaps he was no longer with the theater or the films.

I watched those two crossing rocky, mountainous ground, bare ground, with not a tree anywhere except a few stunted junipers; far away near the ridge murmured the little Reisa. Those two had put their possessions together, were walking together; at the next halt they would be man and wife, and take only one room because it was cheaper.

Suddenly I started up and, moved by some impulse of human sympathy--nay, of duty--I wanted to run across to her, talk to her, say a word of warning: "Don't go on!" I could have done it in a few minutes--a good deed, a duty....

They disappeared behind the shoulder of the hill.

Her name was Ingeborg.

XXVI

And now I, too, must wander on again, for I am the last at the Tore Peak farm. The season is wearing on, and this morning it snowed for the first time--wet, sad snow.

It is very quiet at the farm now, and Josephine might have played the piano again and been friendly to the last guest; but now I am leaving, too. Besides, Josephine has little to play and be cheerful for; things have gone badly this year, and may grow worse as time goes on. The prospect is not a good one. "But something will turn up," says Josephine. She need not worry, for she has money in the bank, and no doubt there is a young man in the offing, on the other side of the fjeld.

Oh, yes, Josephine will always manage; she thinks of everything. The other day, for instance--when Miss Torsen and her friend left. The friend could not pay his bill, and all he said was that he had expected money, but it hadn't come, and he couldn't stay any longer because of his private affairs. That was all very well, but when would the bill be paid? Why, he would send it from the town, of course; that was where he had his money!

"But how do we know we'll get the money?--from him, anyway," said Josephine. "We've had these actor-people here before. And I didn't like the way he swanked about outside, thinking he was as good as anybody, and throwing his stick up in the air and catching it again. And then when Miss Torsen came in to say good-bye, I told her, and I wondered if she couldn't let me have the money for him. Miss Torsen was shocked, and said, 'Hasn't he paid himself?' 'No,' I said, 'he hasn't, and this year being such a bad one, we need every penny.' So then Miss Torsen said of course we should get the money; how much was it? And I told her, and she said she couldn't pay for him now, but she would see the money was sent; we could trust her for that. And I think we can, too. We'll get the money all right, if not from him. I daresay she'll send it herself...."

And Josephine went off to serve me my dinner.

Paul is on his feet now, too. Not that his step is always very steady, but at least he puts his feet to the ground. But he takes no interest in things; he does little more than feeding the horses and chopping some wood. He ought to be clearing the manure out of the summer cow houses for autumn use, but he keeps putting it off, and probably it will not be done at all. So far it hasn't mattered, but this morning's first wet snow has covered the hay outdoors and the maltreated land. And so it will remain till next spring. Poor Paul! He is an easygoing man at heart, but he pushes doggedly on against a whirlwind; sometimes he smiles to himself, knowing how useless it is to struggle--a distorted smile.

   His father, the old man alone in his room, stands sometimes on his threshold, as he used to do, and reflects. He is lost in memories, for he has ninety years behind him. The many houses on the farm confuse him a little; the roofs are all too big for him, and he is afraid they might come down and carry him off. Once he asked Josephine if it was right that his hands and fingers should run away from him every day across the fields. So they put mittens on his hands, but he took to chewing them; in fact he ate everything he was given, and enjoyed a good digestion. So they must be thankful he had his health, Josephine said, and could be up and about.

   I did not follow the others across the field, but returned the way I had come last spring, down toward the woods and the sea. It is fitting that I should go back, always back, never forward again.

   I passed the hut where Solem and I had lived together, and then the Lapps--the two old people and Olga, this strange cross between a human being and a dwarf birch. A stove stood against the peat wall, and a paraffin lamp hung from the roof of their stone-age dwelling. Olga was kind and helpful, but she looked tiny and pathetic, like a ruffled hen; it pained me to watch her flit about the room, tiny and crooked, as she looked for a pair of reindeer cheeses for me.

   Then I reached my own hut of last winter where I had passed so many lonely months. I did not enter it.

   Or rather, I did enter it, for I had to spend the night there. But I shall skip this, so for the sake of brevity, I call it not entering. This morning I wrote something playful about Madame, the mouse I left here last spring; but tonight I am taking it out again because I am no longer in the mood, and because there is no point in it. Perhaps it would have amused you to read it, my friend; but there is no point in amusing you now. I must deject you now and make you listen to me; there is not much more to hear.

   Am I moralizing? I am explaining. No, I am not moralizing; I am explaining. If it is moralizing to see the truth and tell it to you, then I am moralizing. Can I help that? Intuitively I see into what is distant; you do not, for this is something you cannot learn from your little schoolbooks. Do not let this rouse your hatred for me. I shall be merry again with you later, when my strings are tuned to merriment. I have no power over them. Now they are tuned to a chorale....

At dawn, in the bright moonlight, I leave the hut and push on quickly in order to reach the village as soon as possible. But I must have started too early or walked too fast, for at this rate I shall reach the village at high noon. What am I chasing after? Perhaps it is feeling the nearness of the sea that drives me forward. And as I stand on the last high ridge, with the glitter and roar of the sea far beneath, a sweetness darts through me like a greeting from another world. "*Thalatta!*" I cry; and I wipe my eyeglasses tremblingly. The roar from below is sleepless and fierce, a tone of jungle passion, a savage litany. I descend the ridge as though in a trance and reach the first house.

There was no one about, and a few children's faces at a window suddenly disappeared. Everything here was small and poor, though only the barn was of peat; the house was a timbered fisherman's home. As I entered the house, I saw that though it was as poor within as without, the floor was clean and covered with pine twigs. There were many children here. The mother was busy cooking something over the fire.

I was offered a chair, and sitting down, began to chat with a couple of small boys. As I was in no hurry and asked for nothing, the woman said:

"I expect you want a boat?"

"A boat?" I said in my turn, for I had not come by boat on my last visit; I had walked instead over fjelds and valleys many miles from the sea. "Yes, why not?" I said. "But where does it go?"

"I thought you wanted a boat to go to the trading center," she replied, "because that's where the steamer stops. We've rowed over lots of people this year."

Great changes here; the motor traffic in Stordalen must have completely altered all the other traffic since my last visit ten months ago.

"Where can I stop for a few days?" I asked.

"At the trading center, the other side of the islands. Or there's Eilert and Olaus; they're both on this side. You could go there; they've got big houses."

She showed me the two places on this side of the water, close to the shore, and I proceeded thither.

XXVII

A large house, with and upper story of planks built on later, displayed a new signboard on the wall: Room and Board. The barn, as usual, was a peat hut.

As I did not know which was Eilert and which Olaus, and had stopped to consider which road to take, a man came hurrying toward me. Ah, well, the world is a small place; we meet friends and acquaintances everywhere. Here am I, meeting an old acquaintance, the thief of last winter, the pork thief. What luck, what a satisfaction!

This was Eilert. He took in paying guests now.

At first he pretended not to recognize me, but he soon gave that up. Once he had done so, however, he carried the thing off in style:

"Well, well," he said, "what a nice surprise! You are most welcome under my humble roof, and such it is!"

My own response was rather less jaunty, and I stood still collecting my thoughts. When I had asked a few questions, he explained that since the motor traffic had started in Stordalen, many visitors came through this way, and sometimes they wanted to stop over at his house before being rowed across to the steamer. They always came down in the evenings, and it might be fine, or it might not, and at night the fjord was often wild. He had therefore had to arrange to house them, because after all, you can't expect people to spend the night outdoors.

"So you've turned into a hotelkeeper," I said.

"Well, you can joke about it," he returned, "but all I do is to give shelter to the people who come here. That's all the hotel there is to it. My neighbor Olaus can't do any more either, even if he builds a place that's ten times as big. Look over there--now he's building another house--a shed, I'd call it--and he's got three grown men working on it so he can get it done by next summer. But it won't be much bigger than my place at that, and anyhow, the gentry don't want to be bothered walking all that distance to his place when here's my house right at the car stop. And besides it was me that started it, and if I was Olaus I wouldn't have wanted to imitate me like a regular monkey and started keeping boarders which I didn't know the first thing about. But he can't make himself any different from what he is, so he puts up a few old bits of canvas and rugs and cardboard inside his barn and gets people to sleep there. But I'd never ask the gentry to sleep in a barn, a storehouse for fodder and hay for dumb beasts, if you'll excuse my mentioning it! But of course if you've no shame in you and don't know how to behave in company--"

"Lucky I've met you," I said. "Why, I might have gone on down the road to his place!"

We walked on together, with Eilert talking and explaining all the way, and assuring me over and over again that Olaus was a good-for-nothing for copying him as he did.

If I had known what was awaiting me, I should certainly have passed by Eilert's house. But I did not know. I was innocent, though I may not have appeared so. It cannot be helped.

"It's too bad I've got somebody in the best room," said Eilert. "They're gentlefolk from the city. They came down here through Stordalen, and they had to walk because the cars have stopped for the season. They've been in my house for quite some days, and I think they'll be staying on a while yet. I think they're out now, but of course it means I can't let you have my best room."

I looked up, and saw a face in the window. A shiver ran through me-- no, of course not a shiver, far from it, but certainly this was a fresh surprise. What a coincidence! As we were about to enter the door, there was the actor, too--standing there looking at me: the actor from the Tore Peak resort. It was his knees, his coat, and his stick. So I was right--I *had* recognized her face at an upper window. Yes, indeed, the world is small.

The actor and I greeted each other and began to talk. How nice to see me again! And how was Paul, the good fellow--still soaking himself in liquor, he supposed? Funny effect it has sometimes; Paul seemed to think the whole inn was an aquarium and we visitors the goldfish! "Ha, ha, ha, goldfish; I wish we were, I must say!--Well, Eilert, are we getting some fresh haddock for supper? Good!--Really, we like it here very much; we've already been here several days; we want to stay and get a good rest."

As we stood there, a rather stout girl came down from the loft and addressed the actor:

"The missis wants you to come right upstairs."

"Oh? Very well, at once.... Well, see you later. You'll be stopping here, too, I expect?"

He hurried up the stairs.

Eilert and I followed to my room.

As a matter of fact, I went out again with Eilert at once. He had a great deal to tell me and explain to me, and I was not unwilling to listen to him then. Really, Eilert was not too bad, a fine fellow with four ragged, magnificent youngsters by his first wife, who had died two years before, and another child by his second wife. He must have forgotten, as he told me this, the yarn about the sick wife and the ailing children that he had spun for me last winter. The girl who had come down the stairs with the message from the "missis" was no servant, but Eilert's young wife. And she, too, was all right--strong and good, handy about the stables, and pregnant again.

It all looks good to me, Eilert: your wife and everything you tell me about your family.

No one will understand my strange contentment, then; I had been full of an obscure happiness from the moment I came to this house. Probably a mere coincidence, but that did not detract from my satisfactory state of mind; I was pleased with everything, and all things added to my cheerful frame of mind. There were some pigs by the barn, very affectionate pigs, because they were used to the children playing with them and kissing them and riding on their backs. And there was one of the goats, up on the roof of course, standing so far out along the edge that it was a wonder he didn't grow dizzy. Seagulls flew criss-cross over the fields, screaming their own language to one another, and being friends or enemies to the best of their ability. Down by the mouth of the river, just beneath the sunset, began the great road that winds up through the woods and the valley. There is something of the friendliness of a living being about such a forest road.

Eilert was going out in his boat to fish haddock, and I went with him. Actually he should have been getting some meat for us; but he had promised the gentry from the city some fish, and fish was one of the gifts of God. Besides, if he lacked meat, he could always slaughter one of the pigs.

There was a slight wind; but then we wanted some wind, Eilert said, as long as there was not too much of it.

"Not reliable tonight though," he said, looking up into the sky; "the bigger the wind, the stronger the current."

At first I was very brave, and sat on the thwart thinking of Eilert's French words: *travali, prekevary, sutinary, mankémang,* and many others. They've had a long way to travel, coming here by ancient routes via Bergen, and now they're common property.

And then suddenly I lost all interest in French words, and felt extremely ill. It was much too windy, and we got no haddock.

"Pity she's come up so quick," said Eilert; "let's try inshore for a while."

But we got nothing there either, and as the wind increased and the sea rose, "We'd better go home," said Eilert.

The sea had been just right before, remarkably so, but now there was entirely too much of it. Why on earth did I feel so bad? An inner exhaustion, some emotional excitement, would have explained it. But I had experienced no emotional excitement.

We rowed in the foam and feathery jets of spray. "She's rising fast!" cried Eilert, rowing with all his might.

I felt so wretched that Eilert told me to ship my oars; he would manage by himself. But for all my wretchedness, I remembered that they could see me from the shore, and I would not put down my oars. Eilert's wife might see me and laugh at me.

What a revolting business, this seasickness that forced me to put my head over the gunwale and make a pig of myself! I had a moment's relief, and then it began all over again. Charming! I felt as though I were in labor; the wrong way up, of course, through my throat, but it was a delivery nonetheless. It moved up, then stopped, came on again and stopped, came on and stopped once more. It was a lump of iron--iron, did I say? No, steel; I had never felt anything like it before; it was not something I was born with. All my internal mechanism was stopped by it. Then I took a running start far down inside me and began, strangely, to howl with all my strength; but a howl, however successful, cannot break down a lump of steel. The pains continued. My mouth filled with bile. Soon, thank heaven, my chest would burst. O--oh--oh.... Then we rowed inside the islands that served as a breakwater, and I was saved.

Quite suddenly I was well again, and began to play the clown, imitating my own behavior in order to deceive the people ashore. And I assured Eilert, too, that this was the first time I had ever been seasick, so that he should understand it was nothing to gossip about. After all, he had not heard about the great seas I had sailed without the slightest discomfort; once I had been four-and-twenty days on the ocean, with most of the passengers in bed, and even the captain sick in cascades; but not me!

"Yes, I get seasick sometimes, too," says Eilert.

That evening I sat eating alone in the dining room. Since we had not brought back any haddock, the visitors upstairs had no desire to come down. All they wanted, Eilert's wife said, was some bread and butter and milk to be sent up.

XXVIII

Next morning they had gone.

Yes, indeed, they left at four in the morning, at dawn; I heard them perfectly well, for my room was near the stairs. The knight of the plump thighs came first, clumping heavily down the stairs. She hushed him, and her voice sounded angry.

Eilert had just risen too, and they stood outside for some minutes, negotiating with him for the boat--yes, at once; they had changed their minds and wanted to leave, immediately. Then they went down to the boat, Eilert with them. I could see them through the window, chilled by the cold of early morning and short-tempered with each other. There had been a frost during the night; ice lay on the water in the buckets, and the ground was harsh to walk on. Poor things--no food, no coffee; a windy morning, with the sea still running rather high. There they go with their knapsacks on their backs; she is still wearing her red hat.

Well, it was no concern of mine, and I lay down again, intending to sleep till about noon. Nothing was any concern of mine, except myself. I could not see the boat from my bed, so I got up again--just to while the time away--to see how far they had gone. Not very far, though both men were rowing. A little later I got up and looked again--oh, yes, they were getting on. I took up my post by the window. It was really quite interesting to watch the boat getting smaller and smaller; finally I opened the window, even looked through my field-glasses. As it was not yet quite light, I could not see them very clearly, but the red hat was still discernible. Then the boat disappeared behind an island. I dressed and went down. The children were all still in bed, but the wife, Regine, was up. How calmly and naturally she took everything!

"Do you know where your husband is?" I asked her.

"Yes--funny, aren't they?" she replied. "I never saw them till after they'd left--gone down to the fjord. Where do you suppose they're going? Haddock fishing?"

"Maybe," was all I said. But I thought to myself: "They're leaving, all right. They had their knapsacks on their backs."

"Funny couple," Regine resumed. "Nothing to eat, no coffee, not a thing! And the missis not wanting anything to eat last night, neither!"

I merely shook my head and went out. Regine called to me that coffee was nearly ready, so if I'd like a cup--

Of course the only thing I could do in the face of such foolishness was to shake my head and go away. One must take the sensible view. How was it possible to understand such behavior? Nevertheless I, the undersigned, should have gone on to Olaus yesterday, instead of going fishing. That would have been still more sensible. What business had I at this house? Very likely she found it embarrassing to be called the "missis," and this was why she could neither eat last night nor stay here today. So she had beaten a retreat, with her friend and her knapsack.

Well, it was not much to go away with, but perhaps that doesn't matter. As long as one has a reason to go away.

Later in the forenoon Eilert returned home. He was alone, but he came up the path carrying one of the knapsacks--the larger one. He was in a furious temper, and kept saying they'd better not try it on him--no, they'd just better not.

Of course it was the bill again.

"She'll probably have a good deal of this sort of trouble," I thought to myself, "but no doubt she'll get used to it, and take it as nonchalantly as it should be taken. There are worse things."

But the fact remains that it was I that upset them, I that had driven them away without their clothes; perhaps they had really expected some money to be sent here--who knows?

I got hold of Eilert. How big was the bill? What, was that all? "Good heavens! Here you are, here's your money; now row across to them at once with their clothes!"

But it all proved in vain, for the strangers had gone; they had arrived just in time for the boat, and were aboard it at that very moment.

Well, there was no help for it.

"Here's their address," says Eilert. "We can send the clothes next Thursday; that's the next trip the boat goes south again."

I took down the address, but I was most ungracious to Eilert. Why couldn't he have kept the other knapsack--why this particular one?

Eilert replied that it was true the gentleman had offered him the other one, but he could see from the outside that it was not so good as this one.

And I should remember that the money the missis had paid him hadn't covered more than the bill for one of them. So it was only reasonable that he should take the fullest knapsack. As a matter of fact, he had behaved very well, and that was the truth. Because when she gave him the larger knapsack, and wrote the address, she had scolded, but he had kept quiet, and said not another word. And anyway, nobody had better try it on him--they'd better not, or he'd know the reason why!

Eilert shook a long-armed fist at the sky.

When he had eaten, drunk his coffee, and rested for a while, he was not so lively and talkative as on the previous day. He had been brooding and speculating ever since last summer, when the motor traffic started, and did I think it would be a good idea for him to hire three grown men, too, and build a much bigger house than Olaus's?

So he had caught it, too--the great, modern Norwegian disease!

The knapsack was back in her room again; yes, these were her clothes; I recognized her blouses, her skirts and her shoes. I hardly looked at them, of course; just unpacked them, folded them neatly, and put them back in the bag again; because no doubt Eilert had had them all out in a heap. This was really my only reason for unpacking them.

XXIX

Once more I was run into a party of English, the last for this year.

They arrived by steamer in the morning and stopped at the trading station for a few hours, meanwhile sending up a detachment through the valley to order a car to meet them. Stordalen, Stordalen, they said. So they had apparently not yet seen Stordalen--an omission they must repair at once.

And what a sensation they made!

They came across by rowboat from the trading station; we could hear them a long way off, an old man's voice drowning out all the others. Eilert dropped everything he had in hand, and ran down to the landing place in order to be the first on the spot. From Olaus's house, too, a man and a few half-grown boys went down, and from all the houses round swarmed curious and helpful crowds. There were so many spectators at the landing place that the old man with the loud voice drew himself up to his full height in the boat and majestically shouted his English at us, as though his language must of course be ours as well:

"Where's the car? Bring the car down!"

Olaus, who was sharp, guessed what he meant and at once sent his two boys up the valley to meet the car and hurry it on, for the Englishmen had arrived.

They disembarked, they were in a great hurry, they could not understand why the car had not come to meet them: "What was the meaning of this?" There were four of them. "Stordalen!" they said. As they came up past Eilert's house, they looked at their watches and swore because so many minutes were being wasted. Where the devil was the car? The populace followed at some distance, gazing with reverence on these dressed-up fools.

I remember a couple of them: an old man--the one with the loud voice--who wore a pleated kilt on each thigh and a jacket of green canvas with braid and buckles and straps and innumerable pockets all over it. What a man, what a power! His beard, streaming out from under his nose like the northern lights, was greenish-white, and he swore like a madman. Another of the party was tall and bent, a flagpole of sorts, astonishing, stupendous, with sloping shoulders, a tiny cap perched above extravagantly arched eyebrows; he was an upended Roman battering ram, a man on stilts. I measured him with my eyes, and still there was something left over. Yet he was bent and broken, old before his time, quite bald; but his mouth was tight as a tiger's, and he had a madness in his head that kept him on the move.

"Stordalen!" he cried.

England will soon have to open old people's homes for her sons. She desexes her people with sport and obsessive ideas: were not other countries keeping her in perpetual unrest, she would in a couple of generations be converted to pederasty....

Then the horn of the car was heard tooting in the woods, and everyone raced to meet it.

Of course Olaus's two boys had done an honest day's work in meeting the car so far up the road, and urging the driver to hurry; were they not to get any reward? True, they were allowed to sit in the back seat for their return journey and thus enjoyed the drive of a lifetime; but money! They had acquired enough brazenness in the course of the summer not to hesitate, and approached the loud-voiced old man, holding out their palms and clamoring: "Money!" But that did not suit the old man, who entered the car forthwith, urging his companions to hurry. The driver, no doubt thinking of his own tips, felt he would serve his passengers best by driving off with them at once. So off he went. A toot of the horn, and a rapid fanfare--tara-ra-boom-de-ay!

The spectators turned homeward, talking about the illustrious visitors. Foreign lands--ah, no, this country will not bear comparison with them! "Did you see how tall the younger lord was?" "And did you see the other one, the one with the skirts and the northern lights?"

But some of the homeward-turning bumpkins, such as the Olaus family, had more serious matters on their minds. Olaus for the first time understood what he had read in the paper so many times, that the Norwegian elementary school is a worthless institution because it does not teach English to the children of the lower orders. Here were his boys, losing a handsome tip merely because they could not swear back intelligibly at the gentleman with the northern lights. The boys themselves had also something to think about: "That driver, that scoundrel, that southerner! But just wait!" They had heard that bits of broken bottle were very good for tires....